Energy Security in Times of Economic Transition

Energy Security in Times of Economic Transition: Lessons from China

BY

YAO LIXIA

emerald PUBLISHING

United Kingdom – North America – Japan – India – Malaysia – China

2.3 The Quantification of Energy Security: Indicators Identification *32*
2.3.1 Simple Energy Security Indicators *34*
2.3.2 Aggregated Energy Security Indicators *34*
2.3.3 Independent Energy Security Measurement Systems *36*
2.4 Chapter Summary *38*

Chapter 3 Quantitative Analysis of Energy Security in China 39

3.1 Formulation of Indicators to Examine Energy Security in China *39*
3.1.1 Availability (AV) Indicators *42*
3.1.2 Applicability (AP) Indicators *44*
3.1.3 Acceptability (AC) Indicators *49*
3.1.4 Affordability (AF) Indicators *52*
3.2 Data *54*
3.2.1 The AV Data *54*
3.2.2 The AP Data *55*
3.2.3 The AC Data *56*
3.2.4 The AF Data *57*
3.3 Data Coding and the Performance Scoring *58*
3.3.1 Data Coding *58*
3.3.2 Performance Scoring – Area of Rhombus *59*
3.4 Evolution of the 4-As *59*
3.4.1 An Overview *59*
3.4.2 The AV Trend *66*
3.4.3 The AP Trend *68*
3.4.4 The AC Trend *69*
3.4.5 The AF Trend *71*
3.5 Chapter Summary *73*

Chapter 4 Energy Policy in China Since its Reform and Opening Up 75

4.1 Energy Policies from 1949 (Founding of PRC) to 1976 (End of Cultural Revolution) *75*
4.1.1 Energy Polices from 1949 (Founding of PRC) to 1957 (End of the First Five-Year Plan) *75*
4.1.2 Energy Policies During the 'Great Leap Forward' *77*
4.1.3 Energy Policies after the 'Great Leap Forward' (from 1961 to 1966) *79*
4.1.4 Energy Policies During the 'Cultural Revolution' (from 1966 to 1976) *81*
4.2 Energy Policies of the AV Dimension *82*
4.2.1 Coal Production During the Reform Period *82*
4.2.2 China's Oil and Gas Industry *87*
4.2.3 China's Electricity Generation *88*

4.3 Energy Policies of the AP Dimension 90
4.3.1 Energy Conservation and Energy Intensity 90
4.3.2 Advancement of Energy Technologies During the Reform Period 95
4.4 Energy Policies of the AC Dimension 96
4.4.1 Air Pollution Control During the Reform Period 96
4.4.2 Policies on Renewable Energies and Nuclear Power 102
4.5 Energy Policies of the AF Dimension 106
4.5.1 Policies on Coal Price 106
4.5.2 Policies on Electricity Price 108
4.5.3 Policies on Oil Price 110
4.6 Chapter Summary and Further Discussion 111

Chapter 5 The Impact of Economic Reforms on the Energy Sector and Energy Security **113**

5.1 Introduction 114
5.2 Economic Reform and Energy Sector Reform: The Frst Phase (1978–1992) 115
5.2.1 The Initial Period (1978–1984): Planned Economy Dominating, Market Regulation Supplemented 116
5.2.2 From Rural to Urban: Further and Faster Reforms Until 1989 (1984–1989) 119
5.2.3 Adjustment and Recovering of the Economy (1989–1992): Combination of Planned Economy and Market Regulation 124
5.3 Economic Reform and Energy Sector Reform: The Second Phase (1993–2002) 127
5.3.1 Government Structure Reform and Its Impacts on Energy Sector 127
5.3.2 Fiscal and Financial Reforms and Their Impact on Energy Sector 130
5.3.3 SOEs Reform and Its Impact on Energy Sector 132
5.3.4 Western Development Strategy and Its Impacts on Energy Sector 139
5.3.5 A Critical Review of the Economic Reform During the Second Phase and Its Impact on the Energy Sector 141
5.4 Economic Reform and Energy Sector Reform: The Third Phase (2003–2010) 142
5.4.1 Further SOEs Reform 144
5.4.2 Continuing Marketisation 145
5.4.3 Increasing Attention to Environmental Protection 147
5.5 China's Economic Reform and Energy Security: A Chapter Conclusion 149

Chapter 6 Belt and Road Initiative and China's Energy Security: Can China be More Energy Secured? **151**

6.1 Introduction *151*
6.2 BRI Projects in the World's Energy Sector *152*
6.2.1. Central Asia *152*
6.2.2. South Asia *154*
6.2.3. Middle East *156*
6.2.4. Southeast Asia *158*
6.3 Conclusion *159*

Chapter 7 Conclusion **161**

7.1 Contribution of the Book: The Quantitative Methodology *163*
7.2 Contribution of the Book: The Qualitative Methodology *165*
7.3 Contribution of the Book: China's Energy Security Under BRI *170*

Bibliography *171*

Index *193*

Abbreviations

Acceptability by society	**AC**
Affordability of energy prices	**AF**
Analytic hierarchical process	**AHP**
Applicability of technology	**AP**
Asia Pacific Energy Research Centre	**APERC**
Availability of resource	**AV**
Barrels per day	**bpd**
Belt and Road Initiative	**BRI**
Billion cubic metres	**bcm**
British Petroleum	**BP**
Carbon capture and storage	**CCS**
Carbon dioxide	**CO_2**
China Energy Conservation Investment Corporation	**CECIC**
China National Offshore Oil Corporation	**CNOOC**
China National Petroleum Corporation	**CNPC**
China Petrochemical Corporation	**Sinopec**
China Statistical Yearbook	**CSY**
China's National Development and Reform Commission	**NDRC**
China-Pakistan Economic Corridor	**CPEC**
Chinese Academy of Social Sciences	**CASS**
Chinese Communist Party	**CCP**
Coal-bed methane	**CBM**
Coal-mine methane	**CMM**
Contract Responsibility System	**CRS**
Department for Business, Enterprise and Regulatory Reform	**DBERR**
Diversification of primary energy demand	**DoPED**
Driving force–state–response	**DSR**
Energy indicators for sustainable development	**EISD**
Energy Information Administration	**EIA**
European Union	**EU**
Five-Year Plan of economic and social development	**FYP**
Frontier Works Organisation	**FWO**
Global Terrorism Index	**GTI**
Greenhouse gas	**GHG**
Gross domestic product	**GDP**
Gross national product	**GNP**

Introduction

Despite unprecedented energy consumption rates and environmental sustainability threats, China has seen fast economic growth and its energy policy and energy security have gone through decades of transformation. As China's economy shifts from a planned to a market mechanism, it is valuable to find the root reason behind the transformation of the energy policy and energy security situation.

International political economy and security studies on China have yet to explore the interaction among three important factors: its energy policy, its energy security, and macroeconomic reform. This book aims to fill this gap in the literature with a new methodological approach to the study of China's energy security. It applies both quantitative and qualitative analyses to the energy security situation in China during the reform period. With this said, two primary objectives are achieved in this book. The first objective is to examine how the energy security situation in China has evolved during the economic reform period. This book establishes a quantitative framework based on a comprehensive concept of energy security which covers availability of resources, applicability of technologies, acceptability by society, and affordability of prices. The framework analysis shows that China's energy security situation has not improved during the reform period.

The second objective of the book is to explore qualitatively why the energy security situation has not improved. To answer the 'why' question, the book opens up a new perspective by analysing the relationship between energy policies and the macroeconomic reform. It is found that China's macroeconomic reform has restricted the formation of China's energy policies and determined its energy security situation. In essence, China's energy policies are only a reaction to the macroeconomic measures. In other words, China's energy policies are not originally intended to improve energy security, but passive reactions to China's macroeconomic reform. This explains why China did not improve its energy security situation despite 40 years of reform.

In addition, with a separate chapter, it also includes an international perspective by studying the impact of China's Belt and Road Initiative on its energy security situation. This book is not only meaningful for the case of China but also useful to explain energy security in other countries, especially those countries in economic transition.

Acknowledgment

I would like to thank my parents from the bottom of my heart for their dedication and support. They always stand by me whenever I am in difficulty. They are the nicest people in my world.

List of Figures

Fig. 1.1.	The Macro Economy-Driven Energy Security Mechanism	12
Fig. 2.1.	The Energy Security Spectrum	24
Fig. 2.2.	A General Framework Evaluating Energy Security in China	27
Fig. 2.3.	A Detailed Framework Evaluating Energy Security in China	28
Fig. 3.1.	The Concept Behind Sustainability Indicators	40
Fig. 3.2.	Energy Security Status of 1980 (Benchmark for This Study): 68.04 Sq. Units	62
Fig. 3.3.	Energy Security Status of 1985 (the Ending Year of the Sixth FYP Period): 72.52 Sq. Units	62
Fig. 3.4.	Energy Security Status of 1990 (the Ending Year of the Seventh FYP Period): 59 Sq. Units	63
Fig. 3.5.	Energy Security Status of 1995 (the Ending Year of the Eighth FYP Period): 43.92 Sq. Units	63
Fig. 3.6.	Energy Security Status of 2000 (the Ending Year of the Ninth FYP Period): 52.48 Sq. Units	64
Fig. 3.7.	Energy Security Status of 2005 (the Ending Year of the Tenth FYP Period): 70.84 Sq. Units	64
Fig. 3.8.	Energy Security Status of 2010 (the Ending Year of the Eleventh FYP Period): 62.32 Sq. Units	65
Fig. 3.9.	Evolving Trend Timeline for Area of the Rhombuses	66
Fig. 3.10.	Trend Illustration of Average Value for AV	67
Fig. 3.11.	Trend Illustration of Average Value for AP	68
Fig. 3.12.	Trend Illustration of Average Value for AC	70
Fig. 3.13.	Trend Illustration of Average Value for AF	71
Fig. 4.1.	Output Increase by the Centrally Administered State-Owned Mines and TVCMs from 2001 to 2006 (million tons)	86

Chapter 1

Into the Landscape

A country's energy policy and energy security status are closely related and influence each other. Having sound energy policies will improve energy security, whereas less prudent energy policies may worsen its energy security situation. Thus, ensuring energy security is fundamental for domestic prosperity and national security because 'the advent of globalization, the growing gap between rich and poor, the war on terrorism, and the need to safeguard the earth's environment are all intertwined with energy concerns' (Wirth, Gray, & Podesta, 2003, pp. 132–133). China's huge appetite for energy consumption and its massive degradation of the environment have increasingly fostered international concerns. Therefore, analysing the interaction between energy policy and energy security in China is an urgent task and will help address these concerns. This chapter gives a general background, introduces research questions, and explains the research framework and methodology of the book.

1.1. Background

1.1.1. Energy Security and Energy Policy

What makes energy policy and energy security so critical an issue is that the energy sector has specific features. For example, a reliable energy supply is crucial to economies, energy projects involve high capital investment and large risks, and energy production and consumption may result in environmental degradation. These distinctive characteristics of the energy sector require every government to have its own energy policy (Andrews-Speed, 2001). This policy, in turn, has a significant impact on both energy production and consumption. Hence, the security of energy supply has even been deemed as the 'key element for the functionality of the modern societies' (Purhonen, 2005, p. 1).

Energy is an economic commodity, but it has also become a political commodity whereby economics and politics influence the energy sector. Since energy is essential for fuelling the economy, energy resources – especially fossil fuels – have often been a fuse for conflicts and wars. Fossil fuels are the most important source of energy. Therefore, competition for seeking fossil fuels is fierce and prone to tension and conflicts. The historical record shows examples of oil-importing countries that sought to eliminate their oil dependence through military expansion. A case

Energy Security in Times of Economic Transition: Lessons from China, 1–16

doi:10.1108/978-1-83982-464-720201002

the study of energy security and energy policy in China. Unlike the definition of energy security, there is a little variation in the literature on the definition of energy policy. Energy policy is a policy made by the government, industries, or non-governmental organisations to address issues in the energy sector, officially or unofficially (McGowan, 1996). These issues may cover the whole energy sector or deal with a specific subsector, such as coal, oil, renewable energy, energy research and development, and energy conservation.[3] Historical analysis of trends in energy policy shows the change in government thinking about policies on energy, from concentration purely on security of energy supply to greater emphasis on efficient and sustainable energy utilisation (Finon, 1994). This change in policy priority exists in China as well.

1.1.3. The Importance of Analysing China's Energy Policy

The energy industry in China has a number of characteristics that are distinct from other sectors of the economy. First, the ownership of energy resources in China is largely in the hands of the state/government. The government has the right and responsibility to manage these resources. Second, exploration and development of energy resources involve large capital investments, long payback periods, and high risks. It cannot be easily tackled by the private sector. Third, energy production and consumption normally have negative consequences, such as environmental damages at the local, regional, and global levels. These issues need to be addressed by the government, either individually or collectively (Andrews-Speed, 2004). Therefore, these characteristics make energy policy deserving of intensive research.

China's energy industry has gone through 70 years of transformation from the founding of the People's Republic of China (PRC), the Great Leap Forward period, the Cultural Revolution, till the reform era. The energy policy of China, an ultra-large economy and energy consumer, has critical implications not only for its own security situation, but also for the world's. China's energy security situation has increasingly drawn international concerns. One reason for this is the current huge gap between its stagnating domestic energy production and its fast-growing consumption. The combination of China's rising energy demand and its limited indigenous energy resources has prompted its oil companies to acquire stakes in exploration and production projects abroad. Indeed, securing energy supply sources has become the key aim of China's energy and foreign policies. China's rising demand for energy has also raised serious concerns regarding global pollution and other environmental issues. Therefore, it is valuable to identify the way China's energy policy has evolved and its relevant impact on the security situation. It is even more valuable to find the root reason behind the evolution of the energy security situation.

Energy policy stipulates objectives and the means to achieve these objectives, which may change to match a country's economic, political, and social conditions. The means to achieve the objectives are categorised into three groups: command,

[3]For details of the literature on energy policy definitions, see Chapter 2.

market, and persuasion. In a planned economy, command dominates the energy sector. Command, in the form of plans, regulations, and laws, regulates the flow of energy and players' actions. In a liberalised economy, a market mechanism dominates the energy sector. The market determines energy flow and prices. Persuasion, such as education and publicity for policy implementation, is required in both planned and liberalised economies (Andrews-Speed, 2001). As China's economy shifts from planned to market mechanism, it must adjust its energy policy accordingly. Facing the challenges of energy security problems amid rapid economic and social development, China's energy policy objectives have been amended to address emerging issues. The necessary means have been modified to realise these objectives and China's energy policy has evolved correspondingly. Therefore, research on the energy policy of China has both academic and practical significance.

1.2. Research Questions and Key Findings

This book finds solutions for four policy-oriented questions. First, how has China's energy security situation evolved? The answer to this question is a quantitative study based on a framework (the 4-As framework) using indicators to quantify the energy security situation in China, with the conclusion that China's energy security has deteriorated over more than three decades of economic reform. Second, what impact do the energy policies have on China's energy security status? The answer involves a whole chapter that analyses the direct impact of China's energy policies on its security situation. Third, why has China's energy security deteriorated? The answer explores the nature of the evolution of energy policies and their impact on the energy security situation in China. Fourth, whether does China's Belt and Road Initiative (BRI) contribute to improving China's energy security? The answer addresses the impact of BRI on China's energy security.

To put it briefly, this book evaluates the impact made by *past* and *current* energy policies and activities on the energy security status of China. Upon evaluation, it is found that China's energy security situation has not improved over three decades of economic reform. This book gives reasons for the evolution of China's energy security status: China's macroeconomic reform has restricted the formation of China's energy policies. In essence, it is the macroeconomic reform that limits the improvement of China's energy security situation. China's energy policies are only responses to the evolution of macroeconomic measures. In other words, China's energy policies were not originally intended to improve energy security, but only passive responses to macroeconomic reform. This book does not deny or disregard other factors that affect China's energy security situation such as international relations, institutions, interest conflicts, etc., while it finds that the macroeconomic reform is the key driver of China's energy security evolution.

1.3. Existing Discussions on China's Energy Policy and Energy Security

The existing qualitative studies on China's energy security are mostly from the perspective of international relations. They discuss international or geopolitical advantages and challenges for energy security in China and offer suggestions (Wang, 2001; Zhang, 1998 & 2003a; Zweig & Bi, 2005). In the context of international relations theory, the current literature addresses China's energy security and its geopolitical implications through either a realist perspective or a neo-liberal perspective, thus taking an energy perspective of China's foreign relations, which entails either competition or cooperation. Realists take the international system as an anarchical one. Competition and a zero-sum game lead to conflicts. Realists believe peace is achieved through the balance of power between states, whereas neo-liberals believe that peace is achieved through cooperation.

From a realist perspective, China's oil dependence and increased demand for foreign energy resources result in strategic competition between major powers such as the United States (U.S.) and China. The U.S. hegemonic oil strategy in the Middle East had been the root cause of political instability in the region. This strategy has also severely constrained China's ability to secure a stable oil supply in the Middle East (Moran & Russell, 2009; Shu, 2010). Russia too faces fierce competition in its search for energy reserves in the Middle East and Central Asia, which could provoke power warfare on a grand scale. The United States, Russia, and China are trying to bolster their strategic positions and curb the influence of each other, hence a 'three-way geopolitical struggle' has emerged (Klare, 2004, p. 162). Energy reserves in Central Asia provide motives for the United States to secure a position in the region, albeit in competition with the interests of Russia. The latter will undoubtedly try to offset the deepening U.S. penetration in Central Asia. The motive behind Russian–Chinese rapprochement can be traced to China's desires for Central Asia to meet its future oil requirements (Naughten, 2007; Noreng, 2006).

From a neo-liberalist perspective, energy can be a platform for dialogue. Domestically produced coal still dominates China's usage of energy. Therefore, China is less vulnerable to supply shortages than countries that lack domestic energy resources. As major coal producers and exporters, China and the United States share an interest in the development of coal-related technologies. Furthermore, China would prefer investment in expensive oil pipeline projects to conflicts with the United States and its neighbours over sea lanes to ship its oil supplies from the Middle East. China's oil imports from the Middle East offer China an interest in regional stability. It is China's investments in Iran's oil and gas sector that makes China interested in preventing a nuclear Iran (Shaffer, 2009). Since political instability in the Middle East poses high risks for the oil and gas supply from the region, China should work towards a long-term Sino-U.S. energy cooperation rather than risk confrontation in the Middle East (Sun & Pan, 2009). The more China feels threatened by the United States and its allies, the more China will enhance its energy security by seeking alternative options, such as maximising the use of its domestically abundant coal resources, developing expensive oil and gas pipelines, and cultivating relationships with oil-producing states such as Iran (Downs, 2000). As an oil-importing country, China is interested not only in collaborating with Middle-Eastern countries, but also in finding common ground with other oil importers. The oil-importing countries should seek to acknowledge cooperation rather than competition in their search for energy (Jakobson & Zha, 2006).

Neither the realist nor the liberalist perspective gives an assertive evaluation of the evolution of China's energy security situation. Compared to qualitative studies on the energy security situation in China, energy security quantification makes it more operational to evaluate the evolution of China's energy security. Zhang (2007) and Chang (2010) apply the methodology of Analytic Hierarchical Process (AHP) in establishing evaluation frameworks that incorporate indicators to assess China's energy security evolution. Also using the AHP methodology, Shi (2011) makes the same conclusion that China is energy-secure. He analyses general factors that affect the country's energy security and recommends policies. The AHP methodology has also been used to construct a framework to calculate the oil security index and evaluate China's oil security. It concludes that China's oil security has been worsening since 1991 (Zhang & Liu, 2005).

Besides the AHP methodology, other assessment systems can evaluate energy security in China with a more historical view. He, Sheng, and Wang (2011) use 10 key indicators to assess the evolution of energy security in China and conclude that China's energy security situation generally improved from 1988 until 2004, after which it deteriorated. Liu, Shen, Gao, and Liu (2012) review several energy security indices and models and build an assessment model to evaluate China's energy security situation from 1990 to 2008. They conclude that China's energy security situation was the best in 2001 and then began to decrease. Since 2004, the deterioration has accelerated and the energy security situation reached its worst in 2008. However, none of these studies identify the key reason behind the evolution of energy security in China. They only superficially analyse factors that have an impact on energy security in China, such as international relations, domestic energy reserves, economic growth, industry structure, technology, and environment. They fail to identify the key or the most critical reason behind the energy policies and energy security status evolution.[4]

From the qualitative research perspective, study on China's energy policies has gained momentum since economic reform was initiated in 1979. From then on, China's energy policies have been extensively discussed. However, the discussion is either short of a comprehensive overview or lacks combination of energy policies with the country's energy security situation. In 2002, the Strategic Planning Department of the State Power Corporation published *China's Energy in Fifty Years*. This book comprehensively reviewed the achievements in China's energy industry since 1949, summarising the impact of China's energy policies on the energy industry and developments and changes in China's energy structure. It also mentioned China's energy policies, especially the energy policies in the individual energy sectors during the reform era. However, it only covered energy policies in general and omitted details on their evolution.

China's energy situation in the early 1980s is well documented in the *Research Report on China's Energy Policy*. The report extensively reviews past implementation of energy policy and proposes a number of energy policy recommendations. It also points out the major energy challenges China faced in the early 1980s, such

---

[4]For details for energy security measurements, see Chapter 2.

as rural energy shortages and coal transportation difficulties (China's Energy Research Institute, 1982). The report shows the background of China's energy policy formulation in the early 1980s and its dilemma in energy and economic development, but it does not evaluate the effects of China's main energy policies and specific measures on its security situation.

Some works have briefly discussed the evolution of China's energy policy. The evolution is generally categorised into three periods: before the economic reform, from the beginning of the reform to the Tenth Five-Year Plan (FYP) period, and from the Tenth FYP period onwards. The first period is a period of energy self-sufficiency. The second is a period of energy sector reform amid increasing international cooperation. The third is regarded as a period with more 'mature' energy policies where priority is given to energy conservation and sustainable development (Wang, Wang, & Fan, 2012). However, this kind of categorisation only takes a simple view of the change in priority documented by the Chinese government. The actual motivation behind the evolution is ignored. Shi (2005) finds that market reform and an open energy market are 'objective requirements' of energy security in China. She maintains that market liberalisation is directly related to energy security. Perhaps she has some sense of the relationship between market reform and energy security, but she fails to explain how the relationship works. In a later work, she tries to find the motivation behind the energy policy evolution, and she almost gets there with the argument that energy industry reform is a component of Chinese economic system reform. But she argues that the purpose and steps of energy system reform reflect the stepwise process and characteristics of the energy industry, rather than going further to analyse the relationship between energy industry reform and reform of the Chinese economic system. She reviews the processes and contents of the reform in the energy sector from only three aspects – energy pricing mechanism reform, opening of the energy sector to foreign and private investors, and administrative institution reform in the energy sector – and evaluates the effectiveness of the reform (Shi, 2008). The failure to identify the essence of energy policy evolution makes it less possible for her to comprehensively discuss energy policies and the energy security situation with a firm stand.

Traditionally, China's energy policy has a concrete target for each energy sector, such as coal, oil, gas, and power. However, the energy policy lacks coherence (Andrews-Speed, 2004; Smil, 1981). Therefore, most literature tends to address China's energy policy by targeting a specific sector. In this way, China's energy policies can be divided into coal policy, electricity policy, oil policy, renewable energy policy, environmental policy, and energy conservation policy.[5] These works address the policies and their effects in detail, with an analysis of the background of energy policy formulation. They serve as an important reference for this study of China's energy policy, but they are lacking in research on policies throughout the whole energy sector. They also do not relate the policies to the overall energy security situation in China. The gap is filled by this book, which

[5]See Wang (1999), Ma and He (2008), Yeh and Lewis (2004), Li (1984), and Shen (1988).

not only comprehensively researches China's energy policy, but also relates the energy policy to energy security and identifies the essence of their evolution.

To sum up, the existing literature on China's energy policy and energy security does not identify the key reason behind the evolution of energy policy and energy security. Instead, it mostly focuses on quantitatively grading China's energy security status or describing the energy security challenges China is faced with. Most of the challenges and relevant strategies are analysed from an international relations perspective or, for literature focusing on a specific energy sector, without a pan-energy industry view. This book fills the gap by quantitatively portraying the evolution of the energy security situation in China and qualitatively analysing the critical reason behind its evolution from a domestic perspective and a pan-energy industry view.

1.4. Study Value and Contributions to Knowledge

As reviewed in Section 1.3, a number of studies have examined China's energy policies and energy security. However, there are no systematic studies that synthesise the evolution of China's energy policy, energy security status related to energy policy, and macroeconomic reform in a single framework. This book analyses China's energy policy evolution trends accordingly over different periods. China has experienced political changes since its founding in 1949. Different periods have different energy policies and related energy security situations. Taking into account China's distinctive socio-economic adjustments and its national FYP periods of economic and social development, this book discusses China's energy security and energy policy evolution in terms of these FYP periods, analysing the relationship between energy policy and energy security situation in each period. As energy security status directly reflects the effects of energy policy, relating the concept of energy security to energy policy evolution helps to identify the successes and failures of China's energy policies in each specific period, making the study of China's energy policy evolution a more valuable reference for future policymaking. The identification of successful energy policies is meaningful because the degree to which China succeeds or fails in its energy policies is of great significance to the rest of the world. It affects other factors and behaviours such as China's import requirements for different types of energy, the nature and scope of China's diplomatic measures to secure energy supplies, the scale of China's greenhouse gas emissions resulting from the use of energy, and domestic economic and political stability.

International political economy and security studies on China have yet to explore the interaction among three important factors: China's energy policy, its energy security, and macroeconomic reform. This book aims to partially fill this gap in the literature with new methodological approaches to the study of China's energy security and bring a new perspective to China's energy policy and security. To the best of my knowledge, there is no study that combines China's energy policy, energy security situation, and macroeconomic reform with the aim of achieving a comprehensive and detailed understanding of China's energy security. In this sense, this book could be considered an original piece of research.

Energy security is a subject that is equally important to both security and economically oriented researchers and policymakers. This book makes a significant contribution to the literature by focusing on a practical, necessary, and critical issue addressing policy and security. It fills the substantial gap between the quantitative analysis of energy security and qualitative policy relevance in the literature. The contribution of the quantitative methodology and analysis lies in two aspects. First, it provides a new method to quantify energy security in China. The quantification is not only a picture depicting how energy security situation evolved along a timeframe, but also a foundation for qualitative analysis of energy security in China. Second, it provides a very useful method and a valuable reference for energy security quantification in other countries. The contribution of the qualitative methodology is equally prominent. It provides a completely new perspective to analyse energy security in China: the macroeconomic reforms. Other perspectives, such as international relations, have been extensively discussed to explain energy security or insecurity in China. But they failed to 'locate' the key factor that determines energy policy and evolution of energy security in China. This book contributes to the literature with a very powerful instrument to explain and analyse why the energy security in China has evolved in the way it is quantified. More importantly, this new perspective is not only powerful for the China case, but also useful to explain energy security in other countries, especially those countries in economic transition. Besides, this book integrates the quantitative analysis of factors affecting energy security with the qualitative analysis of related policies. Such an integrated analysis is valuable not only because it provides policymakers with information on the performance of past policies, but also because a good understanding of such issues will help to improve policymaking in the future.

At last, this book extends its study beyond the domestic perspective to overseas investment, with an emphasis on the period beginning with the Xi Jinping Administration. In 2013, Chinese President Xi Jinping proposed the building of the New Silk Road Economic Belt and the 21st Century Maritime Silk Road – now collectively called the BRI. The aim of BRI, as communicated by the Chinese government, is to increase connectivity, enhance trade flows, and spur long-term economic growth. Energy plays an important role in China's BRI. Aiming to greatly improve infrastructure interconnectivity, the BRI can greatly reduce logistic costs in bringing foreign energy resources home when more oil and gas pipelines linking China with neighbouring countries would be taken on the horizon. On the one hand, by using BRI to build energy infrastructure, China will be able to source oil, gas, and electricity from the energy-rich countries nearby. On the other hand, the BRI has provided ample opportunities for the Chinese companies to acquire more energy resources abroad. Huge Chinese investments have been devoted to energy projects within and across countries alongside the 'Belt' and the 'Road'. In fact, as the largest energy consumer in the world, China has every reason to secure sufficient and stable energy supplies through energy-related BRI projects in order to ensure energy security, which constitutes an important part of BRI. With this said, by reviewing the BRI projects and by analysing the barriers of the projects implementation, this book looks into energy security of Xi Jinping Administration with an international view to make clear the BRI's relations with China's energy security and explore whether the BRI contributes to enhancing China's energy security or not.

1.5. The 4-As Framework

The 4-As framework is extensively used in this book. The framework incorporates four critical dimensions of energy security: availability of resources, applicability of technology, acceptability by society, and affordability of prices.

Availability of resources (AV) mainly deals with the amount of fossil fuel reserves that China has and the shortage relevant to demand; it also deals with alternative resources, such as renewable energy, that China presently or potentially has. This factor shows how the Chinese government seeks to ensure that China has the energy resources needed for economic growth.

Applicability of technologies (AP) deals with the existing technologies China has and its capability for developing potential technologies that may be relevant to renewable resources, such as hydroelectric power, wind power, and solar power. To sum up, it refers to the exploration of potential resources and efficient use of the already-extracted resources.

Acceptability by society (AC) deals with environmental issues (e.g. emissions control) and measures people take (e.g. harnessing energy from alternative sources) to improve their physical environment. It also addresses the issue of whether local people accept resource exploitation in their area and to what degree they accept it. The extensive use of fossil fuels as the main energy resource in China had led to serious pollution problems. Health effects due to pollution might evolve into strong social critique and public protest. To sum up, acceptability by society addresses the general public's level of tolerance for the possible negative effects of energy exploration and/or use.

Affordability of prices (AF) refers to the purchasing ability of consumers for energy resources. Consumption behaviour should be studied at the personal level and at the commercial level. Affordability should not only involve the 'affordable' factor but also the 'stable' factor of energy prices. Wildly swinging energy prices make it difficult for suppliers to invest prudently. Affordability should also relate to the quality of energy resources. Consumers need high-quality energy with reasonable and stable prices.

Twenty indicators that constitute the 4-As are identified. These indicators cover the four dimensions of energy security: availability, applicability, acceptability, and affordability. Relevant data are collected for each indicator. The data are then converted into ordinal values for energy security status evaluation. For each period of China's energy policy evolution, a rhombus grid is developed. Under the ideal situation, energy security is in the perfect condition and the rhombus will be a perfect square with each 'A' hitting the highest value in its dimension. However, it is difficult to achieve 'perfect' energy security no matter which period the country is in. Therefore, different periods have different shapes and the areas of the different grids indicate the relevant energy security status in that period. The shape and area of the rhombuses indicate the level of China's energy security in each period.[6]

[6]For the construction of the 4-As framework and the development of the rhombuses, see Chapter 2 and Chapter 3, respectively.

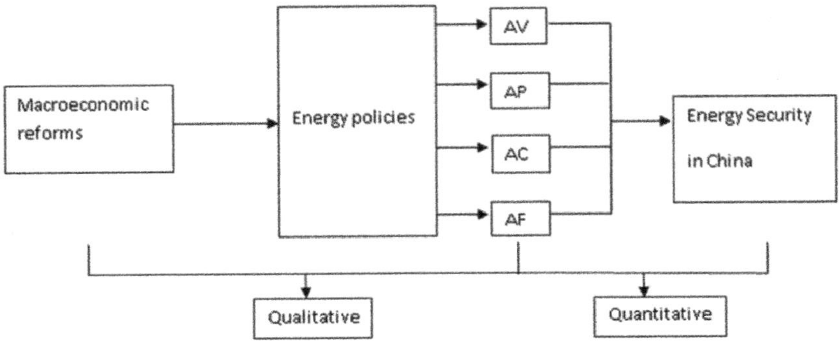

Fig. 1.1. The Macro Economy-driven Energy Security Mechanism.

1.6. Analytical Framework of the Book

This book establishes the Macro Economy-driven Energy Security Mechanism, which is a very useful tool to analyse and explain the evolution of China's energy security. The Macro Economy-driven Energy Security Mechanism is elaborated in Fig. 1.1.

1.6.1. Explanation of the Analytical Framework

The analytical framework identifies the key independent variable that functions in the evolution of China's energy security – macroeconomic reform. Energy security in China is highly dependent on macroeconomic reform. In other words, it is the macroeconomic reform that frames the energy security situation in China. The concept of energy security, as defined in this book, incorporates four dimensions: availability of resources (AV), applicability of technologies (AP), acceptability by society (AC), and affordability of prices (AF). Macroeconomic reform, via its function in the energy sector, improves or worsens each of the four dimensions of energy security. In such way, the causality between macroeconomic reform and energy security is established. The analytical framework does not deny potentially intervening variables, such as international relations, conflict of interest groups, or agencies/actors that have impact on energy security, but it picks out the key variables and provides a new perspective to analyse the energy security of a country, especially one in economic transition.

With regard to the Chinese case, from the very beginning of China's reform and opening up in 1978, the macroeconomic measures began to function as drivers of each dimension of energy security. In the initial reform period, the central government decided to rectify the economic disorder left by the Cultural Revolution and other social chaos. This decision led to the adjustment of energy industry distribution. The coal industry was shifted to coal-rich areas and production efficiency was greatly increased. Also in the initial period, the introduction of the Household Responsibility System made an outlet for the fast development of town and village enterprises, which directly stimulated the spread of town and village coalmines (TVCMs) that greatly contributed to coal production in China. The two-tier pricing system, which typically reflected the Chinese government's cautiousness in introducing 'market force', also covered the energy sector. The in-quota and above-quota coal and oil prices lasted for nearly one decade until the two-tier system was revoked in China.

Of the promulgation and implementation of the mentioned macroeconomic measures and energy sector policies, some intervening variables, such as group interests, might also play a role. For example, the local governments, especially those at the village levels, were very efficient in facilitating the development of TVCMs, which were an important factor for promoting the local economy. The officials who profited from the two-tier pricing system by purchasing at low in-quota prices and selling at high above-quota prices made every possible effort to maintain the system and oppose its abolishment. However, these variables were not the key forces that drove energy policymaking and energy security formation, although their functions cannot be annulled. It was the reform of the national economy and delegation of autonomy that made possible the emergence and development of TVCMs; it was the partial and very careful introduction of 'market forces' that made possible the emergence and development of two-tier pricing of coal and oil. Again, in the early 1990s when the economy was getting better, it was the relaxation of government control over production prices and reduction of the scope of prices administered by the government that finally eliminated the two-tier pricing system of coal and crude oil. Macroeconomic reform was a force too strong to be stopped or reversed. Once initiated, it operates like water rushing out of a floodgate with great energy. Macroeconomic reform thus made itself the key force driving energy policy and forming energy security in China. This key driving force washed away – or at least diminished – all other factors (intervening variables) that may have functioned in China's energy policy promulgation or implementation.

More examples from the 1990s can elaborate on this. For instance, it was the reform measure to save state-owned enterprises (SOEs) that discouraged the development of TVCMs. SOEs reform was one of the key reforms during the time. The aim was to promote the corporatisation of large- and medium-sized SOEs and clarify the property rights, which would facilitate the establishment of a 'market economy'. During the process, the energy sector SOEs were subject to reform as well. In the coal sector, the long-term losses of state coalmines prompted the central government to shut down TVCMs nationwide, which competed with SOEs for resources and markets. As a result, coal production decreased at the turn of the twenty-first century. Many TVCMs, which had long contributed to the Chinese coal supply, were closed down under SOEs reform. Once again, the force of macroeconomic reform dominated. The previous energy policy in the coal sector that had been favourable to the TVCMs and to the coal supply was changed in favour of state coalmines under the reform of SOEs. It is true that conflicts of interest existed and the closure was met with resistance at the local level, as the TVCMs provided an important source of employment and revenue from taxes and fees, but the closure had to be done to provide protection for state mines. At that time, it was SOEs reform that hindered the development of TVCMs. Once again, the 'flood' of macroeconomic reform diminished other (intervening) factors (variables) that might function in energy policy and energy security formation.

Another example that reflects the typical domination of macroeconomic reform is power sector restructuring. In the 1980s, the central government stimulated investments in electricity generation by decentralising the investment authority. Local governments, SOEs, and foreign companies were encouraged to finance and have their own power generation facilities. It is for certain that the introduction of new actors into the electricity sector only changed the Chinese electricity industry from a system exclusively owned and controlled by the central government to a system with dominant central planning and decentralised generation owned by various investors; it did not in any sense shift the underlying corporate governance or regulations in the electricity sector. However, it paved the way for liberalisation in the Chinese electricity market. But, until the 1990s, further liberalisation was blocked by SOEs reform. Instead of injecting the market mechanism further into the electricity sector, reform in the 1990s resulted in the State Power Corporation of China (SPCC) monopolising the sector. Small thermal power plants were shut down to protect state enterprises and the SPCC controlled most of the transmission and distribution assets and half of China's generation assets. SOEs reform in the power sector hindered the creation of a competitive electricity market in China.

To my best knowledge, there is no theory or framework in the relevant discipline that can explain the evolution of energy security in China. Most of the literature on China's energy security, as discussed in Section 1.3, focuses on the international relations perspective, or targets a specific energy sector, without a pan-energy industry view. This literature cannot dynamically explain the 'evolution' of energy security in China along a timeframe. In contrast, the framework of the Macro Economy-driven Energy Security Mechanism provides a completely new perspective that incorporates both quantitative and qualitative analyses that can dynamically explain the 'evolution' of China's energy security along a timeline. This is where the significance of the book lies.

1.6.2. The Scope of the Analytical Framework

The Macro Economy-driven Energy Security Mechanism is an efficient tool for analysing the energy security evolution of a country, particularly countries undergoing economic transition. It incorporates both quantitative and qualitative methodologies that can be extended to other countries. The quantitative methodology is based on well-established economic theories and studies, and is flexible in selecting specific indicators for each dimension of energy security. Therefore, it could be generalised for evaluating the energy policy and energy security of other countries with modified indicators. As long as the key indicators for a country are identified, the energy security situation of that country could be evaluated. The qualitative methodology could also be generalised as every country's macroeconomic policy must, in some way, dominate and manipulate the policies in its specific industrial sector, including the energy sector. The qualitative methodology is new and useful for analysing the energy security of a country from a domestic perspective. It is particularly useful for emerging economies in transition, since they make every effort to utilise reform measures to develop their economies. The macroeconomic reform measure will inevitably cover and affect the country's energy sector, and its energy policies must be subject to the promulgation and implementation of its macroeconomic policies. In this sense, the qualitative analytical framework can also be applied to analyse policies and explain the evolution of other industrial sectors besides the energy sector. This is the contribution of the Macro Economy-driven Energy Security Mechanism as well as the contribution of this book.

1.7. Research Methodology

This study's research and findings are based on information collected from data, reports, journal articles, books, and other scientific works from institutions and think tanks. Additionally, policy documents, such as those issued by the International Energy Agency (IEA), China's State Council, and China's National Development and Reform Commission, are used. A vast amount of data was collected for the research framework. To quantitatively explain China's past energy situation, empirical data were extracted from official reports such as the BP Statistical Review of World Energy, China Statistical Yearbook, China Statistical Yearbook on Science and Technology, and China Energy Statistical Yearbook. Besides printed sources, relevant data were collected online through the websites of international and national institutions. These institutions include but are not limited to the National Bureau of Statistics of China, the U.S. Energy Information Administration, and the IEA. For obvious practical reasons, all empirical data processed in this book are therefore secondary data. However, through different independent empirical sources, objectivity can be extracted for the reliability of these sources.

Extensive quantitative and qualitative research was conducted during my research visits to China. The field research on China's energy security and policies started at Xiamen University in Xiamen, Fujian Province, where I collected data, interviewed scholars, and completed most of the quantitative research. In addition, extensive documentary research was conducted at the National Library of China in Beijing and the Universities Service Centre for China Studies at the Chinese University of Hong Kong. Most of the qualitative part of this book was done at those two places. To describe it in one sentence, the research was conducted by 'digging into the facts' to better answer the proposed research questions.

1.8. Book Structure

The structure of the book is as follows:

Chapter 2 reviews various works related to the concepts, measurements, and frameworks established to quantify energy security in conjunction with an analysis of their contributions to the existing quantitative study of energy security. It also presents an account of the quantitative framework – the 4-As framework. Chapter 3 introduces the respective indicators the 4-As framework uses. It also examines the rigor of the framework and justifies the indicator selection with a discussion of data and measurement issues. Further, it introduces time phases to examine China's energy security and evaluates the security level of each policy period. Chapter 4 explores China's energy policy evolution in detail. A subsection of policy examination from 1949 (founding of the PRC) to 1978 (end of Cultural Revolution) is discussed first. The following subsections within Chapter 4 discuss energy policies from 1981 to 2010 in every possible detail encompassing the Sixth to Eleventh FYPs. The discussion involves an application of the 4-As framework and the quantitative results obtained for each period, which are presented in Chapter 3. The effectiveness of the energy policies in each period is evaluated and a comprehensive picture of China's energy security status throughout history is provided. Chapter 5 gives the reasons for the evolution of China's energy security status and energy policies. It analyses the progress of China's macroeconomic reform during the administrations of Deng Xiaoping, Jiang Zemin, and Hu Jintao, and answers the questions proposed at the beginning of the book. This chapter roots China's energy policies in its macroeconomic reform measures and identifies the key reason behind the evolution of China's energy policies and energy security status. Chapter 6, as an extension of the research, looks into China's energy security situation beyond the domestic perspective. Focusing on the BRI proposed by the Xi Jinping Administration, this chapter explores whether and how the BRI projects can contribute to energy security of China. Chapter 7, the last chapter, reviews the findings, highlights the argument and conclusion, and suggests new areas for future research.

Chapter 2

Energy Security: Concepts, Frameworks and Indicators

This chapter reviews three aspects of research on energy security: the concepts of energy policy and energy security; frameworks established to assess a country's energy security situation; and the indicators used to quantitatively evaluate a country's energy security. Section 2.1 focuses on existing research on the concept of energy policy and energy security. Energy security assessment frameworks in particular are reviewed to establish the 4-As framework used in this book to analyse China's energy security situation. Section 2.2 explains the comprehensive concept of energy security which this book has constructed step by step. Section 2.3 reviews the energy security indicators, based on which China's energy security indicators are selected and constructed in Chapter 3. Section 2.4 gives a brief summary of this chapter.

2.1. Views on Energy Policy and Energy Security

2.1.1. Energy Policy

The concept of 'policy' needs to be clarified before defining 'energy policy'. Policies are 'what governments do or what governments say they do, manifesto commitments or post hoc rationalizations, specific initiatives or by-products of other actions' (McGowan, 1996, p. 132). Energy policy is concerned with energy resources, including renewable and non-renewable resources, and activities to reinforce the efficiency of energy supply and consumption. Energy policies can generally be categorised into official energy policies and unofficial energy policies. Official energy policies are 'clearly elaborated' and 'explicitly formulated' by the government. The official energy policies are normally presented in the form of commitments to particular choices and activity coordination in the energy sector. The unofficial energy policies are those policies that are not dedicated to the energy sector but exert a strong influence in the energy sector, intentionally or incidentally (McGowan, 1996).

Energy policies can also be differentiated by energy policy as a whole and by specific subsets under the general energy policy. Energy policy as a whole refers to a country's policy effort to meet its energy needs. A specific subset, or a specific energy policy, refers to energy policies for an individual energy subsector

Energy Security in Times of Economic Transition: Lessons from China, 17–38

doi:10.1108/978-1-83982-464-720201003

(such as coal, oil, renewable, energy research and development, and energy efficiency) and energy policies dealing with a specific subset such as the welfare of consumers, the environmental impact, safety and health, transportation requirements, employment implications, balance of payments concerns, and geopolitical stresses (Goode, 1980; Prontera, 2009).

2.1.2. Energy Security

Security is an essential prerequisite for the existence and development of a society. The issue of security is a concern that could be extended from the individual to the state, and further to the international community. No matter whose concern it is, security is a sort of 'good' with its value to be protected (Rothschild, 1995). In the twenty-first century, new ways of thinking of security are sought to deal with new threats and new conditions faced by the individuals, states, and international communities. One reason for this is that the function of security has broadened from its military focus to a new perception that encompasses several aspects such as economic, political, environmental, and social ones. Among these aspects, '[e]nergy security is an important component of every country's national security' (Tatalović, 2008, p. 117). Energy insecurity will threaten the functioning of a country's economic, social, and environmental systems, and it is necessary for the country to integrate energy security into its respective national security systems and also formulate energy policies that could guarantee energy security (Tatalović, 2008).

Yet the concept of energy security varies. Due to its polysemic nature, the concept of energy security is 'inherently slippery', hence attempts to clarify the concept of energy security have rarely been made (Chester, 2010). Many academic studies produce definitions for energy security with different components.[1] These definitions can be generally grouped into two categories – the broad sense and the narrow sense. In the broad sense, the common definition for energy security is usually supply oriented[2] and it consists of three elements: reliable supply of energy, adequate supply of energy, and energy supply at reasonable prices. Existing works have attempted to give a systematic and comprehensive definition: the availability of stable and reliable energy supplies at all times in various forms, in sufficient quantities, and at reasonable and/or affordable prices (Bielecki, 2002;

---

[1]Kruyt, van Vuuren, de Vries, and Groenenberg (2009) find that the definitions of energy security have widened over time. Traditionally focusing on physical definition of oil supply, energy security concept began to incorporate the price of energy when oil became a globally traded commodity amid price fluctuations in the world market. When disruptions frequently occurred in the supply chain, energy conversion and transport were mentioned in the concept. The ability to cope with extreme events, such as natural disasters or terrorist actions was sometimes addressed in energy security context. Finally, the political stability of energy supplying appeared in energy security discussions.

[2]In fact, energy security concerns relate equally to energy supply and demand. But most public discussions concentrate on the supply side, especially the external supply sources over which the consuming countries have relatively less control than their domestic supply sources (Bielecki, 2002).

Chang & Lee, 2008; Clingendael International Energy Programme, 2004; IEA, 2007a; Lin, 2009a; Yergin, 1988). However, no energy system, no matter in the short run or in the long run, can be entirely secure. Therefore, energy security can be seen as 'a problem of risk management' which involves 'reducing to an acceptable level the risks and consequences of disruptions and adverse long-term market trends' (IEA, 2007a, p. 161). In this regard, to promote energy security, three key pillars are put forward: energy efficiency, diversification of energy supplies, and minimising energy price volatility (World Bank Group, 2005). Along this line of thought, the three key elements attributed to energy security mentioned earlier have emerged: adequacy, reliability, and a reasonable price. The meaning of adequacy and reliability is easy to understand. It is uninterrupted supply that fully meets the global demand. A reasonable price, however, is less easy to interpret. In general, a reasonable price should be determined by the market which is based on supply–demand balance (Bielecki, 2002). That is to say, a reasonable price is devoid of excessive market power and it does not adversely affect the economic performance of a country (APERC, 2007; Chang & Lee, 2008). Following the three key elements, energy security, in a broad sense, is having an adequate and reliable supply of energy at a reasonable price.

In a narrow sense, energy security refers mainly to primary energy security or oil security which means that it is concerned with the security of primary energy resources, oil in particular (Fried & Trezise, 1993). This oil security focus directs a country's energy security attention to hedge against an 'oil supply crisis', aiming at reducing vulnerability to foreign supply disruption in order to minimise the economic and military costs once such a disruption occurs (Vivoda, 2010). Energy security in the narrow sense mainly covers the economic or national welfare aspect of the disruption of energy supply. It is 'the loss of economic welfare that may occur as a result of a change in the price or availability of energy' (Bohi & Toman, 1996, p. 1). It is the ability of nations to secure supplies of fuels, primarily fossil fuels, especially crude oil and petroleum fuels at reasonable prices, and the capabilities to stave off oil crises (Nautilus Institute for Security and Sustainable Development, 1998).

Energy security issue involves time dimensions generally grouped into short-term energy security and long-term energy security. The short-term energy security deals with the risks of disruption to existing supplies, mainly due to technical problems or sudden political incidents. The long-term energy security covers the issue of investment for potential energy supplies to meet growing energy demand in the long run (Bielecki, 2002). Long-term energy security in the narrow sense is 'a proxy of the certainty level at which the population in a defined area has uninterrupted access to fossil fuels and fossil fuel-based energy carriers in the absence of undue exposure to supply-side market power over a period ahead of 10 years or longer' (Jansen & Seebregts, 2010, p. 1654), which means 'the energy sector does not cause (major) welfare-reducing frictions in the economy at national and global levels' (Loschel et al., 2010, p. 1666). That is to say, long-term strategy for energy supply security must be geared to ensuring the well-being of a country's citizens and the proper functioning of the country's economy (European Commission, 2001).

Although not expressed as completely and explicitly as the broad definition, the narrow sense also includes three elements of energy security: reliability, adequacy, and reasonable price. Hedging against (oil) crisis and making national welfare intact amid the crisis serve as a country's means for achieving energy adequacy, reliability, and reasonable price. These three elements cover several different dimensions.

The first dimension is the economic dimension, which could be depicted by the term availability and affordability. Availability is about energy supply. An implicit factor of availability entails the guaranteed supply and minimum dependence on foreign energy supply at the same time. High level of dependence on foreign energy supply is always a concern for policymakers who are responsible for making energy available to the country (Klare, 2007). Another related aspect of availability which could offset the negative effects of foreign dependency is diversification. To put it simply, this requires a country to diversify its energy sources, energy suppliers, and locations of energy facilities. Affordability is another important principle of energy security. Affordability is generally understood as a reasonable energy price. An important element implied in affordability is that the price should be reasonable to not only the rich people, but also the poor. This requires making access to energy services equitable for everyone. Affordability also requires stability of energy prices and consumers' access to a broad range of high-quality energy services (Sovacool & Brown, 2010).

The second dimension deals with energy efficiency and technology. Energy efficiency, to put it simply, is to maximise production by minimising the input of energy. The efficiency improvements could be realised by substituting fuels or by changing the consumption habits or patterns. This relates energy efficiency to demand-side management. It has been argued that demand-side management is a new factor to be added in the energy security concept. A conventional concept of energy security tends to be supply oriented and assumes that energy demand is given but demand-side risks are not less than the supply side. For example, either demand surges during prosperity or supply surpluses during recession puts pressure on a society's energy balance, hence demand-side management is also a key component of a comprehensive concept of energy security (von Hippel, Suzuki, Williams, Savage, & Hayes, 2011). A key implicit element under this dimension is technology innovation which comprises a set of processes that lead to new or improved energy technologies to amplify energy resources, enhance the quality of energy services, and reduce negative externalities related with energy supply and use (Gallagher, Holdren, & Sagar, 2006). As the world moves towards a technology-based energy society, the concept of energy security must address the various issues associated with technology application and innovation (von Hippel et al., 2011).

On the basis of these two dimensions, a new dimension – the environmental dimension – has been added to the energy security concept as environmental protection increasingly attracts public attention. During the combustion of fossil fuels, energy-related emissions of greenhouse gases have become the main source of environmental deterioration and climate change. To mitigate climate change, the emissions have to be reduced by changing the way energy is produced and utilised (IEA, 2007b). Climate change is a 'threat multiplier' for national security, which is inextricably linked to a country's energy security (CNA Military

Advisory Board, 2007). If environmental problem such as climate change is to be solved, energy security policies must be reformulated. Mitigating climate change and protecting the environment are necessary to guarantee energy security (von Hippel et al., 2011). Definitions of energy security with the environmental factor interpret energy security as a country's ability to guarantee the availability of energy resource supply in a sustainable manner, and at the same time, stressing that the energy price shall be reasonable (APERC, 2007). The European Commission contends that the European Union's long-term strategy for energy security is to ensure uninterrupted physical availability of energy products at an affordable price for both private and industrial consumers, and respect for environmental concerns and sustainable development (European Commission, 2000). The United Nations Development Programme defines energy security as 'the availability of energy at all times in various forms, in sufficient quantities, and at affordable prices, without unacceptable or irreversible impact on the environment' (UNDP, 2004, p. 42).[3] All these definitions incorporate the factor of environmental sustainability in energy security concept.

Apart from these dimensions, some other factors are also identified as new challenges that shall be incorporated as dimensions in the concept of energy security. Social–cultural factors are among them. Not in my backyard (NIMBY) and other environmental justice concerns make it difficult and costly to site power plants and dispose wastes from energy production and utilisation. Opposition to plant siting has forced the government to adjust or reformulate energy policies. Social and cultural factors must be recognised when decisions need to be made (Nautilus Institute for Security and Sustainable Development, 1998; von Hippel et al., 2011). International relations and foreign policies must be counted in as a dimension of energy security. A country shall commit itself to international co-operation on energy-related issues. Although there is no impending threat of another world war, the threats of regional conflicts, nuclear terrorism, and proliferation still exist. These issues need to be addressed by the concept of energy security (Alhajji, 2007; Vivoda, 2010; von Hippel et al., 2011). Human security has also been argued to be incorporated into the concept of energy security which means providing basic energy services such as making electricity accessible to the entire population. Energy security policy and regulation have even been argued as a new dimension: a country without a clearly stated energy security policy may not have the capacity and/or commitment to ensure energy security (Vivoda, 2010). The country should also have legitimate and participatory modes of energy policymaking and its energy consumers should be well informed of the policies (Sovacool & Mukherjee, 2011).

Besides the previous academic discussion on energy security, there are many other conceptions of energy security derived from different points of views. Different energy stakeholders, such as consumers, producers, and policymakers, have different perspectives on energy security (Birol, 2006). For example, from the consumer point of view, energy security for them is simply reasonably priced energy

---

[3]Acceptability to the environment and sustainability are used synonymously here when energy security is defined.

services without disruption. In contrast, from the producer point of view, energy security is about their access to new reserves and the demand for their products. From the politician point of view, energy security is to secure energy resources and infrastructure against terrorism or war. Different national geology and geography may also lead to different conceptions of energy security (Sovacool & Brown, 2010). It appears that the perspectives on energy security vary depending on the beholder's position in the value chain (World Economic Forum, 2006).

It could be seen from the previous discussion that the notions of energy security can be either narrow or broad but drawbacks exist in both senses. The narrow concepts may neglect the comprehensiveness of energy challenges, while the broad concepts may lack precision and coherence. Energy security is an issue so complex that a holistic approach is needed to address it so as to 'capture the complexity of the concept' (Sovacool & Mukherjee, 2011, p. 5346). A few attempts of 'holistic notions' have been put forward. One describes energy security as a situation where five characteristics dominate the whole energy system: surety, survivability, supply, sufficiency, and sustainability (the 'five Ss') (Kleber, 2009).[4] Similar notions are addressed by several 'As': energy resource availability, accessibility barriers, environmental acceptability, and investment cost affordability (APERC, 2007); or availability, adequacy of capacity, affordability, and sustainability (Chester, 2008). Sovacool and Brown (2010) argue that 'energy security should be based on the interconnected factors of availability, affordability, efficiency, and environmental stewardship' (p. 81). In a later work, a 'regulation and governance' dimension has been included so that energy security involves availability, affordability, technology and development efficiency, environmental and social sustainability, and regulation and governance (Sovacool & Mukherjee, 2011). To summarise, energy security is a concept of multiple dimensions that assumes different characteristics depending on the country, energy source, or time frame.

Based on the dimensions of energy security, frameworks could be established to assess a country's energy security performance. The following sub-section discusses the frameworks constructed for the assessment.

2.1.3. Assessment Frameworks for Energy Security

Frameworks for assessing energy security are a kind of new tool for energy security evaluation. These frameworks are created on the basis of the new comprehensive concepts of energy security that incorporate new dimensions.

---

[4]By this description, surety is '[a] condition which provides access to energy and fuel sources'; survivability means 'energy and fuel sources are resilient and durable in the face of potential damage'; supply suggests '[an] identified and available source of energy, whether it is traditional fossil fuels, alternative energy or renewable energy'; sufficiency means 'an adequate quantity of power and fuel from a variety of sources'; and sustainability requires operating practices 'be perpetuated by limiting demand, reducing waste and effectively utilizing alternative energy and renewable resources to the maximum extent possible' (Kleber, 2009).

(1) A 3-A Framework

An early framework, suggested by Chang and Yong (2007), is developed to analyse the perspectives of major oil firms including their perceptions of energy developments and projections of energy potentials. The analytical framework is made up by three As dimensions: availability of resource (AV), applicability of technology (AP), and acceptability by society (AC). Each dimension has three indicators to quantify the dimension. Although the framework is not directly used to assess a country's energy security situation, its reference meaning is obvious.

Among the three As, AV is about oil firms' resource exploration effort. This dimension could also be subsumed in the energy security concept as the resources available for a country include fossil fuels and renewable energy resources. AP is about the oil firms' perspectives on the possibility of a resource switch. This dimension could be subsumed in the energy security concept as technological advancement for harnessing more fossil fuels and new energy resources. AC is about the oil firms' attitude towards the balance between self-interested profit maximisation and desired benefits of using alternative fuels for environmental protection. This dimension could be subsumed in the energy security concept as public's environmental concern and the government's concern about the pollution caused by fossil fuel utilisation.

(2) Four-Dimensional Framework

The classification scheme of the four dimensions to depict energy security is first proposed by APERC (2007), which presents three fundamental elements of energy security: physical energy security, including the availability and accessibility of energy supply; economic energy security, mainly focusing on the affordability of resource acquisition and environmental sustainability. Later, a four-dimensional grid of availability, adequacy of capacity, affordability, and sustainability is proposed to assess the impact of Australia's existing and potential policies and government actions on its energy supply security (Chester, 2008).[5] This approach supposes that all four dimensions contribute to energy security, rather than any one dimension as a primary determinant. Only when all dimensions are considered, implications of such an approach for policymakers can become discernible. This approach is an attempt for 'more holistic conceptualisations of energy security' (Chang & Lee, 2008, p. 110) so that a broader understanding of a country's energy security situation could be achieved.

By applying the four-dimensional framework, Chester (2008) examines Australia's existing and proposed policies that drive the country's energy security in terms of each of the four energy security dimensions. Specific definitions are given for the four dimensions and the impact of Australia's public policies on each of the four dimensions is assessed. The notion of energy security is thus directly and closely connected with a country's public policies that are related with energy. By this methodology, policy impact could be effectively assessed, future projections could be predicted, and the development path to make a country energy secure could be identified. The four-dimensional framework serves as a valuable reference for this study as it connects the notion of energy security with a country's energy policies.

[5]The four-dimensional approach has been reaffirmed by Chester (2010).

This four-dimensional approach is a heuristic one for further research. It directly relates a country's energy policy to the notion of energy security, and it assesses policy by the notion of energy security via the four-dimensional framework. But this approach does not provide any indicators or quantification tools that can directly explain how well a country has been doing on the development/improvement of any one dimension of energy security. The inherent weakness in detecting progress in any dimension has been improved by the methodologies proposed by subsequent researches on energy security assessment frameworks.

(3) Other Four-Dimensional Frameworks: Extension and Application

Based on the four dimensions of energy security established by APERC (2007), Kruyt, van Vuuren, de Vries, and Groenenberg (2009) classify energy security dimensions as follows: availability, accessibility, affordability, and acceptability of energy. With these four dimensions, they allocate indicators for energy security and incorporate these indicators in a model-based scenario analysis. An energy security spectrum has been created based on the different perspectives on globalisation versus regionalisation, and on economic efficiency versus environmental and societal targets, as well as the four dimensions of energy security, which offers a schematic framework for energy security discussion. Fig. 2.1 depicts the spectrum of the framework.

Four different storylines are presented in Fig. 2.1: A1 and B1 represent a situation where a high level of globalisation is expected: A1 focuses on economic efficiency, whereas B1 focuses on environmental and societal targets. A2 and B2 represent a situation where a low level of globalisation is expected: A2 focusing on economic efficiency, whereas B2 focuses on environmental and societal targets.

However, the authors use scenarios for the future analysis rather than directly apply the four different storylines to evaluate energy policy. Their work is not to

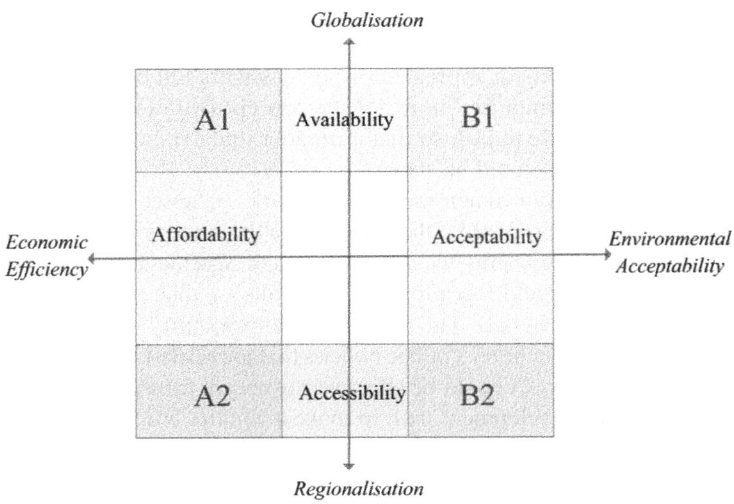

Fig. 2.1. The Energy Security Spectrum. *Source*: Kruyt et al. (2009), Redrawn by the Author.

evaluate the past or current energy policy effectiveness or energy security situation, but to project future energy security situations. With the classified indicators for energy security, they analyse energy security of Western Europe for the next few decades. They explore the applicability of different energy security indicators and assert that it would be better to use a wide range of indicators that cover the different relevant aspects when energy security trends are being assessed.

Their approach is suitable for analysing the future energy security situation and for exploring the applicability of energy security indicators. However, it cannot project an overall multi-faceted energy security situation on the basis of the four dimensional scheme. For this purpose, indicators have to be strictly positioned under individual dimensions so that a comprehensive and overall energy security status could be depicted.

Another four-dimensional framework is based on four interconnected factors of availability, affordability, energy and economic efficiency, and environmental stewardship (see Sovacool & Brown, 2010). A total of 10 indicators, which constitute an Energy Security Index, are developed to measure (the four dimensions of) energy security performance of 22 countries belonging to Organisation for Economic Co-operation and Development (OECD) from 1970 to 2007. Data are collected on these 10 indicators for the 22 countries. Then the relative energy security progress of each country according to each indicator is assessed. The conclusion is that most of the countries have fallen back in their effort to improve their energy security.

Although these 10 indicators, as the authors assert, are 'valid representations' of how well countries have performed with regard to energy security, the indicators 'often highlight not what is most significant or meaningful but merely what is measurable' (Sovacool & Brown, 2010, p. 87). With this kept in mind, the indicators incorporated in such dimensional framework shall not be too many, as this may complicate the concept and lead to double-counting as discussed; whereas the indicators shall not be too few, as this may omit some important aspects of the relevant dimension, such that the notion of the dimension cannot be fully reflected.

This raises the question as to how many indicators should be developed for each dimension. There is no common criterion for this, but it should be kept in mind that the indicators should reflect the notion of the dimension as completely as possible, while at the same time reduce complexity and avoid double-counting. The indicators selected by the Sovacool and Brown (2010)'s four-dimensional framework may not be enough. For example, under the environmental stewardship dimension, only two indicators are selected: SO_2 emissions and CO_2 emissions. Other aspects such as soot emissions and wastes associated with the processing of nuclear fuel are not included. Such omissions make the indicators insufficient and incomplete. These omitted indicators are nonetheless also important energy-related ones as far as the environmental dimension of energy security is concerned.

(4) A Five-Dimensional Framework

Sovacool and Mukherjee (2011) suggested a framework encompassing five dimensions of energy security: availability, affordability, technology development and efficiency, environmental and social sustainability, and regulation and governance.[6] They also suggested 320 simple indicators and 52 complex indicators which could be used to measure a country's energy security performance. This framework synthesises their earlier literature on energy security measurement and quantification into a condensable number of indicators looking at multiple dimensions simultaneously. However, the large set of indicators leads to a weakness of over-quantification as it involves a huge amount of data, making it difficult to find patterns in a country's energy security performance. This eventually leads to cost-ineffectiveness. Another weakness is the overlapping as many of the indicators are mutually non-exclusive, making it impractical for energy security measurement. Further, it is less possible to collect data for all of the proposed energy security indicators, let alone some indicators are overlapping and redundant.

What was suggested in conceptual design of energy security has been finalised and presented by Sovacool, Mukherjee, Drupady, and D'Agostino (2011) in their framework containing 5 dimensions and 20 indicators in total. They try to evaluate national energy security policies and performance of 18 countries across the American, European, and Asian continents. To make the index (scoring of country performance) empirical and relative, all of the collected data points are transformed to a score between 0 and 100. Several indirect indicators were included in the work while as many direct indicators as possible are not included. The indirect indicators here refer to the indicators that are not closely associated with the notion of energy security. For example, as far as environmental sustainability is concerned, forest cover is selected as an evaluating indicator. This indicator, which measures forest area as percent of land area, is not closely related with the direct result of energy production and consumption, which is, as the authors state, only 'loosely connected to issues such as suburbanization, mining, and industrial development' (Sovacool et al., 2011, p. 5849). This study adheres to the principle that key direct indicators should first be selected; indirect indicators should supplement the list when direct indicators are not available. Therefore, some of their indicators are adopted whereas some are rejected.

(5) Frameworks with More Multiple Dimensions

Some scholars use six dimensions to evaluate and measure global energy security (von Hippel et al., 2011). The six dimensions are energy supply, economic, technological, environmental, socio-cultural, and military-security dimensions. They are largely designed to identify the relative benefits and costs of the future energy paths driven by energy policies. Building on these dimensions, an energy security assessment instrument is established to evaluate energy security in the Asia-Pacific region (Vivoda, 2010). To make the instrument more robust and complete, five more dimensions were included to evaluate a country's energy security in addition to the six dimensions created by von Hippel et al. (2011). The five new dimensions are demand management, efficiency, human security, international, and policy (Vivoda, 2010).

[6]This framework is actually an extension of the framework proposed by Sovacool and Brown (2010). The framework has been refined by Sovacool, Mukherjee, Drupady, and D'Agostino (2011).

The problem of over-disaggregation in the dimensions of energy security exists in both frameworks. The framework developed by Vivoda (2010) even has 11 dimensions. In fact, some dimensions are overlapping while some dimensions are not a direct energy security issue. Over-disaggregation only makes the concept of energy security less structured and more complicated. This is destructive not only for indicators selection but also for the formulation of quantitative tools to analyse a country's energy policies and their impact on energy security. Both von Hippel et al. (2011) and Vivoda (2010) frameworks have indicators to measure energy security, but over-disaggregation and the potential overlapping of the dimensions may lead to double-counting when indicators relevant to these dimensions are used to assess a country's energy security. Although both frameworks establish an energy security assessment instrument to analyse energy security of individual countries or regions, they are not applied in the assessment.

(6) Frameworks Evaluating China's Energy Security

Zhang (2007) and Chang (2010) use the Analytic Hierarchical Process (AHP) to establish evaluation frameworks incorporating indicators to assess China's energy security status. Chang (2010)'s framework is built up as Fig. 2.2. The first layer, layer A, reflects the framework's goal to evaluate China's energy security. The second layer, layer B, reflects different dimensions (or consisting of components) of China's energy security. The third layer, layer C, consists of energy security indicators. Zhang (2007)'s framework is similar, except for further categorisation of layer B into two sub-layers, which is illustrated in Fig. 2.3.

As illustrated in Fig. 2.3, Zhang (2007)'s concept of energy security consists of six factors including energy structure (Factor 1), utilisation of renewable energy (Factor 2), energy consumption from foreign sources (Factor 3), international energy transportation (Factor 4), domestic energy reserves (Factor 5), and energy strategic reserves (Factor 6). Under these factors, 11 indicators are selected. They are oil reserve to production ratio (D_{01}), share of oil out of total primary energy (D_{02}), share of independent overseas energy exploitation out of total imports (D_{03}), share of renewable energy consumption (D_{04}), oil import dependence (D_{05}), total energy

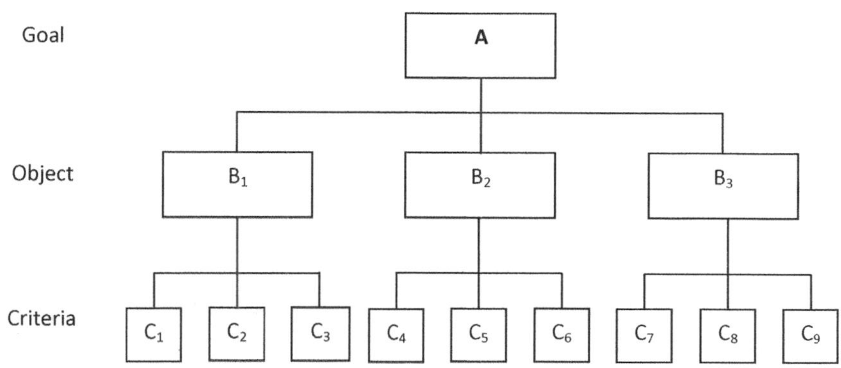

Fig. 2.2. A General Framework Evaluating Energy Security in China.
Source: Chang (2010), Redrawn by the Author.

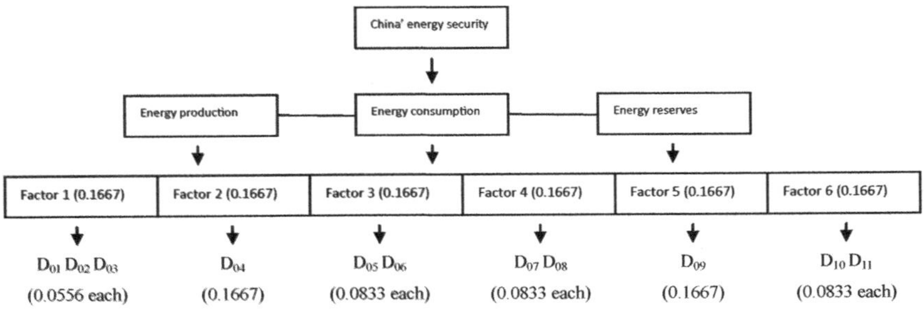

Fig. 2.3. A Detailed Framework Evaluating Energy Security in China.
Source: Zhang (2007), Redrawn by the Author.

imports (D_{06}), import concentration (D_{07}), energy transportation capability (D_{08}), oil consumption per capita (D_{09}), energy reserves (D_{10}), and days of guaranteed energy reserves (oil) (D_{11}). The weight is averagely assigned to the six factors of energy security, which is 0.1667 (1/6) to each factor. Since different number of indicators is allocated to different factors, the weight of each indicator is not the same. D_{01}, D_{02}, and D_{03} are incorporated in the energy structure factor, hence the weight of 0.0556 (0.1667/3) is assigned to each of the three indicators. The utilisation of renewable energy factor only has one indicator, D_{04}. Thus the weight assigned to D_{04} is 0.1667. The rest indicators are allocated weight in the same methodology. The factors and indicators indicate that Zhang (2007)'s framework is obviously constructed on a narrow concept of energy security, which only focuses on the energy supply adequacy.

Chang (2010)'s framework incorporates 24 indicators under six dimensions including energy reserves, energy imports, energy consumption, energy awareness, technology, and environment. The multiple dimensions indicate that his framework is based on a comprehensive concept of energy security. The problem is that several dimensions, such as energy awareness, are too subjective and cannot be normally treated as an energy security dimension. The value of certain indicators such as 'national awareness of energy conservation' and 'national sense of social responsibility' could only be given very subjectively, which may be controversial and involve inaccuracies.

The AHP methodology has also been used to construct the framework to evaluate China's oil security. The framework consists of three layers. The first layer is oil security which comprehensively reflects China's oil security status. The second layer comprises four factors influencing oil security: resource, import, market, and other factors. The third layer has 12 indicators whereby three indicators are assigned to each factor. By assigning value and weight to each indicator, oil security index is calculated. It is concluded that China's oil security has been worsening since 1991 (Zhang & Liu, 2005).

2.2. The Concept of Energy Security – A Need for a Holistic Approach

The previous review on the concept of energy security and the frameworks established to evaluate the level of energy security shows that the notion of energy security has become multi-dimensional. It is noteworthy that different dimensions of energy security are frequently conflicting with each other. A policy which is effective for one dimension of energy security may erode other dimensions. For example, affordability may be competing with applicability and acceptability. Energy price controls which result in artificially low prices may dampen the users' interests in energy conservation and the producers' interests in developing clean energy technologies (Herring, 2006). Empirical examples illustrate the competition between different dimensions of energy security. The transnational energy projects within Thailand, Laos, and Myanmar, including the construction of a gas pipeline and various mega-dam projects enhanced the availability of energy supply. However, such projects benefited mostly the middle class and elite circles in the urban centres and can be environmentally destructive, thus contributing little to the overall energy security for the grassroots (Simpson, 2007). Achievements in one dimension of energy security may impinge on other dimensions while different dimensions of energy security may reinforce each other as well. For example, new technologies and increased energy efficiency may actually lower the implicit price of energy and thus make energy more affordable (Herring, 2006). This may lead to higher energy consumption as well.

The multi-dimensions of energy security make a more comprehensive concept of energy security imperative, as well as a workable framework for energy policy analysis.[7] The comprehensive concept shall include these multiple dimensions, instead of highlighting only one or two aspects of energy security. The functional framework, established on the basis of the comprehensive concept, will be a useful tool for evaluation of a country's energy security performance in a realistic way. This means that achieving energy security in one dimension does not necessarily make a country 'energy secure' in a holistic sense. For example, a country may have enough energy available, but if the energy is not generally affordable, or harnessing or utilising the energy seriously pollutes the environment, the country simply cannot be considered as more 'energy secure'. Therefore, traditional and narrow conceptualisation of energy security cannot help establish a workable framework for the analysis of energy security in a broader and more comprehensive sense (Vivoda, 2010). With this in mind, this research constructs a comprehensive energy security definition as a starting point to examine China's energy security policies. Only a comprehensive view can ensure that all key dimensions are factored into the successful pursuit of energy security.

Section 2.1 has reviewed concepts of energy security and its dimensions. Although the literature on energy security definitions does not have a clear historical line, they exhibit, to some extent, a historical evolution of the concept. First, all definitions, broad or narrow and with whatever dimensions incorporated in the

---

[7]With regard to the mentioned reviewed energy security concepts that are 'polysemic in nature' (Chester, 2010), it is not practical to seek a common definition of energy security, nor does this book try to do so. This research proposes a comprehensive multi-dimensional definition which is suitable for the establishment of an analytical framework for assessing China's overall energy security situation.

concept, stress the economic aspect of energy security. The supply of energy to a nation must be 'adequate' and 'reliable' and energy prices must be 'reasonable' or 'affordable' to the population. To interpret this alternatively, a country must hedge against the risk of inaccessibility to energy resources or fluctuation of energy prices. This is the emergence of the first dimension – the economic dimension – of energy security. Later on, rapid economic development and huge amount of energy consumption require the efficient use of energy. Demand for more energy resources and energy efficiency improvement require technological innovation. Accordingly, the second dimension – the technological dimension – of energy security has been incorporated in the concept. When environmental deterioration began to threat ecosystem and human health, energy harnessing and utilisation had created a major source of environmental pollution. Therefore, environmental protection is taken into account by including the third dimension – the environmental dimension – in the concept of energy security. Nevertheless, it must be noted that these 'dimensions' are only implicitly expressed in the broad and narrow definitions. The notion of 'dimension' (or 'aspect', or 'theme') has only been recently introduced in the interpretation of the concept of energy security.[8]

Along with the social development and change in domestic and international conditions, more dimensions are included in the concept: social factors, international relations, human security, and energy policy and regulations. Continually adding dimensions to the concept makes energy security just 'like a Rorschach inkblot test', and 'you can see whatever you want to see in it' (Sovacool & Mukherjee, 2011, p. 5346). This research, as previously mentioned, constructs a comprehensive definition, but this research does not seek to incorporate as many dimensions that have arisen in the literature as possible but selects an absolutely minimum number of dimensions. As mentioned previously, some dimensions or factors have been too 'disaggregated', which means that they are actually not necessarily to be listed as an individual dimension. For example, social factors have been suggested as a new dimension for the concept of energy security (von Hippel et al., 2011). It is argued that 'NIMBY' and other environmental justice concerns make it necessary for the government to take into account the social and cultural factors in energy policy decision-making. This is another mode of environmental concerns. These two dimensions are merged into one dimension in this research – acceptability by society, which will be discussed later in more detail. Some other dimensions such as the international relations, energy policies, and regulations are, by themselves, not issues in the concept of energy security. They are the 'tools' or 'means' to achieve energy security.

This book maintains that a comprehensive and holistic approach should be taken to define energy security. At the same time, the historical line along the evolution of energy security concept should also be respected. First, fossil fuels face the constraint of a declining rate of production. They will be used in the order of availability; the most cheaply available one is used first (Hotelling, 1931). This means that sometime before or at the ultimate depletion of a fossil fuel,

[8]See APERC (2007), Chang and Yong (2007), Chester (2010), Sovacool and Brown (2010), Sovacool and Mukherjee (2011), Sovacool et al. (2011), Vivoda (2010), and von Hippel et al. (2011).

other fossil fuel or renewable energy resources will replace the existing resource to ensure adequate supply of energy, which is the fundamental requirement to guarantee energy security. This is the first dimension incorporated in the concept of energy security by this research – availability of resources (AV).

Technology is required for harnessing and utilising energy. A more advanced technology is required for harnessing resources which are not readily extractable. Technological advancement in the exploration and production of fossil fuels can expand the recoverable fossil resources base. It can also promote the utilisation of new energy sources by continued research and development of renewable energy technology. Hence, technologies for finding and extracting fossil and renewable resources are also the determining factors for the availability of resources (Nordhaus, 1979; Doriana, Franssen, & Simbeck, 2006). For example, conversion of coal and biomass into liquids offers possible alternative sources of transportation fuel in the future (Chang & Yong, 2007). Applying (advanced) technologies in harnessing and utilising energy resources guarantee (and enhance) the availability of energy resources. This is the second dimension of energy security – applicability of technologies (AP).

Third, energy and the environment are closely connected. While fossil fuels are considered a threat to the environment, especially through the greenhouse effect, using so-called environmentally clean energy resources can harm the environment as well. Utilisation of hydropower will be detrimental to the local ecosystem and nuclear power plants will seriously damage the environment if nuclear and radiation accidents occur. Hence, a more ecological view of energy security is needed (Mulligan, 2010). When environmental protection has become a prominent issue for the international community, the latter will advocate using safer and cleaner energy resources and greener methods of energy production and consumption. Social and environmental concerns are an indispensable element of the contemporary energy regime. This is the third dimension of energy security – acceptability by society (AC).

Fourth and last, all the mentioned dimensions, including objective conditions (availability of resources) and subjective effort (applicability of technologies and acceptability by society), have one common goal – to make energy resources affordable to the population. Affordability comprises three elements: reasonable and stable energy prices, equitable access to energy resources, and high quality of energy resources provided to consumers. This constitutes the fourth dimension of energy security – affordability of energy prices (AF).

Having said these, energy security is a comprehensive notion which encompasses four dimensions of AV, AP, AC, and AF. An 'energy secure' nation is a nation that has affordable energy resources with an adequate reserves of fossil fuels, nuclear energy, and renewable resources, advanced technologies applied to energy harnessing and utilisation, and at the same time, addressing social and environmental concerns. On the basis of these four A-dimensions incorporated in the energy security concept, an analytical framework is established to examine China's energy security level and the effectiveness of its energy policies in achieving energy security. The framework provides a tool for energy policy evaluation from an interdisciplinary perspective: availability, applicability, acceptability, and affordability. It must be noted that though the concept rests on multiple interconnected dimensions, it is more than the sum of these dimensions. The 4-As framework, established on the basis of the concept of energy security, is a dynamic framework whereby all the four dimensions interact with each other. The framework, as Sovacool and Mukherjee (2011) likened, constitutes a comprehensive system akin to an ecosystem comprising individual species interacting with each other within the system. To quantify energy security, each dimension incorporated in the dynamic framework needs to be elaborated by quantitative indicators, which shall reflect each dimension as accurately as possible. Existing literature on energy security indicators is heuristic, serving as a guide in identifying and formulating the indicators under each dimension. The next section discusses the energy security indicators.

2.3. The Quantification of Energy Security: Indicators Identification

Indicators are an instrument that provides information on a specific measurement. Indicators selection could be generally grouped into two categories: identification and formulation. The identification stage involves brainstorming on all the possible or potential indicators. At the formulation stage, indicators are formulated. This section focuses on the identification stage and reviews the existing energy-related indicators.[9] Indicators formulated to examine China's energy security will be addressed in Chapter 3, which focuses on quantitative discussion about the evolution of China's energy security over 30 years' economic reform from 1980 till 2010.

Considering that energy security is closely related to energy policies, it is necessary to 'study the energy security consequences of different development pathways' (Kruyt et al., 2009, p. 2166). To study the consequences/impact of energy policies, energy security indicators are needed to analyse the energy security performance of a country, which is the quantification of energy security. Energy security measure needs to be quantifiable for analytical purposes (DBERR, 2007). Quantification of policy measures is not a new thing. The 1992 Earth Summit has recognised the important role of indicators in helping countries to make informed decisions concerning sustainable development (Vera & Langlois, 2007). Indicators constitute a key tool and are primarily important for making policies and monitoring progress in policy implementation, and evaluating the effectiveness of the policies. The indicators are designed to answer the question: 'How might I know objectively whether things are getting better or getting worse?' (Lawrence, 1997, p. 181). Specifically in quantifying and assessing energy security, the indicators can assess energy policy effectiveness and indicate a desired state of energy security (Scheepers, Seebregts, de Jong, & Maters, 2006; Tönjes & de Jong, 2007). In addition, the indicators condense 'large amounts of complex data into recognizable patterns' so that policymakers and analysts could 'find the best energy solutions'; the indicators could also help us 'understand how dimensions of energy security improve or worsen over time' (Sovacool & Mukherjee, 2011, p. 5346).

[9]The review in this section does not include the indicators adopted by the analysing frameworks reviewed in Section 2.2: Views on energy policy and energy security, but the framework indicators in Section 2.2 also serve as important references during the identification stage of energy security indicators.

Energy security indicators have been gathering momentum within the last two decades. There is plenty of literature on the measurement and indicators of energy security. Several institutions have constructed the quantitative measurement of energy security such as IEA,[10] OECD,[11] UN,[12] IAEA, APERC, HELIO International,[13] and the Clingendael International Energy Programme. Absolute

[10]The IEA has been developing energy indicators since the 1990s. The IEA's first book on the subject is *Indicators of Energy Use and Efficiency: Understanding the link between energy and human activity* (IEA, 1997a). Later, in the book *The Link between Energy and Human Activity*, IEA (1997b) demonstrates how a system of relatively straightforward indicators of energy use has been developed. Indicators in this book describe the links between energy use and human activity in a detailed way. These are the early works IEA has endeavoured to link the indicators of energy use and efficiency to carbon emissions.

[11]The OECD Group on the State of the Environment has developed indicators for the integration of environmental concerns into energy policies, which are called energy–environment indicators and are structured around three themes: sectoral trends of environmental significance, environmental impacts of the energy sector, and economic linkages between energy and the environment (OECD, 1993). These energy–environment indicators are further approved by OECD conference 'Towards Sustainable Development: Indicators to Measure Progress' held in Rome in 1999. This conference shows that these energy–environment indicators that depict aspects of sustainable development have been widely used for policy purposes (OECD, 2000).

[12]In 1998, the Division of Sustainable Development of the United Nations Department of Economic and Social Affairs (DSD) established a set of indicators to measure changes in consumption and production patterns of key resources such as energy, materials, water, and land. In terms of energy, four key indicators are identified. They are annual energy consumption per capita, which monitors energy consumption; intensity of energy use, which monitors energy use per unit of production/service; share of renewable energy in total energy consumption, which monitors the development of renewable energy sources; and energy prices, which monitor energy prices in relation to GDP and disposable income (DSD, 1998).

[13]HELIO International, an international non-governmental network, has undertaken to assess and monitor the contribution of energy policies. For this purpose, HELIO created the Sustainable Energy Watch (SEW) reports, which are based on a set of eight indicators to reflect four aspects of sustainability at the national level: economic, social, technological, and environmental sustainability. According to HELIO, energy systems should be consistent with these four aspects to be conducive to eco-development. In practice, however, not all of these four aspects can be accommodated at the same time. It is important for the government to take into consideration all these aspects in policymaking whereas at the same time trade off the benefits and costs among them. Therefore, indicators are to be designed to measure how these aspects are traded off in a country. Specifically, the SEW reports by HELIO can be used by governments to better promote sustainable development through energy policies and the set of indicators in the reports indicates a country's progress towards energy-related sustainability (HELIO International, 2005/2006). HELIO International indicators therefore constitute an important reference for the indicators selection in this book.

quantification of energy security is still a very complex issue. Every approach to design energy security indicators faces the problem of subjective arbitrariness in defining the relative value of different components in the process of constructing energy security indicators. This section presents the key indicators in the development of energy security quantification. Some are simple indicators dealing with one aspect of energy security; others are aggregated indicators with the attempt to capture several relevant elements in a single indicator.

2.3.1. Simple Energy Security Indicators

Simple indicators are frequently used to measure a particular aspect of energy security. There are many such indicators and they take various forms. For example, energy import dependency, a commonly used simple indicator, shows the extent to which a country relies on imports to meet its energy needs. Energy intensity gives an indication of the effectiveness with which energy is being used to produce added value. Energy self-sufficiency rate deals with the degree that a country does not depend on energy imports. Energy price volatility reflects the impact of fluctuation of energy prices on energy security. A reserve to production ratio indicates the years of production left at current production levels. Energy price indicates the nature of the supply–demand relations and measures the economic impact of energy on energy security. Share of zero-carbon fuels measures a country's effort to switch away from a carbon intensive fuel portfolio (Kruyt et al., 2009). Some other energy security indicators, though not simple, are used to measure security of specific sectors in the energy industry such as the oil sector and the power sector. Examples include the oil vulnerability index (Gupta, 2008), and indicators for adequacy of generation capacity, grid reliability, and reasonable electricity price (Chang & Lee, 2008).

Power sector evaluation also tends to use simple indicators, which mainly measure the security of electricity supply. They are categorised into three groups: adequacy indicators, reliability indicators, and reasonable price indicators. Adequacy indicators measure the amount of spare generation capacity of the peak demand in a system and assess whether a market's peak day demand can be met without a generator in question (adequacy under emergency circumstances). Reliability indicators, measuring the average interruption duration experienced by customers served for a given period and the average number of times that a customer is interrupted during a given period, show how reliable a grid has been during a specific period. Reasonable price indicators measure market power – the extent to which the price exceeds marginal cost (price-cost mark-up) and specifically, the market power of the generator in question (Chang & Lee, 2008).

2.3.2. Aggregated Energy Security Indicators

The most common aggregated energy security indicators are the diversity index and its derivative indicators. The diversity indicator is used to measure the number and evenness of a target object. It is also seen as a basic indicator for energy security, which is frequently used to construct and develop the energy security evaluation index or system. By providing additional options for energy supply sources, diversity is believed to hedge against the risks of supply disruptions. Specifically, in an oil market subject to monopolistic exercises, diversity offers a means to mitigate unfair, disruptive, and other adverse actions. This diversity helps consumers to rely on a variety of mutually disparate options evenly and in a balanced way (Stirling, 1998, 2010). One example of diversity index is the Shannon-Wiener diversity index,[14] an index originally used to measure ecological diversity, which has been modified to construct indicators of energy diversity (Jansen, van Arkel, & Boots, 2004).

The Shannon-Wiener index is extended to construct several other indicators and index systems to assess energy security. IEA (2007b) developed a multi-fossil-fuels approach with a set of two indicators to measure energy security, addressing price and physical availability, respectively. The two indicators are the Energy Security price indicator and the Energy Security physical availability indicator. The Energy Security price indicator (ESIprice) is a sum over the fuels weighted by the share of the respective fuel in the total primary energy supply (TPES).[15] The unique feature of ESIprices is that it takes account of political risk. Energy Security physical availability indicator (ESIvolume) is the share of the net imports of pipe-based gas (purchased through oil-indexed contracts) in a country's total energy demand.[16] Higher values of the IEA energy security indicators mean a lower level of a country's energy security. Although these measures have merits, the IEA energy security indicators have several major drawbacks. First, they only refer to international fossil fuel markets while neglecting other energy sources in the energy consumption. Second, the indicators are complicated to some extent and cannot be readily interpreted by less informed policymakers and other users. Third, the mutual relationship of the two indicators in defining an overall energy security level may puzzle the users (Jansen & Seebregts, 2010, p. 1663).

Also based on the Shannon-Wiener diversity index, APERC (2007) developed an index system with five energy supply indicators applied to APEC countries in order to evaluate energy supply projections. The five indicators are Diversification of Primary Energy Demand (DoPED), Net Energy Import Dependency (NEID), Non-Carbon-based Fuel Portfolio (NCFP), Net Oil Import Dependency (NOID), and Middle East Oil Import Dependency (MEOID). They reflect the potential benefits/risks associated with the diversification of energy resources and import dependencies. DoPED and NEID measure the degree of diversification

---

[14]Shannon-Wiener diversity index is formulated as $I_1 = -\sum_i (c_i^1 p_i \ln p_i)$, where I_1 is energy supply security indicator no. 1; p_i represents the share of primary energy source i in TPES; c_i^1 represents the correction factor to p_i for indicator I_1.

[15]$\mathrm{ESI}_{\mathrm{price}}$ is formulated as $\mathrm{ESIprice} = \sum_f \left[\mathrm{ESMCpol\_f} \left(\frac{Cf}{\mathrm{TPES}} \right) \right]$, where ESMC is Energy Security Market Concentration; $\frac{Cf}{\mathrm{TPES}}$ is the share of fuel *f* in the fuel mix of the consumer country.

[16]$\mathrm{ESI}_{\mathrm{volume}}$ is formulated as $\mathrm{ESI}_{\mathrm{volume}} = \mathrm{Pipe\ Imp(gas)}_{\mathrm{oil\text{-}indexed}}/\mathrm{TPES}$, where Pipe $\mathrm{Imp(gas)}_{\mathrm{oil\text{-}indexed}}$ represents the pipe-based gas imports purchased through oil-indexed contracts.

of a country's energy sources and the impact of both diversification and imports on energy supply security. NCFP, accounting for the share of clean energy in a country's energy demand, measures a country's efforts to switch away from a carbon-intensive fuel portfolio. NOID, considering a country's oil imports and exports, measures the degree of a country's dependence on oil imports. MEOID measures how dependent a country is on the Middle East oil. This index system only addresses a country's energy availability. Yet some of the indicators are overlapping, such as the NOID and MEOID. This makes the energy security assessment complicated and confusing.

Further, Jansen, van Arkel, and Boots (2004) constructed four composite diversity indices of long-term energy security that are also based on Shannon-Wiener index. These indices are diversification of energy sources in energy supply; diversification of imports with respect to imported energy sources; long-term political stability in regions of origin; and the fuel resource base in regions of origin, including the home region/country itself. Each subsequent index accounts for one more factor of energy security. Stepwise, additional aspects of long-term energy supply security are incorporated into the diversity indices. This approach treats all sources equal and thus has its weaknesses because certain sources are exhaustible while others are not. It does not cover any feedback on how demand/consumers respond to the disruptions in energy supply (Jansen & Seebregts, 2010, p. 1659). This weakness is overcome by the Supply/Demand Index (S/D Index), which integrates major underlying supply-side and demand-side factors, such as industry demand, residential demand, and primary energy supply, but the S/D Index still has drawbacks, which are discussed in the following.

2.3.3. Independent Energy Security Measurement Systems

Energy security assessment systems are independent systems that have their own features to describe and evaluate energy security situation. Three major energy security measurement systems are elaborated in the following.

(1) The S/D Index

The S/D Index is a tree diagram integrating major underlying supply-side and demand-side factors with an attempt to cover energy supply and demand balances. It uses four types of inputs to evaluate a country's medium- and long-term energy security. They are the *shares* of different supply and demand categories; the *values* characterising efficiency, adequacy, and reliability in conversion and transport; the *weights* that determine the relative contribution of the different components in the S/D Index; and the *scoring rules* for determining various S/D Index values. In principle, it covers the entire energy system from demand to supply. The complicated system has a couple of drawbacks. First, the aggregation of various inputs has subjective value assignments. Second, the S/D Index tries to catch all possible demand–supply factors. The comprehensiveness of the Index means reduced simplicity, which makes the Index somewhat not readily interpreted. Third, this Index does not capture the geopolitical dimension very well (Scheepers et al., 2006).

(2) The Crisis Capability Index (CC Index)

The CC Index combines Risk Assessment (RA) and Mitigation Assessment (MA) to reflect how well a country is prepared for the short-term energy security problems such as sudden supply interruptions. It deals more with short-term energy security problems by incorporating risk factors such as unforeseen shortfalls of power generation and sudden interruption over oil or gas transport routes. RA deals with the risks of a sudden and unforeseen supply disruption; MA deals with the country's capability to mitigate the negative impact of the sudden disruption on an economy. Both have checklists of factors for assessment. The CC Index could be calculated by assigning values to each factor of RA and MA and then comparing the MA sub-index with RA sub-index. MA sub-index is constituted by assessment factors of emergency stocks, demand restraint and rationing, fuel switch capabilities, reserve capability, and locked-in production. RA sub-index is constituted by assessment factors of domestic primary energy production, energy conversion, independent energy transport, and energy import. If RA sub-index is much higher than MA sub-index, then the country is vulnerable to short-term energy security risks (Scheepers et al., 2006). But the CC Index cannot comprehensively reflect a country's energy security status. A very high MA sub-index does not necessarily mean desirable energy security situation, as the costs to enhance a country's risk mitigation capability may be so high that they exceed the costs of sudden supply disruptions.

(3) The Driving Force–State–Response (DSR) Model

The DSR model is originally used to categorise sustainability indicators (SIs), which are driving force SIs, state SIs, and response SIs. Driving force SIs represent a process that influences state SIs. State SIs describe the state of a specific variable. Response SIs gauge the progress in the response of relevant agents (e.g., the government) to achieve sustainable development. The DSR model is thus a cause-effect model with a causal link: driving force generates the state which requires the response (Bell & Morse, 2008). The DSR model, originally constructed to measure sustainability, has been modified to construct energy security evaluation systems. One derivative is an index system to measure a country's energy security system multi-dimensionally. This index system has six factors that have impact on energy security and three indices correspondent to these factors. The six factors are energy factor, political factor, economic factor, transport factor, military factor, and sustainable development factor, respectively. These six factors are described and explained by the three indices: pressure index, state index, and response index (Chi & Li, 2004).

Another derivative is the set of Indicators for Sustainable Energy Development (ISED) developed by the International Atomic Energy Agency (IAEA) and several other organisations in 1999.[17] The DSR model was applied and a set of

[17]The main collaborating organisations are the UN Committee on Sustainable Energy and the United Nations Work Programme on Indicators of Sustainable Development (WPISD).

41 indicators within the model was constructed. The model and the indicators incorporated three aspects of sustainable development – social, economic, and environmental – together with institutional considerations (IAEA & IEA, 2001). The 41 indicators define the causal relationships among important energy-related factors and link these factors with a set of potentially appropriate policies for increasing energy sustainability. These indicators have also been used to help countries assess the effectiveness of their current energy policies towards sustainable development (Vera, Langlois, Rogner, Jalal, & Toth, 2005).

These 41 indicators were refined to a set of 31 energy indicators published in 2005 by the IAEA in a joint interagency report named 'Energy Indicators for Sustainable Development: Guidelines and Methodologies'. In this report, the original name 'Indicators for sustainable energy development (ISED)' was revised to 'energy indicators for sustainable development (EISD)'. This interagency report is:

> for specialists in energy and the environment, including statisticians, analysts, policy makers and academics—in particular those involved in the development of energy and environmental indicators relevant to sustainable development. (Vera et al., 2005, p. 280)

This study uses the EISD set of indicators as one of its major references when formulating China's energy security indicators. The EISD indicators have already been applied to some developing countries such as Brazil, Cuba, Lithuania, Mexico, Slovakia, and Thailand. The application indicates the flexibility and versatility of the indicators. These indicators could be used to assess energy situations in countries with varied energy and economic conditions (United Nations/IAEA, 2007).

2.4. Chapter Summary

This chapter reviews various studies on energy security in the literature, including notions, assessment frameworks, and measurement indicators. Based on the literature review, this chapter presents the definition of energy security and the 4-As framework. This 4-As framework, which reflects the comprehensive definition of energy security encompassing the dimensions of availability, applicability, acceptability, and affordability, constitutes the foundation of the evaluation of China's energy policy and energy security situation in the following chapters.

Chapter 3

Quantitative Analysis of Energy Security in China[1]

This chapter is devoted to the discussion of the construction of the quantitative tools for assessing the impact of China's energy policies on its energy security status. It provides an insight into China's energy security trends starting from the early period of reform which coincides with the beginning of Deng Xiaoping administration in 1980 and ending with the late period of Hu Jintao administration in 2010. To identify changing policy priorities in China's Five-Year Plans (FYPs) of Economic and Social Development, the timeframe is divided into six periods according to the six FYPs: the Sixth to Eleventh FYP that were drawn up during the administrations of Deng Xiaoping, Jiang Zemin, and Hu Jintao. The key energy policies implemented and their effects on China's energy security will be examined by using the 4-As evaluation framework.

The structure of this chapter is as follows: In Section 3.1, the method of constructing the indicators used for examining China's energy security is explained. In Section 3.2, an introduction to the data selection and China's data problem is provided. Section 3.3 contains an explanation of the method used in coding and converting the original data into ordinal values for analysing the dynamic evolution of China's energy security situation. Section 3.4 contains a brief review of the energy policies that emerged during the six FYP periods and their consequences on China's energy security situation. The conclusion to the chapter is found in Section 3.5.

3.1. Formulation of Indicators to Examine Energy Security in China

Indicators developed in this chapter are scoped by two elements: spatial scale and time scale. The spatial scale refers to the entire country of China and the indicators are used to examine the energy security in China at a national level.

[1] The major part of this chapter has been published in *Energy Policy*, Vol. 67, Lixia Yao and Youngho Chang, Energy security in China: A quantitative analysis and policy implications, Pages 595–604, 2014, with permission from Elsevier.

Energy Security in Times of Economic Transition: Lessons from China, 39–74

doi:10.1108/978-1-83982-464-720201004

The time scale for a study must be sufficiently long to validate the framework against historical data and to depict relevant trends to assist/inform future decision-making (Keirstead, 2007), so the indicators examine China's energy security over 30 years of the three administrations of Deng Xiaoping, Jiang Zemin, and Hu Jintao. The period chosen is not only long enough to validate the 4-As framework constructed in Chapter 2 but also representative enough to detect how and why the status of energy security in China changed.

Sustainability indicators provide a theoretical background for the formulation and application of energy security indicators. To tackle the sustainability problem, many indicators are required to address the excessively broad range of sustainability issues. The values of the indicators are gauged and the results are interpreted to assist policy assessment and policymaking (Bell & Morse, 2008). Fig. 3.1 presents a schematic framework of this mechanism.

Following this schematic framework, energy security indicators are constructed, their values are calculated, and the results are interpreted for policy assessment and policy formulation purposes. The problem is that both sustainability indicators and energy security indicators have to face the 'selection difficulty', which is, to put it simply, 'how many and which indicators to use' (Bell & Morse, 2008, p. 28).

The sustainability indicators reflect the complex processes in sustainability theory in several simple measurements. This means that sustainability could be analysed by a reductionist approach which means breaking sustainability down into components and studying how they work jointly and individually. Clearly, sustainability indicators are quantification tools employing the reductionist approach and they do have limitations. However, it is not possible to deal

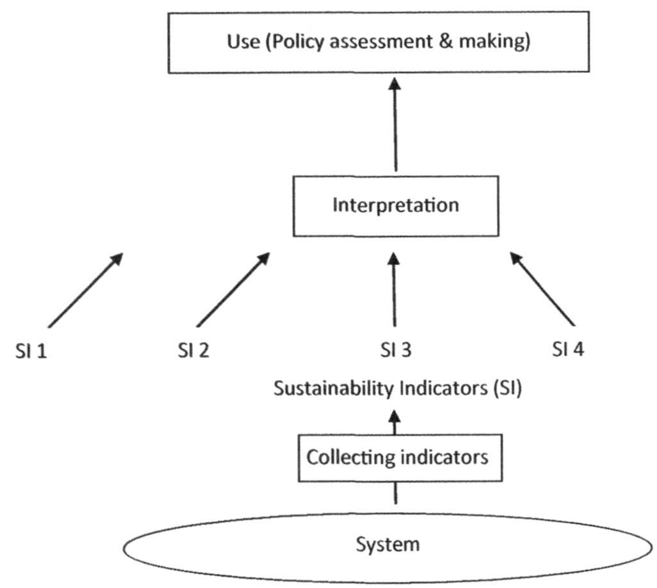

Fig. 3.1. The Concept Behind Sustainability Indicators. *Source*: Bell and Morse (2008), Redrawn by the Author.

with sustainability problems under the conditions of 'real-world complexity' (Bell & Morse, 2008). Thus, a minimum number of variables or indicators should be used if they are good enough to represent or replicate the realty. The same theory also applies to energy security indicators.

The problem lies in the difficulty in setting the acceptable limits of simplification. This involves the issue of indicator selection criteria. When selecting indicators, we should first define the evaluation criteria for the potential indicators. Three basic criteria are considered here: policy relevance and user utility, analytical robustness, and measurability. In terms of policy relevance, indicators should be representative, easy to understand, and provide a basis for comparison, either of different regions or of different time periods. In terms of analytical soundness, indicators should be constructed on the basis of scientific principles and international consensus to ensure their validity. In terms of measurability, data for the indicators should be readily available and frequently updated (OECD, 2003). To sum up, the criteria for constructing indicators ought to address the question: 'Is it possible in practice to measure or judge how well an option performs on these criteria?' (Department for Communities and Local Government, 2009, p. 33). This book adheres to this set of criteria – easily understandable and limited in number – when formulating China's energy security indicators. With this criteria, it is feasible to address the most important energy issues in China to capture as much of the complexity of energy security as possible. The challenge of data availability in China has been taken into account. In fact, many indicator projects are constrained by the availability of reliable data. Most indicators are constructed on the basis of the availability of raw data, which means that some possible 'ideal' indicators may be omitted (Moldan & Dahl, 2007).

Two types of indicators are distinguished in this research: direct indicators and indirect indicators. Direct indicators refer directly to the subject they have been developed for and directly pinpoint the subject of interest; indirect indicators only refer to the subject in an indirect way. In most cases, direct indicators are desirable for measuring the subjects. However, direct indicators may often not be used for two reasons. First, the subject of interest cannot be measured directly; second, even if the subject of interest can be measured directly, the scientifically reliable data may be unavailable or unfeasible to collect. In both cases, indirect indicators will be used, which may very well represent the balance between scientific measurement and data availability.

Given the comprehensive nature of the concept of energy security, this study advocates the construction of a wide range of indicators. These indicators provide a solid foundation for the quantitative description of the overall trend of the evolution of China's energy security situation. To depict the 'big picture' of China's energy security situation, these indicators are incorporated in the 4-As framework developed in Chapter 2, a useful tool that is relevant for policymaking to boost China's energy security. Each indicator is tied to a particular dimension of the 4-As framework. The framework and its indicators make it easy to interpret China's energy security trends and examine how the energy policies affect each dimension of the 4-As framework. These indicators, with their relevant data, present a more complete and accurate picture of changes in China's energy security situation, monitor China's historical trends in energy policymaking, and have implications for current policy decisions. Changes in the values of the indicator over time mark China's progress or setback on energy security. It is noteworthy that these indicators are more useful for dynamically depicting important trends in China's energy security situation than for providing an absolute outcome of the energy security situation.

3.1.1. Availability (AV) Indicators

The actual availability of energy sources is crucial for a country's energy security. The following indicators are direct indicators for the availability dimension of energy security.

AV-1: Coal Reserve-to-Production (R/P) Ratio. The R/P ratio is an indicator widely used for assessing energy resources (Feygin & Satkin, 2004). It is the ratio of energy reserves remaining at the end of a year relative to the production of energy in that year assuming the production rate remains constant for a lifetime. It measures the availability of national energy reserves with respect to corresponding fuel production and estimates the number of years for which current level of production can be sustained by its reserves. It reflects the economic level during a time when the resources have been estimated as exploitable. Therefore, it truly reflects the energy resources available over time (IAEA, 2005).[2] It is one of the energy indicators for sustainable development (EISD) (known as ECO4), and it is also used by Sovacool et al. (2011) to reflect the availability dimension of energy security. Coal is the dominant fossil fuel in China's energy production and consumption. Compared to the other two fossil fuels – oil and natural gas – coal R/P affects China's energy availability the most. It is hence selected as the first AV indicator to describe China's energy availability.

AV-2: Oil Import Dependence Ratio. Besides R/P, the energy import dependence ratio is also used to measure the security level of energy supply (Zou, 2007). It is commonly used as an indicator to depict a country's energy security status in terms of energy availability (i.e. whether there is enough energy for the country). For example, oil dependency served as an important indicator to reflect oil availability and to measure oil security in the United States (Greene, 2010). This indicator is 'a straightforward and insightful indicator that does not require specific expertise to comprehend' (Kruyt et al., 2009, p. 2169). The energy import

[2]Shortcomings of the reserves-to-production ratio indicator are argued as the ratio assumes constant future production rates and only reflects reserves proven at some point of time, while not taking into account fluctuations in energy prices or changes in energy demand. Neither does the ratio reveal anything about the quality of the fuels being produced (Feygin & Satkin, 2004). Nevertheless, the availability of energy supplies is a key aspect of energy security and this indicator can estimate the energy supplies in terms of the availability of energy reserves and the level of production during a specific time period.

dependence ratio expresses the level of exposure in terms of dependence on foreign energy supplies. It is:

> the ratio of net import to total primary energy supply (TPES) in a given year in total and by fuel type such as oil and petroleum products, gas, coal and electricity. (IAEA, 2005, p. 83)

The European Union (EU) defines energy import dependence ratio as the net fuel import as a percentage of gross consumption of the fuel.[3] The EU definition is most suitable for this study because of the data/statistics available on China's energy consumption. In the pursuit of energy security, the core objective of energy policy is the guarantee of a stable supply of energy for the country. The importance of the physical availability of supplies highlights the policies and strategies to prevent the risks of interruptions to energy supply. The physical availability risk is closely related to a country's extent of reliance on imported energy. The costs of reliance, such as the oil dependence costs, could be substantial. High import dependence may be a serious cause of economic vulnerability and also a constraint on a country's defence policy.

Import dependence ratio is commonly used in the energy supply security literature (Bhattacharyya, 2009). For example, it is one of the EISD (ECO15), which measures the extent of a country's reliance on imports to meet its energy requirements. It is also used by the European Environment Agency to address the issue of reducing the EU's dependency on imported fuel and diversifying its energy supply.[4] Sovacool and Mukherjee (2011) list the import dependence ratio separately by fuel type as the first of the three indicators of the dependency component of the availability dimension of energy security.[5]

This book selects the oil import dependence ratio to describe China's energy import dependency. China's accelerating urbanisation and emerging middle class require more energy, particularly oil for the transportation sector. High economic growth and heavy industrialisation make China's continued growth highly dependent on foreign oil (Kong, 2005). China's situation is unique. Within a short period of economic reform, China has transitioned from a net oil-exporting country into a net oil-importing country, and this is reflected by the oil import dependence ratio indicator. This indicator is useful for checking how dependent China is on foreign supplies of oil. A negative value (when China was a net exporter of oil) indicates the time when China did not rely too much on oil imports.

---

[3]For details, see the European Environment Agency website: http://www.eea.europa.eu/data-and-maps/indicators/net-energy-import-dependency#toc-1

[4]For details, see the European Environment Agency website: http://www.eea.europa.eu/data-and-maps/indicators/net-energy-import-dependency#toc-1.

[5]An alternative indicator to reflect import dependency of energy is self-sufficiency, which is 'a useful proxy for evaluating how dependent a country is on foreign sources of fuel or energy imports' (Sovacool et al., 2011, p. 5849). Hence, self-sufficiency is another interpretation for energy dependency.

AV-3: Natural Gas Reserve-to-Consumption Ratio. The reserve-to-consumption ratio is a derivative of R/P ratio and a hybrid of R/P and the import dependency. Compared with the oil production, the natural gas production in China developed relatively slowly whereas its demand for natural gas is projected to increase substantially by 2030. The consumption of natural gas increases faster than any other fossil fuel over the projection period. The main reason for its growing consumption of natural gas is the need for ever more energy to fuel its economic growth and the desire for the diversification of China's energy mix (IEA, 2007a). As a result, the natural gas reserve-to-consumption ratio is more accurate than its R/P for understanding the availability of natural gas resource in China.

The mentioned three indicators represent the availability of fossil fuels in China. Besides these indicators, another major form of energy – electricity – must also be included in the indicators to reflect how electricity is available to the population. Electricity supply is one of the essential inputs for economic activity. Electricity is the dominant form of modern energy for information technology, manufacturing, and services. Top leaders need to take steps to ensure the reliability and sustainability of electrical supply as electricity is practically non-storable and the systems are often affected by fluctuations of the fossil fuel prices. Ensuring that electricity supply remains affordable and reliable is a major energy policy issue (Bhattacharyya, 2009). All these suggest the importance of an availability indicator for electricity. The availability factor, which is calculated as 'actual total generation in MWh/(total installed capacity in MWh times 8,760 hours)', just reflects the electricity availability very well. The electricity availability factor consists of two components: electricity generation and electricity installed capacity. The total amount of electricity generation has major implications for energy dependence, energy prices, and greenhouse gas emissions (IAEA, 2005). It is the maximum output that the generator produced for a specific time and it measures the extent of electricity that is available in a country. Electricity generation alone does not tell the whole story of electricity availability, since the possibility of more power being generated is not considered. This possibility needs to be shown by the total electricity installed capacity, which is the maximum potential that a country's power system could generate electricity. To represent the availability factor more precisely, it is better to distinguish it by the type of electricity. The two availability factors are hence constructed as:

AV-4: Availability Factor of Conventional Thermal Electricity
AV-5: Availability Factor of Non-Thermal Electricity (Including Nuclear and Renewable)

3.1.2. Applicability (AP) Indicators

Applicability indicators are the indicators that reflect China's current technology for harnessing fossil fuels and renewable resources, and improving the efficiency of energy utilisation. They also reflect China's capacity for technological utilisation and innovation. They could be interpreted as energy technology indicators that assess energy efficiency and technology development, and aid in the evaluation of related policies. Energy technology is:

> the means of locating, assessing, harvesting, transporting, processing, and transforming the primary energy forms found in nature (e.g., sunlight, biomass, crude petroleum, coal, uranium-bearing rocks) to yield either direct energy services (e.g., heat from fuel wood or coal) or secondary forms more convenient for human use (e.g., charcoal, gasoline, electricity).

They are also:

> the means of distributing secondary forms to their end-users and the means of converting these forms to energy services (e.g., electricity to light and refrigeration, electricity and gasoline to motive power). (Gallagher et al., 2006, p. 194)

Applicability indicators should reflect the nature of such energy technology.

AP-1: Energy Intensity – Total Primary Energy Consumption Per Dollar of Gross Domestic Product (GDP). The improvement of energy efficiency and energy cost-effective economic development are essential energy security objectives. Several international conventions and agreements, such as the Johannesburg Plan of Implementation agreed at the 2002 World Summit on Sustainable Development, have proposed that energy security and sustainable energy development is largely affected by the application of advanced energy technologies. The extent of the deployment of energy efficiency technologies could be measured by the status of energy efficiency or energy intensity, which indicates the cumulative impact of all the energy efficiency technologies (Gallagher et al., 2006).

Reductions in energy intensity reflect the genuine gains in energy efficiency (Lent & Conklin, 2007). Energy efficiency indicators can be constructed by numerous different formulations to analyse energy efficiency at different levels: from national energy efficiency in general to specific energy efficiency of individual operating units within a plant. The lower the level, the more indicators could be constructed (APERC, 2000). That is to say, energy efficiency indicators can be generated at different levels of aggregation in accordance with different analytical objectives.[6] In this chapter, energy efficiency is analysed at the level of national economy. APERC (2000) defines the energy efficiency indicator as 'energy consumption per unit of GDP' (p. 24), which is actually the concept of energy intensity.[7] Many studies use energy intensity as an index to reflect energy efficiency in

---

[6]IAEA (2005) disaggregated the energy intensity indicator into indicators of energy intensities of several subsectors such as the industrial, agricultural, service/commercial, residential, and transport sectors, which correspond to ECO6, ECO7, ECO8, ECO9, ECO10 indicators in the EISD.

[7]Energy intensity of an economy is calculated by the ratio of energy consumption to GDP, which measures the quantity of energy required to perform an economic activity.

relation with energy security, such as HELIO International (2005/2006), IAEA (2005), IEA (2009), Kemmler and Spreng (2007), Lent and Conklin (2007), and Sovacool et al. (2011).

Energy intensity changes at different rates in different sectors. According to studies on energy intensity in three major sectors of energy use – transport, residential, and manufacturing sectors – technological advancement is ranked as the largest contributor to the causality of energy intensity reduction. In the transport sector, many industrialised countries adopt the fuel mileage as the measure of the efficiency of new car models. This undoubtedly encourages the car manufacturers to improve technology to develop new and more fuel-efficient models. In the residential sector, space heating has the largest share of energy use. The space-heating indicator takes into account the approximate efficiencies of combustion equipment and measures a country's effort to reduce the energy intensity through new technology. This makes technology the key driver behind reducing energy intensity. In the manufacturing sector, the improvement of technology and a change in economic structure may cause energy intensity to decline (Schipper, Unander, & Marie-Lilliu, 2000). A decrease in aggregate energy intensity does not necessarily mean that energy technology has improved because a change within the economic structure can also contribute to the decrease in energy intensity. In China, the emphasis on energy efficiency has gained momentum along with its fast economic growth. There is a growing consensus among scholars that technology improvement has led to reduction in energy intensity.[8]

To sum up, as technology is the key driver for the decline of energy intensity in China, it will be better to categorise it under the technological dimension of energy security. The energy intensity indicator provides useful information on the improvement in energy efficiency and it has been commonly treated as an essential measure of energy efficiency of China's energy security status. In this context, energy intensity serves as a reasonable proxy for energy efficiency (APERC, 2009).

AP-2: Gross Generation Efficiency of Fossil Fuel-Fired Power Plants. After selecting an indicator for evaluating overall energy technological advancement (energy intensity), the next step is to select indicators to depict the application of technology in a particular sector. The electricity generation sector is thus selected. Electricity is a key input to modern production and industrial activities, modern telecommunication in particular. The shortage of electricity, for example, usually means limitations in lighting, telecommunications, and resources for industries (Vera & Langlois, 2007). That is why technological advancement related to electricity generation is always a major concern in the energy industry. The use of advanced technology could improve the efficiency of thermal power plants (IAEA, 2005). The generation efficiency of fossil fuel-fired power plants also depicts technological advancement in thermal power generation – a typical reflection of the applicability dimension. Therefore, the indicator of 'Gross

---

[8]See Fisher-Vanden, Jefferson, Liu, and Tao (2004), Levine, Liu, and Sinton (1992), Lin and Polenske (1995), Sinton and Levine (1994), Sinton, Levine, and Wang (1998), and Zhang (2003a).

generation efficiency of fossil fuel-fired power plants' is adopted. It comes from one of the comprising parts of the indicator 'Efficiency of energy conversion and distribution' (ECO3) of the EISD. The efficiency of energy conversion is also one of the key energy indicators adopted by the National Bureau of Statistics (NBS) of China. It refers to the ratio of the total output of energy products after processing and conversion to the total input of energy for processing and conversion. It shows the conditions of energy processing and conversion equipment and production technology (NBS, 2002). For the power generation sector, the indicator 'generation efficiency of fossil fuel-fired power plants' is 'gross production of electricity (including own use of electricity by power plants) from fossil fuel power plants relative to fossil fuel inputs' (IAEA, 2005, p. 46). A similar indicator, 'average thermal efficiency of power plants', is also used by Sovacool and Mukherjee (2011) as a technology indicator for energy security evaluation. In short, 'generation efficiency of fossil fuel-fired power plants' represents technology advancement in thermal power generation sector.

Besides evaluating the particular sector of thermal power generation, applicability indicators also need to directly measure the technologies that enable China to harness another key energy resource: crude oil. 'Crude Oil Distillation Capacity', as a direct indicator, is a good candidate for this purpose.

AP-3: Crude Oil Distillation Capacity (Thousand Barrels Per Day). '[T]he real technical genius of the oil industry has been to maximize the yield of useful products from a given amount of crude petroleum' (Crabbe, 2003, p. 245). Crude oil cannot be used directly by the consumers. It must be refined via a process of fractionation defined as the separation of the various constituent parts of crude oil by distillation into oil fractions. This is the basis of oil refining. A good indicator to describe this technology is the crude oil distillation capacity. Therefore, it is adopted to reflect the technology of crude oil harnessing.

AP-1 to AP3 refer to applicability indicators related to the overall energy technological advancement, application in the thermal power generation sector, and the harnessing of crude oil. The status in energy technological improvement may also be measured by the supply of human resources – the number of scientists and engineers engaged in the energy sector. But a major drawback is that this indicator does not take the efficiency or work quality into account. The work quality may be poor even though a large number of people are engaged in activities related to energy technological innovation (Gallagher et al., 2006). The indicators related to human resources in the energy sector are hence not adopted.[9] Nevertheless, energy technological innovation could also be further measured by patents of energy technology.

[9]Sovacool and Mukherjee (2011) had selected human resources indicators such as 'Direct employment in the energy sector', 'Indirect employment in the energy sector', 'Induced employment in the energy sector', 'Technical expertise (number of engineers or energy employees)', and 'Unemployment in the energy sector (%)' to evaluate 'technology development and efficiency' dimension of energy security. But in a follow-up work, all these indicators have been dropped (Sovacool et al., 2011).

AP-4: Patents Owned by LME (State-Owned) in Coal Mining and Dressing and Petroleum and Natural Gas Extraction Industries. Patent is a special type of technology document that provides information on technological innovations (Huang et al., 2003). Since patent license is a form of property rights included in technology transfer (Lewis & Wiser, 2007), patents indicate technological innovation and also reflect the pace of technology. Therefore, this indicator shows the technological progress in the fossil fuel industries. Although the patent is not a perfect measure of technological progress, patent counts are still the best available source of data on technological innovation (Johnstone, Hascic, & Popp, 2010).

Patterns of U.S. energy technology patents have been used to examine its Research and Development (R&D) spending on energy technology. The conclusion is that they are highly correlated (Margolis & Kammen, 1999; Nemet & Kammen, 2007). The cutbacks in energy R&D, together with the declining number of energy patents, will probably reduce the capacity of the energy sector to innovate and reduce the pace of energy technological improvement (Margolis & Kammen, 1999). Patents are used to assess the effectiveness of the U.S. R&D investment in emerging energy technologies (Nemet & Kammen, 2007). Patent counts are also used as evidence of the impact of environmental policies on technological innovation in the renewable energy sector. Analysis using patent data on a panel of 25 countries reveals that policy instruments have affected the technological progress of renewable energy sources (Johnstone et al., 2010).[10] With this backdrop, patents are used as an indicator to evaluate the applicability dimension of China's energy security.

AP-5: Energy Industry Technical Updating and Transformation Investment/ Investment in Fixed Assets of State-Owned Units in Energy Industry. Besides patents, investment in energy technological innovation is essential to enable a country to respond to its changing economic and environmental needs. Inadequate investment in energy technological innovation at a national level will have negative effects on the energy sector and the national economy and environment in the long run. A commonly used indicator of status of energy technological innovation is the investments by government and/or the private sector in the energy technology innovation – assuming that there is a strong positive relationship between investment in energy and energy technological innovation (Dooley, 1998; Margolis & Kammen, 1999). When applying this indicator in the case of China, it must be kept in mind that in China, the government budget is only used as a supplementary instrument to boost the development of the energy sector, which is still highly dominated by large SOEs. Under this condition, the energy investments of China's SOEs should be taken as a substitute for the investments by government (Pan & Zhu, 2005/2006). In *China Energy Statistical Yearbook*, investments in fixed assets of state-owned units in energy industry include capital investment as well as upgrading and renovation investment (Pan & Zhu, 2005/2006). AP-5 depicts the share of upgrading and renovation investments in the fixed assets investment of state-owned units in the energy industry. It indirectly reflects the technological advancement in China's energy sector.

---

[10]Besides the energy sector, use of patents for academic research could also be found in Lee and Sorenson's (2001) research on invention and technology; and Huang, et al.'s (2003) research on nanotechnology performance.

3.1.3. Acceptability (AC) Indicators

Energy has a great impact on the environment and is a key element in the study of sustainable development. Fuel combustion is one of the main sources of air pollution. Other energy-related activities such as energy production also have caused water pollution and other environmental problems. The energy–environment relationship has been closely intertwined and indicators are needed to reflect whether such relationship is acknowledged and how well it is reflected in decision-making. For example, air pollutant emissions (ENV3: Air pollutant emissions from energy systems) is used by the IAEA (2005) as one of the environmental dimension indicators of the EISD to track the release of air pollutants into the atmosphere from energy-related activities in order to assess energy sustainability.

Coal will continue to dominate China's energy system in the foreseeable future. Two-thirds of the country's total energy supply comes from coal and 80% of its electricity is generated by coal (Kong, 2005). The use of coal is a major source of air pollution in China. Consequently, the air pollution indicators that directly reflect the impact of the combustion of coal on the environment are selected. These indicators include 'Share of China's CO_2 emissions out of global CO_2 emissions', 'China's SO_2 emissions', and 'the volume of soot emission'. The CO_2 and SO_2 emission levels indicate how far a country has progressed in alleviating air pollution from greenhouse gas emissions and acid rain (Sovacool & Brown, 2010). Soot emissions are commonly used by Chinese scholars as an indicator to depict air pollution in China.[11]

AC-1: Share of China's CO_2 Emissions Out of Global CO_2 Emissions. This indicator measures China's share of the world's total emissions of CO_2 from energy production and consumption. It also provides information on the rising or declining trend of the carbonisation of China's energy system. Fossil-fuel burning produces CO_2, a greenhouse gas associated with climate change. During the twentieth century, the amount of CO_2 increased by more than 30% largely due to the burning of fossil fuels (IAEA, 2005). Consequently, the global environmental impact is conventionally measured by CO_2 emissions (HELIO International, 2005/2006). Typical examples could be found in HELIO International (2005/2006), IAEA (2005), OECD (1993), Pan and Zhu (2005/2006), and Sovacool et al. (2011). The IAEA (2005), in particular, uses this indicator as one of the environmental dimension indicators (ENV1) of EISD to assess energy sustainability. The OECD (1993) measures the levels of CO_2 emissions to assess the environmental impact of energy use to reflect the role of energy and environmental policies in achieving sustainable economic development. This indicator is one of Pan and Zhu (2005/2006)'s environmental sustainability indicators to evaluate China's sustainability and environmental performance. This is also one of the environmental sustainability dimension indicators used by Sovacool et al. (2011) to assess a country's energy security.

[11]I thank Dr. Sun Chuanwang with Xiamen University for this point.

China's high reliance on coal combustion produces huge amounts of CO_2. Its contributions to global CO_2 emissions are already increasingly high because of its fast industrial development and economic growth. The Chinese government has been striving to reduce its carbon intensity[12] and its share of the world's emission of CO_2. In 2007, China released its First National Climate Change Assessment which sets the goal of reducing China's carbon intensity by 40% by 2020, and 80% by 2050 (Herzog, 2007). By the end of 2009, as a participant in the Copenhagen Accord, China committed to reduce its carbon intensity by 40–45% by 2020 compared to 2005 levels (Cohen-Tanugi, 2010, p. 1). In order to achieve the long-term goal, the Twelfth FYP (2011–2015) sets the target to reduce carbon intensity by 17%. Reflecting the mentioned elaboration, the indicator 'Share of China's CO_2 emissions out of global CO_2 emissions' is selected to demonstrate the historical evolution of one environmental aspect of the country's energy system: the CO_2 emissions.

AC-2: China's SO_2 Emissions. An increase in the pollutants from the burning of coal also causes acid rain that harms ecological systems. Therefore, SO_2 emissions, the source of acid rain, are selected to evaluate the impact of air pollution on the environmental sustainability dimension of a country's energy security (Sovacool et al., 2011). The level of SO_2 emissions is adopted by OECD (1993) to measure environmental effects of energy use to reflect energy and environmental policies designed for economic sustainability. The combination of the concentration of particulates in an urban area with the SO_2 concentrations is the most significant energy-related local pollutant(s) selected for China by HELIO International (2005/2006). As the SO_2 is more region specific, its absolute amount (rather than a global share) of emissions is selected.

Given China's heavy reliance on coal and particularly its direct use of coal, it is no surprise that coal burning contributes more than 85% of SO_2 in China. The correlation coefficient between coal consumption and increased SO_2 level is above 95% (He, Huo, & Zhang, 2002, p. 410). Therefore, the emission of SO_2 is a key indicator of China's air pollution.

AC-3: Volume of Soot Emissions. The burning of coal releases soot and smoke to the atmosphere. Soot emissions are a major source of pollution from the energy industry (especially coal in China) and cause significant health risks. Besides CO_2 and SO_2 emissions, soot emissions are also identified as one of the main pollutants in the air (Heymann, 2006). The empirical study on China's air pollution often includes three air pollutants: SO_2, industrial soot emissions, and dust emissions (Shi, 2009). The indicator of soot volume is used to evaluate both the air pollution situation and the air pollution control in China (Chen & Xu, 2010; Hu & Jiang, 2007).[13] The 'volume of soot emissions' is hence selected, together with CO_2 and SO_2, as one of the acceptability indicators.

---

[12]Carbon intensity is the ratio of carbon emissions to GDP.

[13]Another commonly used indicator for air quality evaluation is the suspended particular matter concentration level: PM_{10} emissions, mainly the result of industrial process, of which coal mining and burning constitutes a major source. Data on PM_{10} emissions in China, however, are not readily available.

In addition to air pollution indicators, there are some indicators that indirectly measure the effects of energy production and consumption on the acceptability dimension of energy security. For example, the share of zero-carbon fuels in energy mix is used as an indicator of the acceptability (environmental) dimension of energy security (APERC, 2007; Sovacool & Mukherjee, 2011). Formulated as the share of renewables and nuclear in total primary energy supply (TPES), this indicator measures the extent/status of a country's effort to move away from a carbon-intensive fuel portfolio (Kruyt et al., 2009). It quantifies a country's progress in utilising alternative energy sources by increasing the share of clean energy resources to meet their energy demand.

A fuel mix in electricity generation is the most critical contributor to the variation in the carbon factor.[14] Since nuclear and hydro energy resources have little carbon emissions, a country with a high share of these energies in electricity generation will naturally have a low carbon factor (Ang, 1999). China has been working hard to increase the share of electricity use in end-use sectors. The expansion of electricity use makes Chinese electricity generation a global-scale industry. Large power stations (including coal-fired power plants, hydroelectric facilities, and nuclear power stations) have been constructed. Electricity generation itself is, however, a polluting industry in China, since coal contributes more than half of the sources of electricity generation. To alleviate environmental pollution, China must expand the construction of nuclear power stations and also the renewable power generation facilities in order to raise the share of nuclear energy and renewables in electricity generation.

A share of renewable energy, no matter in energy consumption or energy supply, reflects a type of energy mix. This percentage gives information on renewable resources exploitation as well as the status of market penetration of various alternative energy sources and reveals consumer preferences for different energy sources. Both the indicator 'renewable energy deployment' of HELIO International Indicators (2005/2006) and the indicator 'Renewable energy share in energy and electricity' (ECO13) of the EISD highlight the status of the renewable share in environmental improvement.[15] Besides the renewable energy resources, the use of other new energy resources (such as substituting fossil fuels with nuclear energy) may lead to negative environmental effects which are markedly different from the air pollution caused by fossil fuel utilisation. Therefore, how the population accepts nuclear energy in

---

[14]The carbon factor, also referred to as the carbonisation index, is the energy-related carbon emissions per unit of energy consumption (Ang, 1999).

[15]Actually, the percentage of renewable energy in TPES is a good indicator to reflect the level of harnessing renewable energy. Renewable energy is normally used to generate electricity or produce biofuels. However, consumption and production of biofuel started only in 2001, and biofuel consumption and production make up only a very small share of China's total renewable energy consumption or supply. Therefore, the contribution of biofuel in the renewable energy supply is omitted. The indicator 'share of renewable energy out of total electricity generation' is used as a proxy of 'percentage of renewable energy in total primary energy supply (TPES)'.

their community needs to be reflected. Accordingly, two specific indicators to depict China's non-carbon shares in energy mix are adopted in this research:

AC-4: Share of Renewable Energy Out of Total Electricity Generation
AC-5: Share of Nuclear Energy Out of Total Electricity Generation

3.1.4. Affordability (AF) Indicators

Energy pricing is a key driving factor in energy consumption. It also measures the economic impact and reflects the scarcity of energy resources as well. For example, as a dominant energy carrier, oil pricing is considered a crucial energy security indicator (Kruyt et al., 2009). Energy pricing must reflect whether and how the population can afford to pay for energy consumption. For this purpose, the growth rate of ex-factory price index for coal, petroleum, and electricity prices is adopted. The growth rate is calculated over a five-year period on the basis of ex-factory price index with the previous year's equal to 100.

Coal is the dominant fossil fuel in China's energy mix and its consumption is still growing rapidly. Eighty per cent of China's electricity is generated by coal. The majority of rural residents in China still use coal as a fuel for daily activities such as cooking and heating (Gan & Yu, 2008). Therefore, changes in coal pricing affect the energy costs of large numbers of industries and consumers in China.

Besides using coal, China's oil demand is growing fast as people's disposable income rises and as more households opt for cars. The pricing of oil directly affects the consumers' daily life. Further, in an emerging economy like China, sustained economic growth requires an expanding electrical power sector to support industries and commercial activities as well as to raise the people's living standards (Andrews-Speed, 2004). Electricity prices are thus critical to people's daily life and to the nation as a whole. In view of these, the following three AF indicators are selected[16]:

AF-1: Growth Rate of Ex-factory Price Index (previous year=100) for Coal (over five-year period)
AF-2: Growth Rate of Ex-factory Price Index (previous year=100) for Petroleum (over five-year period)

---

[16]Sovacool and Brown (2010) use two indicators to measure affordability: retail electricity prices and retail gasoline/petrol prices. In a refined subsequent work, Sovacool et al. (2011) use only the retail price of gasoline/petrol as a direct price indicator to measure affordability. The electricity pricing indicator is adjusted as 'percentage that retail electricity prices have changed every five years' to measure the stability of electricity prices. This study uses three direct price indicators. Coal price is included in addition to electricity and prices of petroleum products. This is because coal is a major source of China's energy mix. The gas price is not included in the AF indicators. Although the piped gas supply has a long history in China, its development was slow until the early twenty-first century when large hikes in oil prices caused many enterprises to switch fuel to natural gas (Wong, 2010).

AF-3: Growth Rate of Ex-factory Price Index (previous year=100) for Electricity (over Five-year Period)

In addition, the volatility component of the affordability dimension can be measured by the 'stability of electricity prices' (Sovacool et al., 2011). In this study, the 'volatility of coal prices' is used as a proxy to measure energy price stability in China:

AF-4: Volatility of Coal Prices. The 'volatility of coal prices' measures how the ex-factory price index (previous year=100) for coal has changed every five years. The 'volatility of coal prices' is used rather than the 'stability of electricity prices' because electricity pricing is still kept artificially low, and thus relatively stable in China. In contrast, the coal sector has been fully liberalised in China and its pricing is subject to the forces of demand–supply. Therefore, the 'volatility of coal prices' (instead of the 'stability of electricity prices') is selected for study.[17]

AF-5: Energy Consumption Per Capita: Non-Productive Use. Affordability indicators need to reflect the energy consumers' sensitivity to price changes. The energy consumption per capita can indirectly reflect the affordability of energy to the population. It measures the level of energy consumption on a per capita basis and reflects the changing patterns of a country's energy consumption over time. By using a global level of average consumption as a benchmark, the higher the level, the more people can afford to pay for more energy consumption; the lower the level, the fewer people can afford to sustain a decent level of energy consumption. In the developing countries where the per capita consumption of energy is much lower than that of the developed countries, having lower energy consumption than what is required to sustain a decent level poses a serious constraint on economic development. This indicator refers to consumption in the end-use sectors, thus excluding energy consumed, or losses incurred, in the conversion, transformation, and distribution of energy resources (IAEA, 2005).

It is noteworthy that the indicators constructed to evaluate China's energy security could also be used to measure that of other countries. Given that the selection of indicators in this chapter is subject to data availability in China, one could alternate or tweak some of the indicators to evaluate the energy security of other countries. The indicators listed in this chapter are not exhaustive but they are the best and most suitable key indicators, considering the limited data available to evaluate China's energy policy and security. These energy security indicators can be further developed for any other country by adding or reducing the listed indicators.

---

[17]The 'stability of electricity prices' refers to the percentage that retail electricity prices have changed every five years (Sovacool et al., 2011). Following this definition, this book selects five years as the time interval measure for the 'volatility of coal prices' indicator.

3.2. Data

This section contains an explanation of the method of data collection and extrapolation for the indicators for the period 1980–2010 in five-year increments. The energy databases used in this book primarily include NBS of China, China Statistical Yearbook (CSY), China Energy Statistical Yearbook, the U.S. Energy Information Administration (EIA), the Lawrence Berkeley National Laboratory (LBNL), and the BP Statistical Review of World Energy (BP).

3.2.1. The AV Data

This section explains how the data for the indicators are chosen, collected, and calculated. As mentioned earlier, there are five AV indicators:

AV-1: Coal R/P Ratio
AV-2: Oil Import Dependence Ratio
AV-3: Natural Gas Reserve-to-consumption Ratio
AV-4: Availability Factor of Conventional Thermal Electricity
AV-5: Availability Factor of Non-thermal Electricity (Including Nuclear and Renewable)

China's Coal Reserves. It is noteworthy that even though the CSY has extensive data for coal reserves and production, the statistical coverage has changed since 2002. Before 2002, the CSY used 'ensured reserves' (*Baoyou Chuliang* in Chinese). Since 2002, the CSY used 'basic reserves' (*Jichu Chuliang* in Chinese). In fact, there is no consensus on the precise reserves of China's coal resources. Estimates vary among the international and Chinese sources (Aden, Fridley, & Zheng, 2009).

With a series of extensive national resource surveys, China reported to the World Energy Council (WEC) that their coal reserves totalled 114,500 million tons in 1992. This coal reserves estimate was often cited in subsequent years and in other references such as the annual BP Statistical Review of World Energy (Aden et al., 2009). This could be verified in WEC's published reports. In its *2010 Survey of Energy Resources*, the WEC reported that China's proved recoverable coal reserves at the end of 2008 was 114,500 million tons and its coal production was 2,782 million tons (World Energy Council, 2010, p. 16), with the R/P ratio of coal 41 years in 2008. The BP has the same figure, i.e., 41 years in 2008. Therefore, when extrapolating China's coal R/P ratio, the author uses the WEC estimate of coal reserves, i.e., 114,500 million tons. Table 3.1 shows China's coal R/P ratio.

The coal production data are sourced from *BP Statistical Review of World Energy June 2011*. Since the *BP Statistical Review of World Energy* began to record coal production from 1981, the 1980 data on coal production, 620.1 Mt, is retrieved from the EIA. The EIA figures of coal production are very similar to those of the BP in the other years. It is noteworthy that discrepancy exists in *BP Statistical Reviews* of various years. This book adopts the *BP Statistical Review of 2011*, which is the year immediately after the ending year in analysis.

Data of AV-2 are retrieved from the NBS, AV-3 from the *BP Statistical Review of World Energy June 2011*, and AV-4 and AV-5 from the EIA. AV-4 and AV-5,

Table 3.1. China's Coal Reserve (Mt), Coal Production (Mt), and Coal R/P Ratio (Years).

Year	1980	1985	1990	1995	2000	2005	2010
Coal Reserve	114,500	114,500	114,500	114,500	114,500	114,500	114,500[18]
Coal Production	620.1	872.3	1,079.9	1,360.7	1,384.2	2,349.5	3,240.0
AV-1	185	131	106	84	83	49	35

Table 3.2. AV Data for Each Ending Year of the FYP Periods.

Year	1980	1985	1990	1995	2000	2005	2010
AV-1	185	131	106	84	83	49	35
AV-2	–0.1406	–0.3158	–0.1791	–0.0076	0.2824	0.3947	0.5473
AV-3	49.3	67.4	65.5	94.1	55.8	32.8	25.7
AV-4	0.571	0.563	0.521	0.531	0.500	0.561	0.495
AV-5	0.324	0.395	0.396	0.416	0.331	0.401	0.361

the availability factor, are calculated as 'actual total generation in MWh/(total installed capacity in MWh times 8,760 hours)'. Table 3.2 presents the collected data for AV indicators.

3.2.2. The AP Data

This section explains how the data for AP indicators are chosen, collected, and calculated. As illustrated in Section 3.2.2, the AP indicators include the following:

AP-1: Energy intensity – Total Primary Energy Consumption Per Dollar of GDP (Btu Per Year 2005 US Dollars (Purchasing Power Parities))
AP-2: Gross Generation Efficiency of Fossil Fuel-fired Power Plants
AP-3: Crude Oil Distillation Capacity (Thousand Barrels Per Day)
AP-4: Patents Owned by LME (State-owned) in Coal Mining and Dressing and Petroleum and Natural Gas Extraction Industries
AP-5: Energy Industry Technical Updating and Transformation Investment/ Investment in Fixed Assets of State-owned Units in Energy Industry.

The data of AP-1 are retrieved from the EIA. The EIA only has data on China's energy intensity until 2008. The 2010 figure is calculated on the basis of the 2005 figure and the actual energy intensity reduction. In its Eleventh FYP, the Chinese

[18]The reason why the WEC's coal reserve estimate is frozen is that coal resource has been converted into reserve at a rate equal to annual consumption (Aden et al., 2009).

government set the target of reducing energy intensity by 2010 by 20% from 2005. From 2005, China's energy intensity began to decrease after a steady three-year rise. The Climate Group (2011) claimed that China achieved a reduction of 19.1% in 2010. With the 2005 energy intensity of 12,546.7 Btu/GDP, and the real reduction figure at 19.1%, the 2010 energy intensity is calculated as 10,150.3 Btu/GDP.

The data of AP-2 are sourced from the LBNL. The LBNL only has the data of China's gross generation efficiency of fossil fuel-fired power plants until 2006. The 2010 figure, 0.373, is extrapolated on the basis of the average annual increasing rate of gross generation efficiency of fossil fuel-fired power plants over the latest period based on data available from 2002 till 2006.

The data of AP-3 are sourced from the EIA.

For AP-4, the data are sourced from the *China Statistical Yearbook on Science and Technology* of various years. This yearbook has records on patents owned by the LME (state-owned) from the year 1996 until 2008. The 1980, 1985, and 1990 data are thus taken as zero. From 2009, there is a change of statistical coverage. The statistics previously recorded as 'patents owned' by LME was changed to 'patents in force' by LME. As a result, the data from 2009 onwards are not used. There is no regular change in the number of patents owned by LME. In general, patents owned by LME since 2004 are more than those in the period before 2004. This book uses the 1996 figure to represent the 1995 figure, and the 2008 figure to represent the 2010 figure.

The data of AP-5 are sourced from LBNL and the *China Energy Statistical Yearbook*. The LBNL only has data on the 'energy industry technical updating & transformation investment' until 2003. The *China Energy Statistical Yearbook* has these data recorded until 2002 and the data of 'investment in fixed assets of state-owned units in energy industry' until 2010. The LBNL has the data on 'energy industry technical updating & transformation investment' as from 1981. In fact, the *China Statistical Yearbook* was first published in 1982, which marked the beginning of the regular release of official statistical data in China. The first one is the 1981 issue, which covers only 1981 data. The second one is the 1983 issue, from which the most recent data in each issue are on the previous year (Holz & Lin, 2001). This book uses the data of 1981, i.e., 0.330, to represent the 1980 data. The 2005 figure is extrapolated on the basis of the average annual increasing rate of the technical updating and transformation investment of energy industry over the years from 1999 till 2003. The 2010 figure is also extrapolated on the basis of the data over the years from 1999 to 2003. Table 3.3 presents the collected data for AP indicators.

3.2.3. The AC Data

The AC indicators include the following five. This section explains how the data for these AC indicators are chosen, collected, and calculated.

AC-1: Share of China's CO_2 Emissions Out of Global CO_2 Emissions
AC-2: China's SO_2 Emissions (10,000 Tons)
AC-3: The Volume of Soot Emissions (10,000 Tons)
AC-4: Share of Renewable Energy Out of Total Electricity Generation
AC-5: Share of Nuclear Energy Out of Total Electricity Generation

Table 3.3. AP Data for Each Ending Year of the FYP Periods.

Year	1980	1985	1990	1995	2000	2005	2010
AP-1	33,161.7	25,364.3	21,310.4	15,385.0	10,644.3	12,546.7	10,150.3
AP-2	0.298	0.309	0.314	0.325	0.339	0.359	0.373
AP-3	1,600	2,150	2,200	2,867	4,346.8	4,649.6	6,806
AP-4	0	0	0	314	199	828	808
AP-5	0.330	0.153	0.152	0.223	0.322	0.357	0.290

Table 3.4. AC Data for Each Ending Year of the FYP Periods.

Year	1980	1985	1990	1995	2000	2005	2010
AC-1	0.078	0.093	0.109	0.139	0.143	0.199	0.251
AC-2	1,325	1,325	1,494	1,891	1,995.1	2,549.4	2,185.1
AC-3	1,324	1,324	1,324	1,478	1,165.4	1,182.5	829.1
AC-4	0.202	0.234	0.212	0.196	0.174	0.168	0.193
AC-5	0	0	0	0.0129	0.0124	0.0212	0.0177

Table 3.4 presents the collected data for AC indicators. AC-1 data are sourced from the *BP Statistical Review of World Energy June 2011*. AC-2 data are sourced from the *China Statistical Yearbook*. The data include emissions by the industry and emissions by daily consumption. The *China Statistical Yearbook* began to record SO_2 emissions from 1985. The 1980 figure is taken as the same with that of 1985. The AC-3 data come from two sources. From 1995 onwards, the data are sourced from the *China Statistical Yearbook* of various years. China began to keep records of soot discharges from 1992. The *China Environment Yearbook* began to keep data of soot discharges in 1990. The 1980 and 1985 data are taken as the same as the 1990 data. Both AC-4 and AC-5 data are sourced from the EIA. China began to generate nuclear power in 1992.

3.2.4. The AF Data

This section explains how the data for AF indicators are chosen, collected, and calculated. The AF indicators include:

AF-1: Growth Rate of Ex-factory Price Index (Previous Year=100) for Coal (Over Five-year Period)
AF-2: Growth Rate of Ex-factory Price Index (Previous Year=100) for Petroleum (Over Five-year Period)
AF-3: Growth Rate of Ex-factory Price Index (Previous Year=100) for Electricity (Over Five-year Period)

AF-4: Volatility of Coal Prices (Measured by New Formula)
AF-5: Energy Consumption Per Capita: Non-productive Use (SCE* Kg)

Table 3.5. AF Data for Each Ending Year of the FYP Periods.

Year	1980	1985	1990	1995	2000	2005	2010
AF-1	0	5.24%	5.72%	20.48%	2.24%	11.84%	10.4%
AF-2	0	5.06%	6.18%	35.06%	11.78%	9.3%	10%
AF-3	0	2.32%	4.1%	22.12%	7.18%	2.12%	2.22%
AF-4	0	122.95	160.53	338.27	541.29	696.55	1,202.99
AF-5	112.26	126.71	139.18	130.68	123.66	194.1	258.34

Table 3.5 presents the collected data for AF indicators. Data AF-1, AF-2, AF-3, and AF-4 are all sourced from the *China Statistical Yearbook* of various years. To account for changing relative energy prices, the relative energy price indices of ex-factory prices for coal, petroleum, and electricity are adopted. These relative ex-factory price indices are calculated on the basis of the previous year figure equal to 100. The growth rate is calculated over a five-year period. There is no data about energy price index available in the 1970s. It was in the early 1980s that a two-tier pricing system (the beginning of price liberalisation) was adopted. Prior to that (i.e. 1976–1980), the energy pricing was under the strict control of the government and also damaged by the Cultural Revolution. Therefore, the period 1976–1980 is taken as no price growth and volatility. The 1980 figure is thus zero. The AF-5 data are sourced from the NBS. Coal price volatility is calculated by the following standard deviation model:

$$\sigma = \sqrt{\frac{1}{n-1}\sum_{t=1}^{n}(r_t - \mu)^2}$$

where r_t is the logarithmic return: $r_t = \ln\frac{P_t}{P_{t-1}}$

μ is expected return given by:

$$\mu = \frac{1}{n}\sum_{t=1}^{n}P_t$$

P_t is the yearly price index and n is 5.

3.3. Data Coding and the Performance Scoring

3.3.1. Data Coding

To make the gathered data comparable, the data are coded and normalised on a scale of ordinal values. This section contains an explanation for the coding of

*Standard Coal Equivalent.

the raw data (i.e. conversion of the raw data into ordinal values). It is noteworthy that when coding data, the indicators are made unidirectional, which means that higher values correspond to better energy security performance. The scores are not designed to reflect the dichotomy between energy insecurity and energy security. Instead, the scoring for the specific years just reflects a dynamic change of China's energy security status (i.e. whether the situation has improved or deteriorated). The scoring range is scaled from 1 to 10. The higher score, the better the energy security situation.[19] Table 3.6 presents the scoring scale of data and Table 3.7 presents the ordinal values of each indicator.

3.3.2. Performance Scoring – Area of Rhombus

This section depicts China's energy security status in each FYP period. Seven rhombuses are drawn to represent the status. Figs. 3.2–3.8 illustrate the rhombuses and their relevant energy security situation. Fig. 3.2 is the energy security situation in 1980, the original situation and also the benchmark for analysis. Figs. 3.3–3.8 show the energy security situation of the ending year of each FYP period. Table 3.8 lists total area of the rhombus of each period.

Besides the total rhombus area, the energy security performance of each period is depicted by an imbalance index as well, which is defined as (area of a diamond taking the highest A score – actual total area)/area of a diamond taking the highest A score. The lower the index, the more balanced the four dimensions of each period. Table 3.9 indicates the imbalance index of the ending year of FYP.

3.4. Evolution of the 4-As[20]

3.4.1. An Overview

China's energy security evolution is studied in terms of its FYPs, as the analytical framework is based on the study of energy policy decisions according to specific time periods to assess the entire energy security evolution. This book presents seven timing points to mark the ending year of the FYP over 30 years to reveal significant trends in China's energy security situation. A total of six FYPs are covered – from the Sixth FYP till the Eleventh FYP – which also coincides with the period of China's early economic reform to its transition to market liberalisation. The 1980 rhombus marks the beginning of the period under study, which is also the beginning of economic reform and China's recovery from the 'Cultural Revolution'. The lagging economy and low level energy demand made China a net energy export country. Besides, its underdeveloped electricity generation capacity was accompanied by low levels of technology, environmental pollution, and energy pricing under strict government control. The AV, AC, and AF scored

[19]This is a second best methodology to depict the energy security situation. The ideal methodology would be identifying the absolute highest and lowest possible values for each indicator. If such values are identified, absolute ranges for the indicators can be constructed.

[20]For data source of this section, see Section 3.2 except otherwise specified.

Table 3.6. Scoring Scale for Data Converted into Ordinal Values.

Indicator	Ordinal Value									
	1	2	3	4	5	6	7	8	9	10
AV-1	30–46	46–62	62–78	78–94	94–110	110–126	126–142	142–158	158–174	174–190
AV-2	0.5–0.6	0.4–0.5	0.3–0.4	0.2–0.3	0.1–0.2	0–0.1	(−0.1)–0	(−0.2)–(−0.1)	(−0.3)–(−0.2)	(−0.4)–(−0.3)
AV-3	25–32	32–39	39–46	46–53	53–60	60–67	67–74	74–81	81–88	88–95
AV-4	0.495–0.503	0.503–0,511	0.511–0.519	0.519–0.527	0.527–0.535	0.535–0.543	0.543–0.551	0.551–0.559	0.559–0.567	0.567–0.575
AV-5	0.32–0.33	0.33–0.34	0.34–0.35	0.35–0.36	0.36–0.37	0.37–0.38	0.38–0.39	0.39–0.40	0.40–0.41	0.41–0.42
AP-1	31,600–34,000	29,200–31,600	26,800–29,200	24,400–26,800	22,000–24,400	19,600–22,000	17,200–19,600	14,800–17,200	12,400–14,800	10,000–12,400
AP-2	0.290–0.299	0.299–0.308	0.308–0.317	0.317–0.326	0.326–0.335	0.335–0.344	0.344–0.353	0.353–0.362	0.362–0.371	0.371–0.380
AP-3	1,600–2,130	2,130–2,660	2,660–3,190	3,190–3,720	3,720–4,250	4,250–4,780	4,780–5,310	5,310–5,840	5,840–6,370	6,370–6,900
AP-4	0–84	84–168	168–252	252–336	336–420	420–504	504–588	588–672	672–756	756–840
AP-5	0.150–0.171	0.171–0.192	0.192–0.213	0.213–0.234	0.234–0.255	0.255–0.276	0.276–0.297	0.297–0.318	0.318–0.339	0.339–0.360
AC-1	0.241–0.260	0.222–0.241	0.203–0.222	0.184–0.203	0.165–0.184	0.146–0.165	0.127–0.146	0.108–0.127	0.089–0.108	0.070–0.089
AC-2	2,470–2,600	2,340–2,470	2,210–2,340	2,080–2,210	1,950–2,080	1,820–1,950	1,690–1,820	1,560–1,690	1,430–1,560	1,300–1,430
AC-3	1,432–1,500	1,364–1,432	1,296–1,364	1,228–1,296	1,160–1,228	1,092–1,160	1,024–1,092	956–1,024	888–956	820–888
AC-4	0.160–0.168	0.168–0.176	0.176–0.184	0.184–0.192	0.192–0.200	0.200–0.208	0.208–0.216	0.216–0.224	0.224–0.232	0.232–0.240
AC-5	0–0.0022	0.0022–0.0044	0.00440.0066	0.0066–0.0088	0.0088–0.0110	0.0110–0.0132	0.0132–0.0154	0.0154–0.0176	0.0176–0.0198	0.0198–0.0220
AF-1	18.9%–21%	16.8%–18.9%	14.7%–16.8%	12.6%–14.7%	10.5%–12.6%	8.4%–10.5%	6.3%–8.4%	4.2%–6.3%	2.1%–4.2%	0–2.1%
AF-2	32.4%–36.0%	28.8%–32.4%	25.2%–28.8%	21.6%–25.2%	18.0%–21.6%	14.4%–18.0%	10.8%–14.4%	7.2%–10.8%	3.6%–7.2%	0–3.6%
AF-3	20.7%–23.0%	18.4%–20.7%	16.1%–18.4%	13.8%–16.1%	11.5%–13.8%	9.2%–11.5%	6.9%–9.2%	4.6%–6.9%	2.3%–4.6%	0–2.3%
AF-4	1125–1250	1000–1125	875–1000	750–875	625–750	500–625	375–500	250–375	125–250	0–125
AF-5	110–125	125–140	140–155	155–170	170–185	185–200	200–215	215–230	230–245	245–260

Table 3.7. The 4-As Indicators in Ordinal Values.

Indicators	**Years**						
	1980	**1985**	**1990**	**1995**	**2000**	**2005**	**2010**
AV-1	10	7	5	4	4	2	1
AV-2	8	10	8	7	4	3	1
AV-3	4	7	6	10	5	2	1
AV-4	10	9	4	5	1	9	1
AV-5	1	8	8	10	2	9	5
Average value	6.6	8.2	6.2	7.2	3.2	5.0	1.8
AP-1	1	4	6	8	10	9	10
AP-2	1	3	3	4	6	8	10
AP-3	1	2	2	3	6	6	10
AP-4	1	1	1	4	3	10	10
AP-5	9	1	1	4	9	10	7
Average value	2.6	2.2	2.6	4.6	6.8	8.6	9.4
AC-1	10	9	8	7	7	4	1
AC-2	10	10	9	6	5	1	4
AC-3	3	3	3	1	5	5	10
AC-4	6	10	7	5	2	1	5
AC-5	1	1	1	6	6	10	9
Average value	6.0	6.6	5.6	5.0	5.0	4.2	5.8
AF-1	10	8	8	1	9	5	6
AF-2	10	9	9	1	7	8	8
AF-3	10	9	9	1	7	10	10
AF-4	10	10	9	8	6	5	1
AF-5	1	2	2	2	1	6	10
Average value	8.2	7.6	7.4	2.6	6.0	6.8	7.0

high in 1980 whereas the AP score was pretty low. The 1980 rhombus covers 68.04 sq. units, which is also a relatively high score among the seven rhombuses. This shows that at the very beginning of China's economic reform, its energy security status was favourable compared to that of subsequent years.

The target of the country's economic plan was to speed up growth in its industries that were damaged during the 'Cultural Revolution'. During the Sixth FYP period (1981–1985), energy shortage was the key obstacle to the nation's economic development. To fuel the economy, the Sixth FYP highlighted the expansion of energy supply. It specified the targets for coal, oil, and electricity

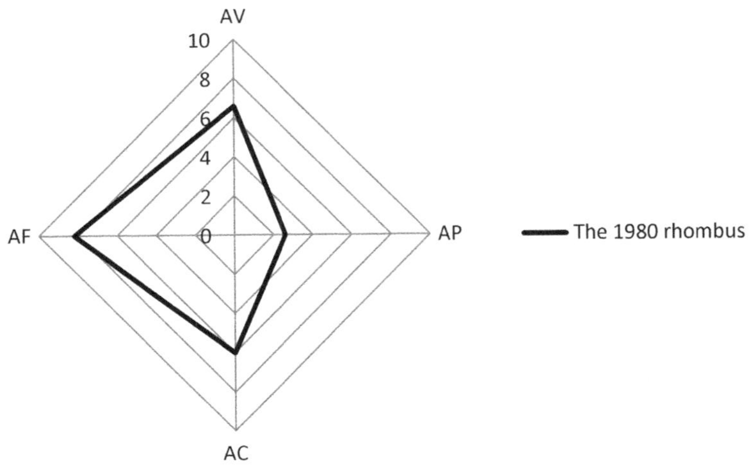

Fig. 3.2. Energy Security Status of 1980 (Benchmark for This Study): 68.04 Sq. Units.

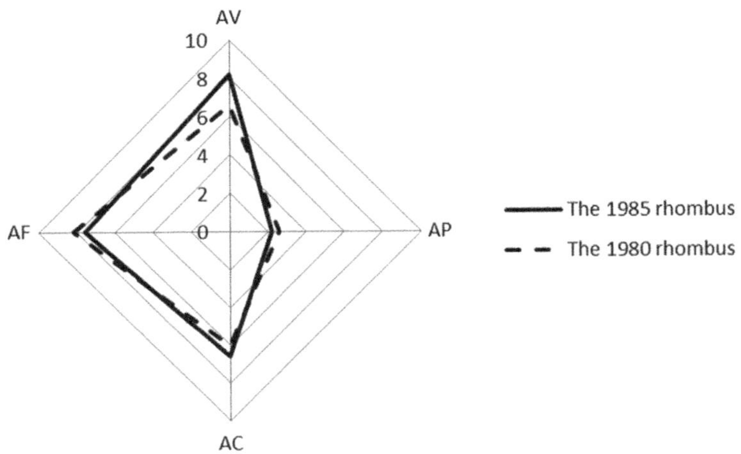

Fig. 3.3. Energy Security Status of 1985 (the Ending Year of the Sixth FYP Period): 72.52 Sq. Units.

production. Considering the scale of the national economic development goal, the government forged ahead to promote the development of renewable energy, hydropower in particular, and called for energy conservation to compensate for restrictions caused by the low level of energy technology. All energy policies during this period showed an obvious emphasis on the availability dimension.

The energy security situation improved a little during the Seventh FYP period. The 1985 rhombus covers 72.52 sq. units, which is the biggest area among the seven rhombuses. The 1985 rhombus shows that the negative impact of the low level of technology on the status of energy security of China was offset by relatively low

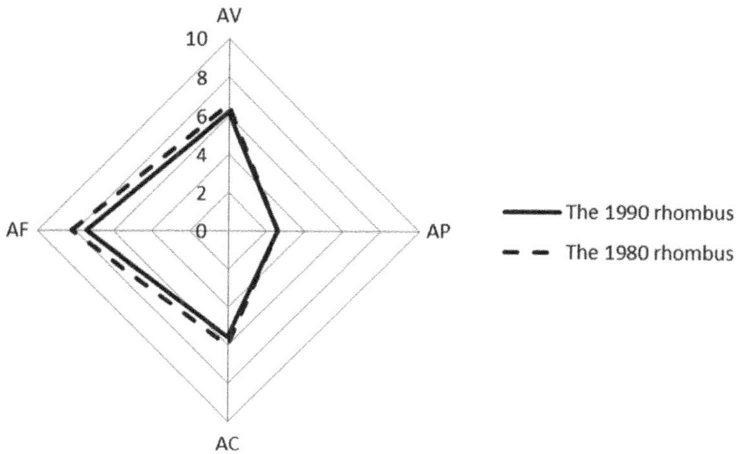

Fig. 3.4. Energy Security Status of 1990 (the Ending Year of the Seventh FYP Period): 59 Sq. Units.

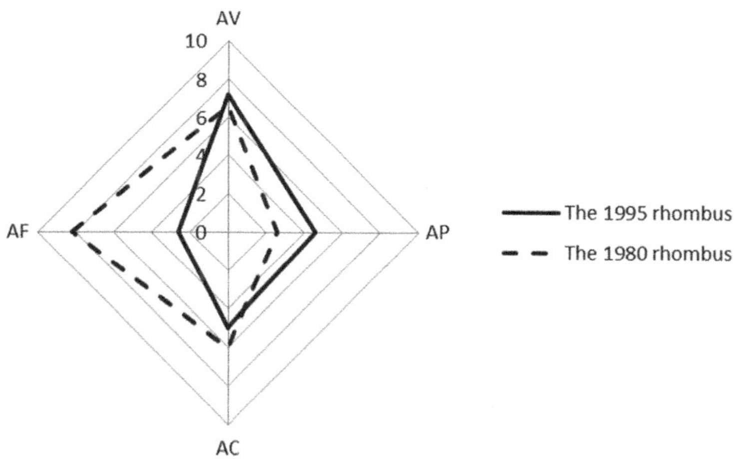

Fig. 3.5. Energy Security Status of 1995 (the Ending Year of the Eighth FYP Period): 43.92 Sq. Units.

volatility in energy prices and by the cleaner environment. Taking into account the imbalance index, which is the second lowest among the seven years in calculation, the Sixth FYP period shows a relatively good energy security situation. More energy reserves, cleaner environment, and stable prices contributed to relatively balanced development of the four dimensions of energy security in China.

Since the industrial production growth was much faster than originally planned, the development of the energy industry was clearly defined during the Seventh FYP period (1986–1990). The government emphasised supply expansion to meet the expected surging demand for energy. The planned annual growth in total primary energy production was targeted at 3.4% (NDRC, 1986, p. 18).

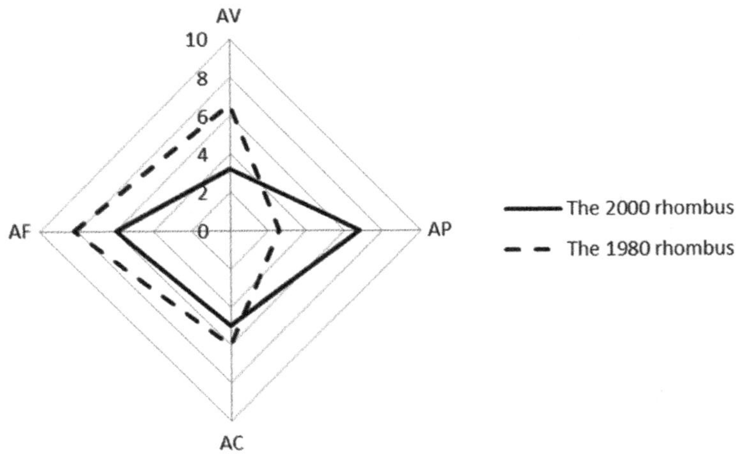

Fig. 3.6. Energy Security Status of 2000 (the Ending Year of the Ninth FYP Period): 52.48 Sq. Units.

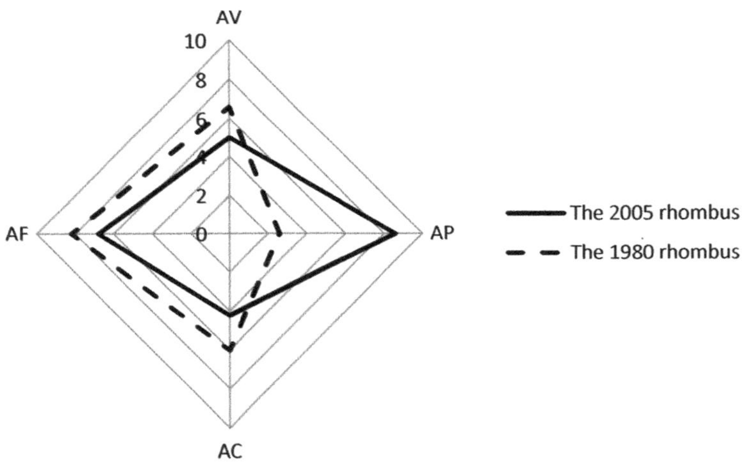

Fig. 3.7. Energy Security Status of 2005 (the Ending Year of the Tenth FYP Period): 70.84 Sq. Units.

The power industry was highlighted as the most critical sector to be developed. It was clearly stipulated in the suggestions on the Seventh FYP that power industry should be the centre of energy industry development: China shall 'actively develop thermal power' and 'vigorously develop hydropower' (NDRC, 1985). But the energy security situation did not improve. The 1990 rhombus covers 59 sq. units, indicating a deteriorating situation.

China's energy security continued to deteriorate in the 1990s, a period characterised by 'deepening reform and broadening opening up', resulting in its drastic economic transformation and an insatiable hunger for energy. The 1995 rhombus

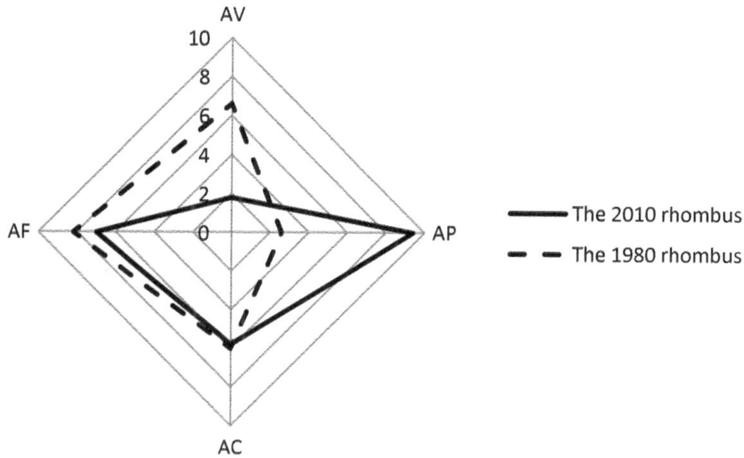

Fig. 3.8. Energy Security Status of 2010 (the Ending Year of the Eleventh FYP Period): 62.32 Sq. Units.

Table 3.8. Total Rhombus Area of Ending Year of FYP.

Year	1980	1985	1990	1995	2000	2005	2010
Area (sq. units)	68.04	72.52	59	43.92	52.48	70.84	62.32

Table 3.9. Imbalance Index of Ending Year of FYP.

Year	1980	1985	1990	1995	2000	2005	2010
Imbalance index	0.49	0.46	0.46	0.58	0.43	0.52	0.65

is the smallest and its relevant imbalance index, 0.58, is the second highest among the years in calculation, suggesting an obvious imbalanced development of the four dimensions of energy security. This period was marked by expanding energy production, fluctuating energy prices, and deteriorating environmental conditions.

The Ninth FYP (1996–2000) continued to rank power as the centre of energy development. Its annual growth in production was targeted at 7% over the Plan period. The coal industry was selected as the key sector for development. Its development principle was to stabilise the production in eastern areas and accelerate development in north-western regions. Energy technologies – the clean coal technology and long distance power transmission technology – were highlighted in the Plan. The state coalmines were expected to improve their production efficiency and raise profits by making technological progress. Nevertheless, the drastic economic reform measures and the untiringly pursuit of the economic goal only worsened the overall of energy security situation. The 1995 and 2000

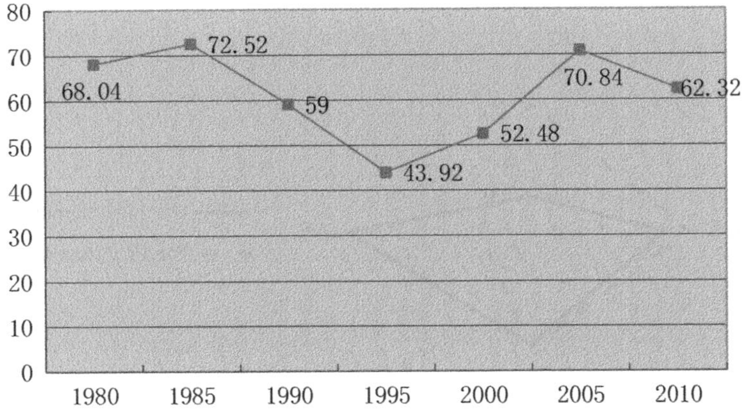

Fig. 3.9. Evolving Trend Timeline for Area of the Rhombuses.

rhombuses cover 43.92 and 52.48 sq. units, respectively, indicating a relatively worse energy security situation in the 1990s.

The Tenth FYP (2001–2005) specified that the energy sector had to continue to undergo marketisation. The AP and AF dimensions began to attract increasing attention and improved to some extent. The 2005 rhombus covers 70.84 sq. units, an area much larger than the 2000 rhombus of 52.48 sq. units, indicating an improved energy security situation. However, during the Eleventh FYP (2006–2010), the energy availability reached its worst situation in all the years under study. The 2010 rhombus covers 62.32 sq. units. Taking the panoramic view of China's 30 years of economic reform, the Sixth FYP period had the best energy security situation and it coincided with the early reform period. Although the overall situation was better in the first decade of the new millennium than in the 1990s, it did not catch up with the Sixth FYP period. Fig. 3.9 shows the evolving trend timeline for area of the rhombuses.

3.4.2. The AV Trend

The average ordinal value peaks in 1985 at 8.2 and hits the lowest in 2010 at 1.8. Fig. 3.10 shows a downward trend of the availability dimension.

China's economic development, accelerated by a series of economic reforms, required high levels of energy production. Since 1980, the expansion of energy supply has been vital to China's energy policy. The policy changes were evidently related with energy supply as the nature/roles of policies swing between two extremes: policies gave incentives to push for energy production during times of shortages of energy; policies imposed harsh restrictions when the economy was overheated. Since the early 1980s, the government began to encourage the development of town and village coalmines (TVCMs) to alleviate energy shortages even though some TVCMs were shut down in the late 1990s due to the pressure to enhance environmental protection and to protect the state-owned coalmines. The steady growth of coal production led to a decreased coal R/P

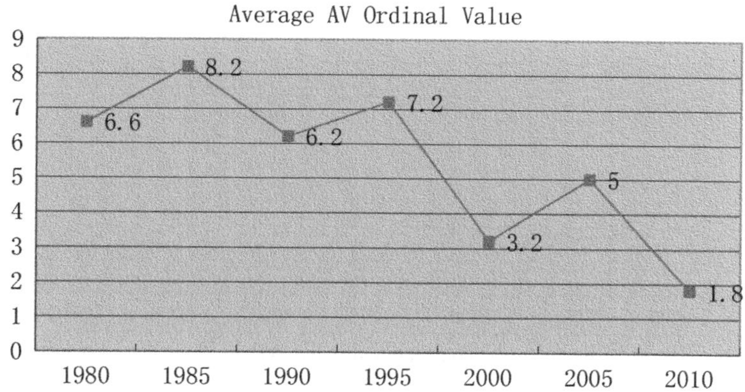

Fig. 3.10. Trend Illustration of Average Value for AV.

ratio. Similarly, the growth rate of natural gas consumption increased faster than that of its proved reserves. The natural gas reserves-to-consumption ratio began to decrease in the mid-1990s. China was a net exporter of energy resources. The oil import dependence ratio was –31.58% in 1985, which was the decisive factor that made the AV dimension the highest ordinal value in 1985. The huge demand for energy, along with a fast pace of economic development, made China a net importer of oil in 1993, a net importer of natural gas in 2007, and a net importer of coal in 2009.

The power sector is vital to China's energy security due to its key role in both industry and daily life. It was stipulated in the Seventh FYP that the power industry should be the centre of the country's energy industry development. Since then, the electricity generation and the installed capacity of generation had grown steadily. Reforms in the power sector accelerated the expansion. The first stage of the power-sector reform was initiated in 1986. The reform partially decentralised the investment authority in the generation sector. Various investors, including local governments, SOEs, and private and foreign companies were invited to build new power plants to supplement power generation to meet the increasing demand for electricity. Since Deng Xiaoping's 1992 Southern Tour, China accelerated its transformation to the market economy. This gave birth to the second stage of the power-sector reform beginning in 1997. This wave of reform aimed at separating the government administration from the business operations of the power plants and power grids (Zhang & Heller, 2004). Market competition was gradually injected into the power sector to hasten the pace of economic expansion of both electricity generation and installed capacity of China's power industry. The pace of the expansion of the power industry was so fast that by the end of the Eleventh FYP in 2010, China generated about 4,000 billion kWh of electricity with a total installed capacity of about 1,000 million kW, at least a tenfold increase compared to the early reform period. In general, the installed capacity in the conventional thermal electricity sector expanded faster than the actual generation, especially in 2000 and 2010, when the government rushed to shut down small and inefficient thermal plants to protect state-owned ones in a concerted effort to improve the environment. This makes the

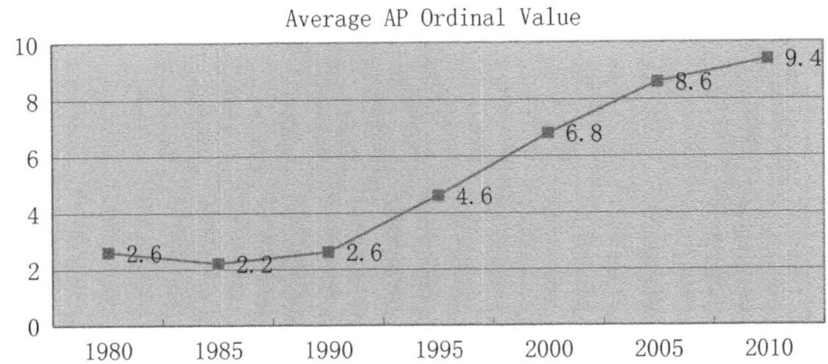

Fig. 3.11. Trend Illustration of Average Value for AP.

ordinal value of the availability factor of conventional thermal electricity the lowest in 2000 and 2010. The availability factor of 1985, 1995, and 2005 scores relatively high, which drives up the average AV ordinal value in these three years, respectively.

3.4.3. The AP Trend

China's energy-related technology generally improved over time. Fig. 3.11 shows that there is a general upward trend of the ordinal value during the 30 years of economic reform except for the slight outlier in 1985. But since then, the trend takes an upward turn until 2010. The ordinal value hits the highest at 9.4 in 2010 and the lowest at 2.2 in 1985.

China's energy intensity decreased steadily and consistently between the 1980s and 1990s, with the government's awareness of the need to reduce its energy intensity and improve energy efficiency. Since 2001, fast economic growth and huge consumption of energy triggered the rise of energy intensity. In response to the surge in energy demand during the Tenth FYP period, the government set the goal to reduce the country's energy intensity by 20% during the Eleventh FYP period and made structural adjustments to move the economy away from energy-intensive production (IEA, 2007b). Consequently, by the end of 2010, China 'saw a last-minute rush to meet targets' amid social and economic disruption including blackouts, forced factory closures, and the disrupted residential heating (The Climate Group, 2011, p. 8). With much awkwardness, China managed to achieve its goal of energy intensity reduction. The relevant ordinal value increases from 9 in 2005 to 10 in 2010.

The increase of generation efficiency of thermal power plants reflected China's success in improving its power generation technology. This helped to push up the AP ordinal value particularly since 1990, the starting year of the steady rise of the AP ordinal value. Coal is the dominant fossil fuel for electricity generation. China has been actively conducting R&D of various forms of advanced coal-burning technologies including supercritical and ultra-supercritical systems, circulating fluidised beds, and flue gas desulfurisation (Wu, Pineau, & Caporossi, 2010). Although the development of supercritical and ultra-supercritical systems in China started relatively late, it made rapid progress. The first application of supercritical boilers, imported from Switzerland and the U.S., was at the Shanghai Shidongkou

Second Power Plant, operated by the China Huaneng Group in 1992. During the Eleventh FYP period, there were two more power plants using ultra-supercritical pressure boilers: China Huaneng Group's Yuhuan power plant in Zhejiang Province and China Huadian Corporation's Zouxian power plant in Shandong Province. Both had high-efficiency dust removal and desulphurisation equipment that could meet international standards. By 2010, supercritical and ultra-supercritical units accounted for more than 40% of the newly built thermal power generating units (Chen & Xu, 2010, p. 2126). These units greatly helped to reduce the energy consumption per kilowatt hour electricity supply. Other advanced power generation technologies such as supercritical and ultra-supercritical systems, circulating fluidised beds, and flue gas desulphurisation were rapidly developed during this period. The generation efficiency of thermal power plants grew very fast, with its ordinal value going up from 4 in 1995 to 8 in 2005, and 10 in 2010.

In the oil sector, the introduction of foreign technology and capital along with the opening up of China's offshore oilfields to international oil companies during the Sixth FYP period sped up China's oil harnessing technology. International oil companies were also allowed to be involved in China's onshore oilfields in the coastal provinces in July 1985. The modernisation and maintenance of onshore oilfields accelerated oil technological advancement and oil production (Locatelli, 1989). China's oil distillation capacity increased steadily from 1,600 thousand barrels per day in 1980 to 6,806 thousand barrels per day in 2010. This contributes to the steady rise of the AP ordinal values since 1985.

Patents owned by coal mining and dressing and petroleum and natural gas extraction industries grew very fast during the Tenth and Eleventh FYP periods. These industries focused on technological advancement, which contributes the most to the fast and steady increase of AP ordinal values since 2000. To boost the development of the energy industry, the government implemented a series of measures to attract domestic and foreign investments since 1990. From then on, energy investments had expanded. The milestone of investment in Chinese energy industry was in 2004. The State Council issued the *Decision about Investment Regime Reform*, which specified the principle that 'whomever makes the investment shall be the decision-maker, the beneficiary, and the risk undertaker of the investment' (Pan & Zhu, 2005/2006, p. 45). The *Decision* prospered technical updating and transformation investment in the energy industry.

3.4.4. The AC Trend

Fig. 3.12 shows that there is a steady declining trend in the AC ordinal values from 1985 to 2005. The ordinal value declines from 6.6 in 1985, the ending year of the Sixth FYP, to 4.2 in 2005, the ending year of the Tenth FYP. The worsening situation took a turn for the better during the Eleventh FYP period, when the ordinal value rebounded to 5.8.

Fossil fuels are the key sources of CO_2 and SO_2 emissions, with coal alone accounting for a major part. Continued growth in energy production and consumption led to steady increases in the CO_2 and SO_2 emissions in China. China had been addressing the air pollution problems since the 1980s. Starting in 1982,

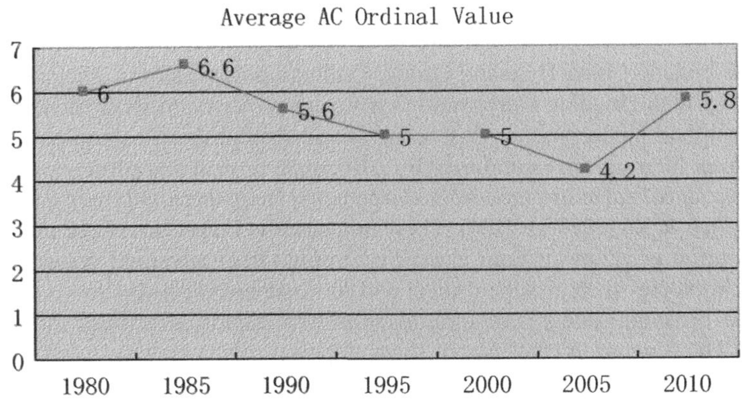

Fig. 3.12. Trend Illustration of Average Value for AC.

the government ordered the industries to pay a 0.04 Yuan for every 10 m^3 of SO_2 emitted in excess of standards. However, most enterprises preferred to pay the charges instead of reducing emissions, due to the high cost of emissions abatement (Yun, 1998). Environmental problems had been serious in China since the 1990s. Although environmental protection began to exert its full presence on China's political agenda during this period, the enforcement was at odds. China's share of global total CO_2 emissions increased from 7.8% in 1980 to 25.1% in 2010. The government's effort in controlling SO_2 emissions was effective in the Eleventh FYP period. The SO_2 emissions rose steadily and reached a peak of 25,494 thousand tons at the end of the Tenth FYP period in 2005, before falling back to 21,851 thousand tons in 2010 – partly as a result of the requirement of installing more desulphurisation equipment at thermal power plants. The total volume of soot discharges deceased from 11,825 thousand tons in 2005 to 8,291 thousand tons in 2010, which proved to be the most effective soot discharge control over 30 years of economic reform. The promotion of environmental protection proved fruitful during the Eleventh FYP and contributed to the climbing up of the AC ordinal value in 2010.

In the renewable energy sector, China had shown strong willingness to support the deployment of renewable energy since the early 1990s when the *China's Agenda 21* was issued. Several policies on renewable energy technological development were made. In 1994, the State Planning Commission formulated the *Brightness Program and Ride the Wind Program*. In 1996, the State Economic and Trade Commission (SETC) advanced the *Ninth Five-Year Plan of Industrialization of New and Renewable Energy*. In 2001, the SETC proposed the *Tenth Five-Year Plan for New and Renewable Energy Commercialization Development*. In 2003, the *Renewable Energy Promotion Law* was promulgated (National Renewable Energy Laboratory, 2004). All these policies promoted the renewable energy technological development in China, but the development pace lagged behind the enlarging appetite for energy. Although the electricity generated by renewable energy resources increased on a yearly basis, the share of renewable energy out of total electricity generation decreased steadily from 23.4% in 1985 to 16.8% in 2005. Several economic, political, and social barriers delayed the progress of renewable energy development.[21]

To alleviate the environmental pollution, several programs were set up during the Eleventh FYP to promote renewable energy development in China. *Renewable Energy Law* and *Circular Economy Law* took effect in 2006 and in 2007, respectively. According to the *Renewable Energy Law*, the National Development and Reform Commission (NDRC) announced *Plans on Medium- and Long-term Development of Renewable Energy Resources* in 2007 (NDRC, 2007b). All these measures contributed to the small rebound of the renewable energy resources share in total electricity generation from 16.8% in 2005 to 19.3% in 2010. The exploitation and development of renewable energy became more effective during the Eleventh FYP period.

A favourable factor that may have helped the development of nuclear energy in China was the willingness of the Chinese people to embrace the role that nuclear technologies will play in the country's continued economic development (Zhou, 2010). Since 1992, nuclear power has been utilised and generally, it has an increasing share of total electricity generation despite slight decreases in some years. In 2005, the nuclear share peaked at 2.12% in China's total net electricity generation. Over the Eleventh FYP period, the increase rate of nuclear share went down, but the share still remained at 1.77%, much higher than in the 1990s. The Chinese people's acceptability of nuclear power dilutes the declining trend of AC ordinal values.

3.4.5. The AF Trend

Fig. 3.13 shows that there is a slight dip of AF ordinal values with the year 1995 as an outstanding outlier. The highest ordinal value 8.2 is in 1980, showing the best affordability situation in China. The outlier 1995 only has the ordinal value

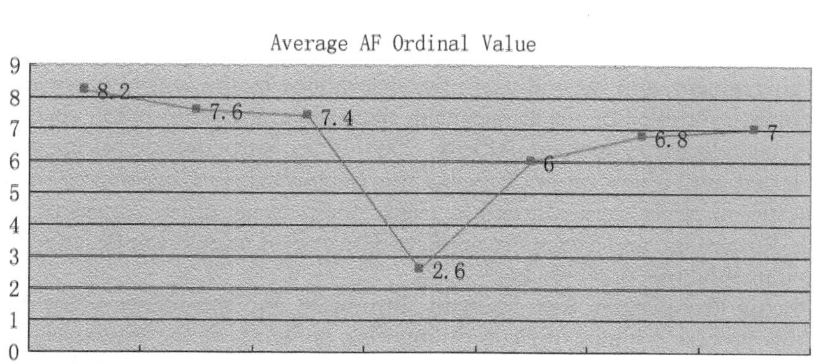

Fig. 3.13. Trend Illustration of Average Value for AF.

[21]For detailed discussion on barriers of renewable energy development in China, see Section 4.4.2.

of 2.6, the lowest one among the seven years in calculation, due to the high growth rate of coal, oil, and electricity prices in that year.

Before the economic reform, China's energy industry operated within the planned economy system. Energy prices were decided by the central government, which intentionally kept the prices low to fuel the economy. The low and stable prices led to a relatively favourable situation that enhanced affordability in the country. Little progress was made in liberalising energy pricing in the 1980s except the introduction of a two-tier pricing system in the coal sector.

Since 1984, local state mines were allowed to sell coal output in excess of their official quotas at a premium and all non-state mines were allowed to sell their products at market prices. In 1986, the central state mines were also allowed similar concessions for their over-quota output (Wright, 1996). The coal sector was the sector with the earliest pricing liberalisation, albeit not in a full scale. China's explicit target to establish a socialist market economic system after Deng Xiaoping's 1992 Southern Tour accelerated the deregulation of coal pricing. Since then, the market mechanism had been gradually injected into energy pricing. In 2002, the 'supervised prices' imposed on thermal coal consumed by power plants was revoked. The liberalisation of coal pricing was finally completed in the coal sector in 2009, when the NDRC approved of direct negotiation between coal enterprises and power plants on thermal coal contracts (Tu, 2011). The liberalisation of coal pricing during the Eleventh FYP period led to the highest volatility of coal prices in 2010.

The electricity pricing reform preceded the oil pricing reform and progressed rapidly. In the early 1990s, electricity tariffs were allowed to fluctuate according to the prices of primary energy and other production materials (Yang & Yu, 1996). Relevant pricing policies made the electricity tariffs very complex. In 2002, the separation between the enterprises of power generation and the enterprises of power grid stimulated the electricity tariff reform. The pricing system was designed to be more market oriented, with three categories: the generation price based on generator status; the transmission and distribution price set by the central government; and the end-user price determined by the central government. Although controlled by the government, these prices are set to reflect costs and to manage electricity demand (APERC, 2008). The control over oil pricing generally lasted until a new oil price regime was established. In November 2001, the domestic oil prices were adjusted to peg to the package price – prices of New York, Rotterdam, and Singapore markets. The market mechanism began to play a fundamental role in oil pricing.

Pricing liberalisation was gradually introduced into the energy sector. During this process, China experienced mounting pressures of the excessively high growth rate of energy prices in 1995 and the worst affordability situation. Only in the later periods when the market mechanism in energy pricing gradually became relatively mature did the situation begin to improve, which is reflected in the upward trend during the Ninth FYP, and the flat and smooth slope shown in the Tenth and Eleventh FYP periods. The 1995 high-energy price growth rate is inextricable from Deng's 1992 Southern Tour and the central government's goal to establish a socialist market economy. Driven by Deng's tour and the reform to construct a socialist market economy, China's national economy grew very fast between 1992 and 1993. At the same time, excessive price increases and inflation pressures rose again (Peng and Chen, 2011b). The overheated economy during the Eighth FYP period made the rise in energy prices steep in 1995. After that, the sustained transition to marketisation brought about a relatively mature pricing mechanism in the energy sector. The AF dimension had gradually improved since 1995.

3.5. Chapter Summary

In this chapter, the author uses the comprehensive concept of energy security and the indicators within the 4-As framework to measure China's energy security over 30 years of economic reform. The energy policies are reviewed to analyse the extent of their impact on energy security.

The 4-As framework is constructed by four dimensions – the availability of energy resources, the applicability of technology, the societal acceptability, and the affordability of energy resources. Unlike other existing quantitative frameworks and measurements of energy security, the 4-As framework uses the least number of indicators but is comprehensive enough to accurately represent the nature of energy security. Ordinal values are converted from the statistical data of 20 indicators under the 4-As for seven years in calculation: 1980, 1985, 1990, 1995, 2000, 2005, and 2010. They are then plotted into seven rhombuses, respectively, to illustrate the energy security situation by measuring the area of these rhombuses. A bigger area indicates that a higher level of energy security is brought about by the energy policies that were implemented in a particular FYP. The analysis shows that China's overall energy security situation had not improved since its reform in 1980. The status of energy security appears to be the best in 1985 and the worst in 1995. Since then, the situation improved until 2005, but still fell short of its peak in 1985. From 2005 to 2010, the situation deteriorated. The emphasis on the energy development plan had affected the status of energy security directly and deeply. In the early reform period, the Chinese economy was still directly under government control and prices were still stable. The energy resources were not extensively exploited so the environment was relatively not so polluted. However, the reform package introduced in 1994 had an immediate adverse impact on the 1995 energy security status. Amid the expanding energy production, deteriorating environment, and fluctuating energy prices, the energy security situation in China hit the bottom in 1995, as depicted by the smallest rhombus in the study.

China's insatiable hunger for energy resources caused the quantitative value of the availability dimension to decline while the environmental (acceptability) dimension deteriorated along with the energy utilisation. However, there were signs of slight improvement in the late 2000s. The affordability dimension improved after it hit the worst status in 1995. China's technology progressed steadily but the applicability dimension did not make sufficient progress to make the overall energy security status reach the early reform period level. In 2010, the deteriorating energy security status was accompanied by the worst availability situation. Along with the injection of the market force into the energy industry in China, the sectors of coal, oil, and electricity experienced reforms that either improved or diminished the relevant 'A' dimension, and affected the overall energy security in China. The next chapter provides a detailed review on the impact of the energy policies on the energy security situation in China.

Chapter 4

Energy Policy in China Since its Reform and Opening Up

China's energy policies are a diversified mix of government mandates, industry stipulations, and company activities. This chapter contains a discussion of these policies and an analysis of their impact on China's energy security situation which is evaluated in Chapter 3.

4.1. Energy Policies from 1949 (Founding of PRC) to 1976 (End of Cultural Revolution)

4.1.1. Energy Polices from 1949 (Founding of PRC) to 1957 (End of the First Five-Year Plan)

In the early days after the founding of People's Republic of China (PRC), the first task of the energy industry was to restore the normal production of the existing coalmines, oil fields, and power plants. To do this, the Ministry of Fuel Industry was established in October 1949 to manage the Coal Mine Bureau, the Oil Bureau, and the Electrical Industry Bureau (Yu, 2010). Acting as China's energy industry authority, the Ministry of Fuel Industry was to take the lead to develop the coal industry, power industry, and oil industry in order to meet domestic demand. It developed the energy production plan and interfered with the individual enterprises' production and management matters such as production planning, technology, and even workers' wages. The establishment of the Ministry of Fuel Industry fully reflected the role of the planned economy of that period (CASS, 1996).

Immediately after the founding of PRC, the Ministry of Fuel Industry held three national professional meetings to address the management of coal, electricity, and oil. The meeting on coal management was the most important as it established the key aim for the coal industry in China. The aim was to recover the coal production and at the same time build several new mines with new technology and equipment in order to guarantee supply for future industrial development (Chi, 2005). In 1949, the central government established and exercised control over new institutions to stabilise the prices of key resources such as coal. By 1952, due to the threat of the Korean War, the central government further improved the allocation of important materials, 12 (including coal) of which were under direct

Energy Security in Times of Economic Transition: Lessons from China, 75–112

doi:10.1108/978-1-83982-464-720201005

central control (Chen, 1992). The existing energy industry was taken over by the central government. The foreign investment and bureaucratic capital left behind by the Kuomintang (KMT) government were confiscated to form a large part of China's energy industry (Su, 1999).

4.1.1.1. Investment. In 1951, the first National Industrial Conference set out a plan for industrial production. The total investment in coal, electricity, and petroleum industries represented 18% of the total national infrastructure investment (Li, 1992, p. 306). The investment in the energy industry made up a relatively high proportion of the country's total investment in infrastructure. During the First FYP (1953–1957), the industrial projects were randomly distributed. Key projects were scattered across the country, and were mostly concentrated around the cities. Most of the coal and power industries were located in coal-rich regions of Northeast and North China. The industrial investment in these two regions accounted for 70% of the national total between 1953 and 1955. In 1954 and 1955, the output of coal and electricity of these two regions accounted for 84.4% and 66% of country's total output, respectively (Liu, 1995, p. 8). During the five years, the fuel industry[1] accounted for 25.5% of the national industrial infrastructure investment. This is higher than the heavy industry (24.4%) and only slightly lower than the machinery industry (26%) (CCP Central Committee's Literature Research Center, 1993a, p. 416). In contrast, the investment in coal still kept a high proportion. Within five years, 31 coal enterprises were constructed and accounted for more than one million tons of coal per annum (Li, 1993). The central government realised that energy development must remain top priority for the development of other industries. However, during the First FYP period, the unexpected rapid heavy industrial development resulted in a shortage of energy supply. To meet the demand for coal, measures such as inventory reduction, sales control, and energy conservation were adopted (CCP Central Committee's Literature Research Center, 1993b).

4.1.1.2. Reform of Energy Enterprises. Both coal and power sectors had to undergo reform during this period. The coal industry experienced three types of reforms: production, management, and technology. The coal industry followed the former Soviet Union production model. The cadres at all levels in the Party, the government officials, and the workers were required to cooperate under the leadership of the Party committee. Both coal mining and transportation adopted mechanisation. The reform of the coal sector helped to reduce accidents and casualties, save resources, and improve productivity. The reform of the power industry upgraded its technology to the Soviet model to solve practical problems. It focused on the workers' use of innovative tools. Plenty of suggestions and proposals were submitted by workers to increase efficiency. In the meantime,

[1]In the early days of China's energy production and consumption pattern, coal was the major one. Exploration of oil and gas was very low. This situation lasted for more than a decade until the exploitation of Daqing and other oil fields which greatly improved the structure of energy production and consumption. This means that in the early days of China's national economic plan, fuel industry mainly refers to the coal sector.

the heavy equipment maintenance technology improved significantly. The safety of power supply was enhanced. The management system of the power industry, which played an important role in saving manpower and resources, also improved (CASS, 1996). The coal and power sectors were reformed in a planned and systematic manner under the centralised planned system.

4.1.1.3. Policy Effects. From 1950 to 1952, China saw the restoration of its coal, power, and petroleum industries. The recovery of the power industry was the most remarkable. Years of war had ravaged the power industry. After the restoration of the existing old equipment, the growth rate of the power industry became impressive. In 1952, the total electricity generation was 7.3 billion kWh. The growth rate of power production was 26.3% (Woodard, 1980, p. 462). Production efficiency rose. During the recovery period, China had largely restored the war-torn energy industry and upgraded the technology of the energy industry. During the First FYP period, the production of energy industry increased but still lagged far behind the soaring demand for coal. This demand–supply gap also existed in the oil and electricity sectors (CASS, 1998; Chen, 1993).

4.1.2. Energy Policies During the 'Great Leap Forward'

China's attempt to a quick transition to heavy industrialisation forced it to develop heavy industries promptly, even though its energy and raw material industries were not mature enough. Focusing on heavy industry made China rapidly establish its energy industry but at the same time undermined the development of other sectors such as the agricultural development. This phenomenon was especially prominent during the 'Great Leap Forward', a period marked by the rampant practice of incorrect economic development guidelines (Zhao, 2010). As China's heavy industry development (mainly the iron and steel industry) was essential for national industrialisation and economic development (Shi, 1996), it became the key focus of its energy production plan.

In 1957, the Chinese leaders had unprecedented confidence in pursuing rapid economic development because they achieved the target of their First FYP ahead of schedule. In 1958, the 'Great Leap Forward' was introduced to strengthen China's industrial power via increasing steel and iron production. However, the movement disrupted the national economy and wasted resources. The mass steel and iron smelting campaign had a direct negative impact on the energy production and consumption. The campaign was also the major reference for the government energy policymaking. The following subsections have a discussion in detail.

4.1.2.1 'Great Leap Forward' of Coal Industry. In 1958, the Second FYP set its target to turn China into a socialist country by modernising its industry, agriculture, and science and culture. Therefore, the central government highlighted the importance of steel production and ordered that industrial production meet the needs of the mass steel and iron smelting campaign. The expected target, by the end of the Second FYP, was as follows: by 1962, if the production of steel was 80 million tons, then the corresponding key energy indicators would include 300 billion kilowatt-hour of electricity, 900 million tons of raw coal, and 50 million tons of crude oil (CCP Central Committee's Literature Research

Center, 1995, p. 432). Subsequent modifications to the energy production plan were subject to the adjustment of the steel and iron production plan. In order to meet the needs of the national mass steel and iron smelting campaign, the Ministry of Coal Industry proposed the slogan of 'Whole Nation Put Great Effort to Build Coalmines'. The Ministry of Coal Industry adjusted the production plan's target to 380 million tons in 1959 and 520 million tons in 1962 (Editorial Board of 'Contemporary China', 1988, p. 44). As the production plan departed from the coal mining production capacity, the coal production was seriously affected. Since May 1960, the national coal production continued to fall significantly (Editorial Board of 'Contemporary China', 1988). It was estimated that China's raw coal production was around 280–425 million metric tons in 1960 (Woodard, 1980, pp. 408–409). But in 1962, this figure fell in the range of 180–254 million metric tons. It is difficult to make estimates for the 'Great Leap Forward' period due to the over-reporting at that time. One thing that was certain was that in the early 1960s, China's coal industry was sluggish. New mines were not constructed, and the output of the existing mines remained at low levels (Woodard, 1980).

4.1.2.2 'Great Leap Forward' of Power and Oil Industries. Soon after the 'Great Leap Forward' began, the development of the steel and iron industry led to a huge demand for electricity, creating a severe shortage of it. One reason was the severe shortage of power generation equipment. Therefore, under the 'Great Leap Forward', the central government ordered all power generation equipment to be installed immediately. It also ordered factories to do everything possible to manufacture more power generation equipment. However, the shortage of large castings caused the delay of most of the equipment-producing projects (State Economic and Trade Commission, 2000).

Besides, it was stipulated in the *Report on Draft of 1958 National Economic Plan* that:

> the future development of the power industry should resolutely implement the Central Committee's proposal—dominated by hydropower while supplemented by thermal power. Central authorities should help the local governments build small hydropower stations. (Bo, 1958)

Consequently, the central government handed some power plants to the local governments. The Ministries of Electric Power and Hydro Conservancy were merged to form the Ministry of Hydro Conservancy and Electric Power (Yu, 2010). This 'hydropower-based' development approach, which did not take into account the local realities, damaged the power industry. Hydropower-based development needed water-rich terrain and thus not suitable for all parts of the country. For example, Northeast and North China did not have much water resources for the hydropower development. This approach impaired the development of the power industry in these areas (State Economic and Trade Commission, 2000).

At the beginning of the Second FYP, Deng Xiaoping pointed out that the oil exploration effort should primarily concentrate on regions such as Songliao, North China, East China, Sichuan, and Ordos. Since then, the focus on oil exploration shifted from the west to the east (Wang & Zhang, 1997). By that time, China had increased the production of the oil industry equipment according to the Soviet model. The Soviet Union had also provided extensive aid in carrying out seismic surveys, which had led to the identification of some important oilfields including the Daqing oilfield (Congress of the United States, 1979). The eastward industrial shift and the discovery of the Daqing oilfield helped to ease the oil crisis in China after the Sino-Soviet relations worsened.

4.1.2.3 Impact of 'Great Leap Forward' on Energy Industry. During the 'Great Leap Forward' (1958–1960), governments at all levels, from the central to the local, invested heavily in the construction of the energy industry. The production of energy, including coal, oil, and electricity, had risen. However, the disadvantages outweighed the advantages. The negative impact of the 'Great Leap Forward' on China's energy industry can be categorised into three aspects. First, energy production was increased at the expense of massive resource wastage. For example, in the coal industry, most of the coal produced were of inferior quality and wasted in the campaign of steel and iron smelting in the families' or communities' 'backyard' furnaces (Smil, 2010). The construction for power-generating equipment was blindly carried out, resulting in great wastage and long-term shortage of energy supply in subsequent years. Second, the mass steel and iron smelting campaign resulted in low efficiency in energy production and utilisation. Third, huge investments in the energy industry yielded far less return. The hydropower-based development approach regardless of the local differences in the actual situation resulted in severe power shortage and massive wastage of resources (CCP Central Committee's Literature Research Center, 1997, p. 264).

4.1.3. Energy Policies after the 'Great Leap Forward' (from 1961 to 1966)

After the end of the 'Great Leap Forward', the central government attempted to adjust energy policies to get the economy back on track. Its energy policies focused on three aspects: adjustment of the energy investments, adjustment of the energy industry management system, and construction of the Third Front.

4.1.3.1 Adjustment of Investments in Energy Industry. The ratio of the industrial sector investment was adjusted. Investments in coal, wood, non-ferrous metals, and oil accounted for 30.6% of the total heavy industry investment in 1960, 45.5% in 1961, and 58.8% in 1962 (Li, 1997, p. 494). Specifically, it was mentioned in Li Fuchun's *Report on the Adjustment and Implementation of the Last Two Years of the Second Five-Year Plan* that 'it is absolutely necessary to largely reduce infrastructure investments and projects' (Li, 1997, p. 494). It could be seen that the central government reduced its investments in the heavy industry but increased its investments in the energy industry. In the past, the increased investments in the energy industry infrastructure were used to expand production scale. Later, it was used to provide equipment for the enterprises. As a result, between 1961 and 1962, there was a positive increase in production. The power plants' installed capacity increased 1.13 million kilowatts; natural oil output increased 3.15 million tons; and coal output increased 13 million tons (Li, 1997, p. 495).

attempt in southern China delayed the coalmine construction in the coal-rich regions of Northeast, North and East China, which were more suitable for coal mining development (National Electric Power Corporation, 2001).

The energy policy during the Cultural Revolution was a continuation and intensification of the energy policy developed during the 'Great Leap Forward' and 'Third Front' construction. The construction of both small-scale local energy industry and coalmines in southern China was typically influenced by the political ideology of the 'Great Leap Forward'. Energy production, important for producing war weaponry, was given high priority during the Cultural Revolution. This was clearly affected by the 'Third Front' construction strategy. To sum up, regardless of China's actual energy resources and construction capabilities, these energy policies resulted in high costs and low rewards.

Despite the chaos and destruction brought about by the Cultural Revolution, the Chinese government persevered in its FYP and reaped some achievements that promoted the future development strategy for the country. Heavy investments led industrial growth to average 13.5% nationally between 1969 and 1976 (Fairbank & Goldman, 1998, p. 400). Investments in the energy industry in the 'Third Front' area had developed energy resources in the western parts of China, especially coal resource. This made the western parts of China the main source of coal production. The development of the Daqing oilfield was a major breakthrough in China's oil exploration which formed the base for rapid development in the energy industry in the following years.

Since 1979, a variety of energy policies have been introduced. In general, the energy policies in China recognise the importance of expanding energy supply and simultaneously, prioritising energy efficiency and energy conservation across the country (Asian Development Bank, 2009). The energy policies are primarily guided by the successive FYPs for China's macroeconomic and social development. China's energy policies from 1979 to 2010 in terms of the FYPs under the administrations of Deng Xiaoping, Jiang Zemin, and Hu Jintao are discussed in the following sections.[2] The discussion is categorised according to the 4-As framework presented in Chapter 2 and 3 and offers a timeline for various energy policies in relation to the '4 As'.

4.2. Energy Policies of the AV Dimension[3]

4.2.1. Coal Production During the Reform Period

4.2.1.1. Adjustment of Coal Industry Distribution and Development of Coal Production. With intensive production during the reform period, the coal reserve-to-production ratio steadily decreased from 185 years in 1980 to 35 years

[2]China's FYPs establish the overall development framework for the national economy. As these FYPs provide macroeconomic guidance for detailed policymaking, these documents are valuable in understanding China's energy development trends and its energy security status.

[3]For data source of this section, see Section 3.2 except otherwise specified.

in 2010. The Sixth FYP had a chapter on 'energy', which mainly focused on energy supply. In the coal sector, the planned annual growth in production was 2.5%. The main measures to expand production included expanding the productivity in existing mines through mechanisation and development of new mines in coal-rich areas such as Shanxi and Hebei. The development of the new mines materialised through adjusting the distribution of the energy industry. Before the reform and opening up, energy industries were developed and distributed in a 'balanced' way. The construction of the 'Third Front' and local small coalmines had intensified the decentralisation of the distribution of the energy industry. The development of coalmines in southern China had further reinforced this trend. This development strategy greatly undermined the economic efficiency and violated the comparative advantage principle.

Therefore, since the reform and opening up in the late 1970s, the central government changed the strategy of economic development. Preferential development strategy was implemented to make full use of comparative advantages of local resources. This policy shift also affected the distribution of the energy industry, which was typically reflected by the coal industry distribution. To address the chaotic management of the coal industry, coal production was adjusted at the beginning of the Sixth FYP. The production was shifted to the coal-rich areas especially Shanxi, Hebei, and eastern Inner Mongolia. Energy infrastructure was also constructed accordingly. For example, the railway construction focused on enhancing its coal transporting capacity. In order to develop the coalmines in Shanxi and Inner Mongolia, the Sixth FYP enhanced railway construction around these areas (NDRC, 1982). The intensive development of coalmines rapidly increased coal production and improved the energy supply system in China.

Coal production increased rapidly and met the Sixth FYP target in 1983, two years ahead of schedule. In 1984, the upward trend continued. In 1985, the coal production increased drastically to 872.3 million tons. The AV-1 ordinal value decreased from 10 in 1980 to 7 in 1985. Besides the adjustment of the coal industry distribution, the government support for the town and village coalmines (TVCMs) development also contributed to the fast increase in coal production (the decrease in AV-1). In the wake of the liberalisation of the coal sector, coal was permitted to be transacted in the market and transported freely throughout the country since the mid-1980s. In 1985, the central government implemented the 'General Contract Program'. The program set specific targets for coal production which was directly related to the economic benefits of the relevant coal production department. By 1990, coal production reached 1,079.9 million tons.

In the Eighth FYP period from 1991 to 1995, the government stressed the construction of key state-owned coalmines and the promotion of transformation and improvement of local mines, and mines operated by townships (NDRC, 1991). The rural coalmines experienced initial reform and consolidation. A total of 13,000 small coalmines without certification were closed down (Chen & Chen, 2007, p. 2041). In 1995, the marketing balance between supply and demand began to replace the conventional state-fixed-yields policy that had dominated the coal industry. At the end of the Eighth FYP in 1995, the coal production increased to 1,360.7 million tons. The coal production stabilised during the Ninth FYP period from 1996 to 2000, as reflected by the same AV-1 ordinal values of 4 both in 1995 and 2000. In 1998, 94 key state coalmines were transferred to the local governments. Since then, no production plans or breakeven indices prescribed by the State Coal Industry Bureau were needed any more. In the same year, the TVCMs closure campaign resulted in a reduction in production by the TVCMs in the subsequent years until 2001. In 1999, the '14.40 Project' helped to adjust the basic structure of the coal industry. Fourteen coal enterprises went bankrupt and 40 inferior and resource-depleted coalmines were closed down. At the end of the Ninth FYP, the coal industry was rectified by the government. The macro-control policies and the rectification of coal extraction and processing, together with the decontrolling of coal pricing in the 1990s, contributed the coal enterprises' rising profits. The rise in international oil prices also accounted for the increase in the production and profits of the coal enterprises (Lin, 2010). Since 2000, coal production increased very fast. During the Tenth FYP from 2001 to 2005, the coal industry focused on improving efficiency and productivity of large state coalmines. Coal supply and demand was more balanced, and coal production rebounded to 2,349.5 million tons in 2005.

During the Eleventh FYP from 2006 to 2010, China's economy developed very fast. This raised the production and consumption of coal. To guarantee the efficient exploration and rational use of coal resources, the Ministry of Land and Resources issued a series of policies: the *Notice on Further Strengthening the Management of Coal Resource Prospecting and Mining* (24 January 2006), the *Notice on Strengthening the Management of Mineral Resources and the Collection of Compensation Fees to Improve Coal Recovery Rates* (28 April 2006), and the *Notice on Strengthening the Management of Comprehensive Exploitation of Coal and Coalbed Methane (CBM) Resources* (17 April 2007). More large modern coalmines were constructed. Coal production rocketed to 3,240.0 million tons in 2010. The AV-1 ordinal value finally decreased from 2 in 2005 to 1 in 2010.

4.2.1.2. Contribution of China's TVCMs to Coal Production. The economic reform provided the opportunity for small-scale coalmines to flourish by meeting the demand where the large state-owned coalmines could not do so. In China, the small-scale coalmines were normally the TVCMs. In the early 1980s, several measures were designed to promote such coalmines. In 1981, the Ministry of Coal Industry formulated new policies to provide subsidies for small-scale coalmines and funds for their maintenance (Andrews-Speed, 2004).

In March 1983, the *Eight Measures on Accelerating the Development of Township and Village Coalmines* document was issued by the State Council. It stated that the government would bear responsibility for the strategy, while the people (enterprises) would bear responsibility for the operation of the coalmines. In January 1985, the state developed a new coal industry development strategy, which required both the state and the individuals to engage themselves not only in the large coalmines, but also in the medium and small ones (*guojia, jiti, geren yiqishang; dazhongxiaoxing meikuang yiqigao* in Chinese) (Pan, Pu, & Xiang, 2002). In 1987, Vice Prime Minister Li Peng reaffirmed this strategy in the national coal work conference to raise output (People's Daily, 1987). These measures were successful in raising the output of domestic coal to sustain China's fast economic development.

However, the coal sector evolved to a sector so diverse and dispersed that it was difficult to manage. On 20 March 1990, at the third meeting of the Seventh National People's Congress (NPC), Prime Minister Li Peng drew attention to the government work report *Struggle for Further Stabilization of China's Political, Economic and Social Development*. He highlighted the government's determination to manage the chaos in the coal market.[4] Since the early 1990s, a series of measures, regulations, and laws were issued to manage the TVCM sector, such as *Administrative Measures for the Coal Production License* (*meitan shengchan xukezheng guanli banfa* in Chinese) effective from 20 December 1994, and *Management Regulations of Township and Village Coalmines* (*xiangzhen meikuang guanli tiaoli* in Chinese), effective from 20 December 1994. These two documents were taken as the legal basis for rectifying and regulating the TVCMs. However, these measures, regulations, and laws were uncoordinated and hence ineffective. Small coalmines were still exploited within the key state coalmines. Some owners even declared that their ancestors had been mining in the region since the Ming Dynasty. Some coalmine management departments arbitrarily issued licenses regardless of losses incurred by the key state mines (Zheng, 1995). The situation began to improve in 1998, which marked a turning point for China's coal industry for two reasons. First, the government carried out a package of reforms for restructuring institutions and industries, including the coal sector. The Ministry of Coal Industry was abolished and state coalmines were transferred to local governments. The production plan was no longer needed. Second, the drop in demand for coal during the 1997 Asian Financial Crisis continued, resulting in substantial oversupply of coal (Andrews-Speed, 2004). This posed a threat to the large state coalmines which held huge amounts of government investments. As the TVCMs had sold coal at prices below the costs of the state coalmines, the government had to close TVCMs to protect the large state coalmines.

All these factors led to the TVCMs closure campaign in 1998 to shut down illegal and hazardous TVCMs and to rationalise the structure of coal production (Andrews-Speed, 2004).[5] Many TVCMs were shut down between 1998 and 2002. In 1998 alone, 25,000 small, non-state coalmines and 40 state-owned mines, accounting for about 250 million tons of annual output, were shut down (Sinton & Fridley, 2000, p. 674). The 1998 TVCMs closure campaign was seen as 'the first systematic attempt by central government to bring order to a chaotic sector across the whole country' (Andrews-Speed, 2004, p. 96). The campaign was effective in shutting down the TVCMs and in controlling coal production. As discussed in Chapter 3, the indicator AV-1 in 2000 maintained the same ordinal value as in 1995, which indicated little expansion of coal production in 2000 compared to 1995.

---

[4]For the details of the report, see *Struggle for further stabilization of China's political, economic and social development: the government work report at the third meeting of the Seventh National People's Congress on 20 March 1990*, published by People's Publishing House in 1990.

[5]For the details of the TVCMs closure policy, see the 1998 State Council Document No. 43 *Notice Concerning the Closure of Illegal and Irrationally Distributed Coalmines*.

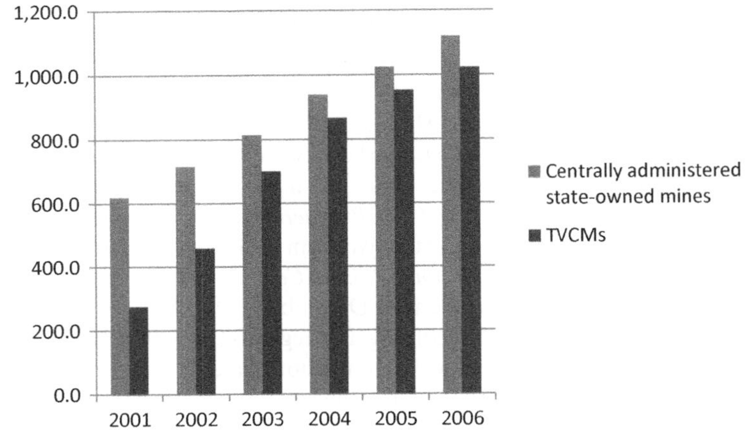

Fig. 4.1. Output Increase by the Centrally Administered State-Owned Mines and TVCMs from 2001 to 2006 (million tons). *Source*: China Energy Data Book of LBNL (2008).

China in the early twenty-first century saw its economy enter a fast track after its recovery from the Asian Financial Crisis. Pushed by the increasing energy demand in the energy-consuming industrial sectors, the coal production increased dramatically. By 2006, the total raw coal production was about 2,332 million tons. Of the output, the share contributed by TVCMs increased very quickly. From 2001 to 2006, the output by TVCMs increased by 271% while the centrally administered state-owned mines increased only by 81%. In 2006, the output of TVCMs peaked at 1,023 Mt, amounting to 44% of total output in China.[6] Fig. 4.1 presents the comparison of output increase by the centrally administered state-owned mines and TVCMs from 2001 to 2006.

The leading role of key state-owned coalmines had been strengthened through the TVCMs closure campaign beginning in 1998, but the system of regulations and laws made it hard to maintain this favourable condition. For example, the *Law of the People's Republic of China on the Coal Industry*, which came into effect in 1996, explicitly states that:

> [w]ith regard to township coal mines, the State shall adopt the policies of support, transformation, rectification, merging and upgrading, so that they shall exploit the resources in a regular and rational manner and in good order. (Article 6)[7]

This law legitimates the survival of TVCMs without specifying the requirements for operation or management. The governmental system within the

[6]Data source: China Energy Data Book of LBNL (2008).

[7]*Law of the People's Republic of China on the Coal Industry*, website: http://www.npc.gov.cn/zgrdw/englishnpc/Law/2007-12/11/content_1383585.htm

energy sector was so weak that it could not coordinate the interests of state mines, TVCMs, and local governments and other parties. In the absence of a system of regulations and laws that can establish a rational relationship between the state mines and TVCMs, and without efficient institutional administration, the central government's effort to guarantee the healthy development of state-owned coalmines was largely reversed by the booming local government-backed TVCMs in subsequent years (Andrews-Speed, 2004).

4.2.2. China's Oil and Gas Industry

4.2.2.1. China's Oil Balance. During the Sixth FYP, the government established a rationing system and stabilised the level of crude oil production at above 100 million tons, in which 94.5% was unified-planned (Chen & Chen, 2007, p. 2043). The Ministry of Petroleum Industry contracted with the state to produce 100 million tons of crude oil. The surplus output over the lump sum was 'overcapacity crude oil', which was permitted to be exported or sold at higher domestic prices (SETC, 2000). This also led to an increase in the amount of crude oil exports. In 1985, the oil import dependence ratio was –31.58%, indicating a higher independence of oil supply in China compared to 1980's ratio of –14.06%. The AV-2 ordinal value hit 10 in 1985, the highest among the years in calculation.

Since 1985, the AV-2 indicator deteriorated steadily. Oil independence disappeared quickly due to China's growing appetite for oil to sustain its fast economic growth. Most of the oil basins in China were well explored. The oldest and largest oil fields in northeastern China, which provided the bulk of China's domestic oil supply, were experiencing a decline in production due to insufficient oil exploration investment and storage capacity. China's upstream oil industry had to face the challenge of declining output (Chen & Chen, 2007; Wang, 1999). In 1993, China became a net importer of oil products. In 1996, it became a net importer of crude oil. Facing the domestic supply–demand gap, the Chinese government had endeavoured to reduce its dependence on foreign oil. It tried to stabilise the eastern oilfields output and explore and develop the Western oilfields while at the same time, make rational use of international resources (NDRC, 1991). In 1998, the oil industry was restructured. The formation of three national oil companies strengthened the capability of Chinese oil companies to invest in international resources. However, the formation of the companies was initiated by the government, not caused by capital accumulation or market competition (Shao, 1999).[8] The 1990s policies did not reduce the country's dependence on foreign oil. The oil import dependence ratio increased from –17.91% in 1990 to 28.24% in 2000.

During the Tenth FYP from 2001 to 2005, the concept of 'energy security' was officially introduced in official documents as the government began to place great strategic importance on the oil industry. The government took all possible measures to accelerate oil exploration and exploitation, and make effective use of overseas resources. In 2003, the Chinese government released the policy of *Twenty-First*

---

[8]The restructuring of the oil sector in 1998 is discussed in Chapter 5.

Century Oil Strategy, a key theme in China's Tenth FYP. This policy allocated 100 billion USD for a 'futuristic strategic oil system' in China (Miller, 2006, p. 39). In June 2004, the State Council adopted the *Medium and Long-term Energy Development Program* from 2004 to 2020, which emphasised the diversification of oil supply, building of strategic oil reserves, and regional cooperation of energy production. Yet these policies did not stop China's increasing dependence on foreign oil. Since 2000, the country's oil import dependence increased even more sharply.

4.2.2.2. Development of Natural Gas in China. China's first natural gas reservoir started operating in Daqing in 1980. Although the Seventh FYP put the natural gas development on the agenda to optimise the energy consumption and production structure (NDRC, 1986), the progress of natural gas exploitation and development was very slow until 1995. Few investments and heavy taxes hindered the development of natural gas consumption and production. The combined mechanism of market regulation and government planning within the natural gas industry also impeded its development. The raw materials for the natural gas industry were regulated by the market, while the gas production was decided by the government. This resulted in financial losses, making it impossible for the natural gas industry to develop rapidly.

There was a turning point during the Eighth FYP period (1991–1995) when marketisation was accelerated and new gas fields were discovered. The new gas fields included Shaanxi–Gansu–Ningxia, Eastern Sichuan, and Xinjiang reserves (Chen & Chen, 2007, p. 2045). This caused AV-3 in 1995 to hit 94.1, the highest among the years in calculation. With the discovery of new reserves, the Ninth FYP led to the accelerated exploration of natural gas resources in order to maintain a steady increase in natural gas production and consumption. Offshore development of oil and gas took priority. It was also planned to construct oil and gas pipelines (NDRC, 1996). Since the late 1990s, China's city gas industry developed rapidly and increased its consumption level (Wong, 2010). Domestic pipelines were under construction. The first Liquefied Natural Gas (LNG) terminal was constructed in Guangdong Province and received its first shipload of LNG in May 2006. The need for more energy to fuel its economic growth and the desire for the diversification of China's energy mix spurred China's demand for natural gas (IEA, 2007a). The rapid growth of natural gas consumption resulted in an ever-decreasing AV-3 value since 1995.

4.2.3. China's Electricity Generation

During the Sixth FYP, the government increased the installed capacity by constructing mine-mouth thermal generation plants in coal-rich areas, and large- and medium-sized hydropower stations in water-rich regions. At the end of the Sixth FYP period, the gap widened between power supply and demand. Power shortage expanded from the coastal areas to the west and seriously constrained agricultural and industrial production (National Electric Power Corporation, 2001). During this period, primary energy had been converted into electricity at a lower level in China. The share of electricity in China's energy production and consumption was small. The proportion of electricity in the total energy consumption was regarded an important symbol of a country's technological and economic development and its people's living standards (Ma, 1988). Therefore, during the Seventh FYP, the power industry was singled out as the most critical sector for development to meet the soaring demand for energy. It was clearly stipulated in the suggestions on the Seventh FYP that the power industry should be the centre of energy industry development: China should 'actively develop thermal power', 'vigorously develop hydropower', and construct nuclear power plants step by step (NDRC, 1985). The power industry-centred energy policy was proposed. To develop power industry, the central government planned to build many thermal power plants in the major coal-producing areas and coastal areas. Large-scale hydropower plants were to be built in the region adjacent to the Yellow River and the Yangtze River (NDRC, 1986). However, these policies increased the installed capacity without simultaneous growth of thermal power generation. As discussed in Chapter 3, the availability factor of conventional thermal electricity (AV-4) decreased from 0.571 in 1980 to 0.521 in 1990. A direct reason was the dramatic increase in the demand for coal for non-power generation. The coal for power generation was not supplied as scheduled. The accumulated shortage of thermal coal exceeded 8 million tons. Without enough coal to generate electricity, many generators were forced to shut down (People's Daily, 1989).

During the 1990s, the Chinese government developed thermal power and hydropower progressively. Thermal power plants were planned to be constructed especially at the mine-mouth, in coastal areas, and along railroads. When constructing hydropower, particular attention was given to areas with abundant hydropower resources. In addition, nuclear power was expected to undergo proper development as well (NDRC, 1991). The Ninth FYP continued to emphasise the development of thermal and hydropower. The Plan also called for further development of mine-mouth power stations in order to alleviate the pressure of coal transport (NDRC, 1996). In the 1990s, two key legal documents served as the foundation to guarantee adequate electricity supply. One was the *Electrical Power Law of the People's Republic of China* (effective from 1 April 1996); the other was the *Regulations on Electric Power Supply and Consumption* (effective from 1 September 1996). The *Electrical Power Law*, as a series of policy expressions, required the electricity supplier to supply qualified electricity to consumers in its operational area, so did the *Regulations* (Andrews-Speed, 2004). Both installed capacity and electricity generation increased in the 1990s.

There was a turning point in 1999, when the central government decided to advance the restructuring of state-owned enterprises (SOEs). The decision was to shut down inferior and technologically backward, polluting, and resource-wasting small enterprises involved in coal mining, oil refining, and thermal power generating (People's Daily, 1999). Although small thermal power enterprises were explicitly restricted by the central government since 1995, many provinces continued to construct them. During the Ninth FYP period, about 3 million kilowatts of small thermal power plants were built each year. A key reason was that these projects could be constructed only upon approval of the local planning department, rather than the central government (People's Daily, 2001). The policy priority to expand energy supply encouraged investment expansion not only in small thermal power plants but also in the state energy enterprises. However, during the Asian Financial Crisis, growing investment resulted in an inevitable surplus of electricity supply. Consequently, the investment in large-scale power stations was banned between 1999 and 2002 (Meidan, Andrews-Speed, & Ma, 2009). The closure of the small thermal power plants and the prohibition of investment in large-scale power stations drove the availability factor of electricity very low. The ordinal value of indicator AV-4 and AV-5 only scored 1 and 2, respectively, in 2000, which were fairly low values among the seven years in calculation.

Energy supply surplus in the late 1990s came to an end in 2002, when fuel shortages and blackouts became widespread. The enlarging supply-demand gap was a serious threat to China's economy. Since 2002, China's energy consumption grew at a faster rate than its GDP growth, due to high economic growth driven by the demand for energy-intensive materials to support the development of the industrial sector (CASS, 2005). Therefore, China saw the growth of large-scale mine-mouth thermal power plants during the Tenth FYP. The AV-4 indicated the lowest ordinal value '1' again in 2010.

The shortage of power supply also forced the government to develop the renewable resources. In February 2005, the *Renewable Energy Law* was passed to give legal backing for China's renewable energy development. For the first time, the central government legalised renewable electricity generation and connection to the grid. The government drafted the long-term renewable energy development strategy as well. Both the *Medium and Long-term Renewable Energy Development Plan* released in 2007 and the *Eleventh Five-Year Plan of Renewable Energy Development* issued in 2008 set mandatory targets for renewable energy development in the national supply of energy. The Chinese government made heavy investments in renewable energy resources during the Eleventh FYP period. In 2010, China's investment of 54.4 billion USD in the renewable industry made it the biggest investor in clean energy resources. Until 2010, China had the highest installed hydro capacity and the largest installed wind power capacity in the world (Betz, 2013, p. 16). In addition to renewable resources, China also sped up its nuclear power construction to expand utilisation. By 2005, China had a total installed nuclear capacity of 6.958 million kilowatts, which made up 1.34% of the total installed power generation capacity in the country.[9] The Chinese government had planned to greatly speed up its nuclear power construction to achieve a total nuclear power capacity of 36 million kilowatts by 2020 (People's Daily Online, 2004). The AV-5 indicator hit '5' in 2010, a moderate one of the years in calculation.

4.3. Energy Policies of the AP Dimension[10]

4.3.1. Energy Conservation and Energy Intensity

China has a long history of pursuing energy conservation to support its economic development. In the late 1970s, the Chinese government had listed energy

---

[9]The data are sourced from EIA website and calculated by the author. Data source is available at: http://www.eia.gov

[10]For data source of this section, see Section 3.2 except otherwise specified.

conservation as an important part of domestic energy policy since the potential for energy saving was enormous (Smil, 1981). The Chinese government incorporated energy conservation into its Sixth FYP and issued numerous supporting regulations and policies to encourage energy conservation. The regulations and policies include both administrative measures and financial incentives. During the 1980s, systematic policy measures such as the establishment of energy conservation technology centres, low interest loans, and tax credits for investment in energy conservation were adopted to improve energy efficiency (Andrews-Speed, 2009). However, deepening marketisation and emergence of market forces in more sections of the economy since the 1990s had not improved energy conservation as effectively as in the 1980s.

In January 1980, the National Economic Commission held a special meeting to carry out energy conservation throughout the year. The target savings set for 1980 included 23 million tons of coal, 3 million tons of gasoline and diesel, 1.5 million tons of fuel oil, 1.5 million tons of coke, and 70 million kilowatt-hour of electricity. Energy production enterprises were expected to focus on saving energy consumption and reducing energy loss (People's Daily, 1980). It was explicitly stated in the Sixth FYP that the total production of national primary energy was expected to grow at an average annual rate of 1.4%. While during this period, the average annual industrial production growth rate was targeted at 4%, which had to be achieved mainly by energy conservation. During the Sixth FYP period, the Chinese government initiated an investment plan for the energy-saving programs. These cost-effective investments were estimated to reduce the annual energy consumption growth by 3% by 1985 (Levine, Liu, & Sinton, 1992, p. 427). Several projects were identified by the government for energy conservation, and an amount of 10 billion Yuan was allocated to these projects (Levine et al., 1992, p. 428). This was the first time that the Chinese government devoted specific funds to energy conservation.

During the Seventh FYP period, the central government was very active in promoting energy conservation. It planned to save energy resources equivalent to 100 million tons of standard coal (NDRC, 1985). To do so, it issued numerous new efficiency policies to limit energy consumption in industrial production. In 1986, the State Council released the *Provisional Regulations Regarding Energy Conservation Management* to regulate energy consumption in the industrial and residential sectors. Regulations on efficient technology development were also included in the document. This energy conservation policy expanded the scope of the government's role to promote energy conservation. It established an energy-saving management system, which required that all key enterprises that consumed energy above 10,000 tons of coal equivalent (tce) to have a person responsible for the energy conservation work. The amount of energy savings was also a criterion for evaluating the work of an enterprise's manager (State Council, 1986a). Later in the same year, the State Council passed the specified requirements of the enterprise evaluating system in the *State Council Decisions Regarding Problems in Strengthening Management of Industrial Enterprises*. The evaluation was based on product quality and materials consumption, and in particular, the energy consumption of the enterprise. Thus, energy conservation was linked to the overall performance of enterprises and became an indispensable part of successful management (State Council, 1986b).[11] In 1987, the State Council approved the *Several Regulations Regarding Further Strengthening Electricity Savings*. This document required departments in charge of enterprises and electricity distribution to set electricity-consumption quotas for the enterprises and to implement the award and penalty system to encourage electricity savings. Enterprises consuming electricity below the quota would be awarded while the enterprises with electricity consumed in excess of the quota would be subject to electricity price 5–10 times of the regular price for the part of excessive electricity consumption (State Council, 1987).

To guarantee that actual work be done for energy conservation, a variety of meetings were held to issue general guidelines for energy conservation and to monitor and promote energy-saving activities (Levine et al., 1992). In general, the energy conservation policies during the 1980s were successful in reducing energy intensity. The central government made direct investments in many energy conservation projects, including the installation of efficient equipment and the support of research and development. Substantial savings were achieved. It is estimated that during the Sixth and Seventh FYP, about 280 million tce was achieved as a result of energy conservation policies (Byrne, Shen, & Li, 1996, p. 459). As the administrative measures were very effective for energy conservation, the ordinal value of AP-1 increased from 1 in 1980 to 6 in 1990.

Facing rapid energy demand growth, the Eighth FYP specified that '(the country shall) adhere to the principle of both energy development and energy conservation, but give prominence to conservation'. Since the annual growth of total primary energy supply was targeted at 2.4% whereas the annual economic growth rate was targeted at 6%, energy conservation continued to be a heavy task (NDRC, 1991). The Ninth FYP made energy conservation top priority and highlighted the principle of conserving and developing energy simultaneously. The ordinal value of AP-1 continued to increase from 6 in 1990 to 10 in 2000.

It is noteworthy that even though the energy intensity kept on decreasing (continuous increasing in AP-1), the central government had the tendency to overlook energy conservation. In 1996, China's total investment in energy conservation projects dropped considerably for the first time in the reform period, and remained low until 1999, when the investment was restored to the 1995 level. The ratio of energy conservation investment to the energy supply investment dropped from about 7% in 1995 to about 3% in 1996. The ratio remained low throughout the entire Ninth FYP period. Energy conservation investment as a percentage of the total energy investment declined in importance (Lin, 2007, p. 920). This was largely because of the changes in investment vehicles. The financing program managed by the China Energy Conservation Investment Corporation that offered preferential loans for energy conservation and promoted investments in energy efficiency was phased out during government restructuring in the 1990s. Instead, market-oriented financing mechanisms through commercial banks emerged. Consequently, the former

[11]This evaluating system was later considered as an awkward and expensive way to manage energy use and was dismantled in 1992 by State Economic and Trade Commission (Liu, Sinton, Yang, Levine, & Ting, 1994).

preferential loan interests were not available for energy-efficiency investments. As China was in transition to a more market-based economy, policies to support energy conservation investments weakened. The reforms 'stipulated the wholesale scrapping of older sets of codes and regulations, including measures intended to stimulate efficiency investment' (Sinton, Levine, & Wang, 1998, p. 827).[12]

China's transition to market economy affected technical service and training centres as well. Throughout the ministerial systems, energy-efficiency technical service and training centres were established in all major cities in China. These centres provided aid in technical matters. However, the market reform package during the 1990s weakened China's bureaucratic energy management apparatus severely. These energy-efficiency technical service and training centres gradually lost their government funding. Therefore, the capacity of the institutions to enhance energy efficiency and the investments in energy conservation rapidly diminished (Lin, 2007). Therefore, energy conservation in the 1990s was mainly conducted via international assistance. Announcements on energy-efficiency standards for international cooperation were made for refrigerators, ballasts for fluorescent lamps, and air conditioners. For example, the China Green Lights Program, launched in 1996, benefited from the United States and other international aid. This program contributed significantly to the widespread application of energy-efficient lighting technologies in China. Another internationally funded program was the CFC-Free Energy-Efficient Refrigerator Project, which aimed to improve the energy efficiency of the Chinese refrigerators (Sinton, Levine, Fridley, Yang, & Lin, 1999, p. 6). However, the energy-efficiency gains were largely offset by the rapid growth in the energy-intensive sectors during the Tenth FYP period, a result of industrial policies at that time. The policies paid little attention to structural adjustments across industrial sectors and there had been a structural shift towards energy-intensive sectors. The rapid development in the energy-intensive industrial sectors became the most important driver behind China's energy-intensity increase (Andrews-Speed, 2009; Zhao, Ma, & Hong, 2010). Ordinal value of AP-1 decreased in 2005, after its steady increase from 1980 to 2000.

Power shortages during the early new century left the central and local governments anxious to bring energy conservation to the policy agenda again. During Hu administration, reducing energy intensity was a top priority in the government's policy agenda. In 2004, the NDRC drafted *China's Medium and Long Term Energy Conservation Plan*. It set the target of quadrupling China's GDP at the national level in order to reduce energy intensity in various sectors by 2020 and also identified a number of projects to achieve significant energy savings (Cheng, 2008; Yang, 2008). The Plan indicated the central government's desire to integrate energy conservation into long-term economic development. The medium- and long-term energy conservation projects outlined in the Plan covered the industry, construction, transport, residential, commercial, and other sectors in the economy.

In May 2005, the NDRC initiated 10 major energy conservation projects to implement the 2004 *China's Medium and Long Term Energy Conservation Plan*.

---

[12]For detailed discussion, see Section 5.3.2.

Energy conservation in the construction industry was bolstered. All buildings constructed after 2006 were required to embrace the new technology to reduce 50% of their energy consumption during the Eleventh FYP (2006–2010) compared to the 2005 level (Wang, 2005). High fuel-efficiency standards were imposed on automakers, which were compelled to produce cars that consume less fuel (Kong, 2005). China's steel industry, as an energy-intensive industry, received much attention for its success in energy saving. In July 2005, the NDRC released the *Steel Industry Development Policy*, which specified that the comprehensive energy consumption per ton of steel should be reduced to 0.73 ton of standard coal and below by 2010, and to 0.7 ton and below by 2020 (Cheng, 2008, p. 309). In addition to the administrative measures, the market mechanisms were also adopted. The electricity prices increased twice in 2004 and 2005, respectively. In June 2004, the average price of electricity increased by 0.022 yuan per kilowatt/hour in the south, east, central, and north of China. To contain the careless expansion of energy-intensive industries, differentiating electricity pricing was adopted for some energy-intensive sectors. Extra charges were imposed on enterprises that failed to meet the energy conservation requirements. In May 2005, electricity prices rose again by another 0.022 yuan per kilowatt/hour (Kong, 2005, p. 32).

These policies began to show their effectiveness at the end of the Eleventh FYP, when the energy intensity decreased again after a rapid rise of energy consumption in China during the Tenth FYP period. During the Eleventh FYP, the government identified the rise in domestic energy consumption as a great obstacle to the goal of economic development. On the one hand, it began to improve the energy efficiency of the sectors that would yield the greatest short-term benefits. On the other hand, it began applying the most effective policy instruments. Policy apparatus was created to design and implement energy-efficiency policies throughout the country. In August 2006, the State Council issued the *Decision of the State Council on Strengthening Energy Conservation Work*, which stated that China must put energy conservation at a more prominent strategic position (State Council, 2006b). The government set a specific target to reduce the energy intensity by 20% (compared to late 2005) by the end of 2010. This was the first time China listed energy conservation as a national development goal. The numerical energy industry targets for the efficiency of major industrial products and equipment were specified. For example, in order to discourage exports that relied heavily on energy and resources, China started levying export taxes on energy-intensive products. From July 2007, China eliminated export tax rebates on many low value-added but high energy-consuming exported items. In April 2006, the NDRC focused on key energy-consuming enterprises and launched the *Top 1,000 Enterprises Energy Conservation Action Implementation Plan* to save about 100 million tce in the industrial sectors by 2010. The 1,000 enterprises accounted for the major energy-consuming sectors, and their combined energy consumption was about 670 million tce in 2004, accounting for 33% of total energy consumption and 47% of industrial energy consumption in the year (Zhang, 2010, p. S48).[13]

[13]The data are cited directly from the *Top 1,000 Enterprises Energy Conservation Action Implementation Plan.*

The top 1,000 enterprises took the lead in improving energy efficiency. All the participating enterprises signed energy conservation contracts with provincial governments. These enterprises enjoyed several funding opportunities subject to the amount of energy they saved (Price, Wang, & Jiang, 2010). To further cut energy consumption, the State Council issued the *The Limit of Project Approves* and authorised the National Environmental Protection Agency (NEPA) to implement this policy. Under this policy, the NEPA re-audited the energy-intensive projects/plants. If a plant's energy consumption and emissions exceeded the limits, the plant must be shut down. In January 2007, 82 large, energy-inefficient, and high-polluting projects/plants in energy-intensive industries were forced to stop operations (Yang, 2008, p. 565). These policies proved very effective for China to cut down the energy intensity. The ordinal value of AP-1 increased from 9 in 2005 to 10 in 2010.

To summarise, with strong policy support and attractive financial incentives, energy intensity decreased rapidly between 1980 and 2000. However, after the taxation reform in 1994, China saw the weakening of most financial incentives, and the slowdown in the decrease of energy intensity from 1995. As a result of rapid expansion of the energy-intensive heavy industries and rapid rise of energy consumption, energy intensity began to increase since 2000. When energy conservation and energy efficiency were at the core of China's energy policies during the Eleventh FYP, energy intensity decreased again, with the lowest level in 2010 among the years in calculation.

4.3.2. Advancement of Energy Technologies During the Reform Period

In general, economic reform led to the improvement in energy technology and energy efficiency. The introduction of imported machinery in the mid-1980s opened the door for industrial technology advancement to take off. A variety of financial incentives also fostered the development of energy technologies. Government-sponsored programs created better technologies. Most importantly, macroeconomic reform created a microeconomic environment where the enterprises require the adoption of advanced energy and equipment.

The SOEs reform during the 1990s made fast technology advancement possible. The SOEs, as the major force of technology R&D, stimulated the development of energy technology. This could be seen in the contrast of the technology advancement in the power sector in the 1980s and 1990s. In the 1980s, the less-efficient small thermal power plants constrained the technology advancement of electricity generation. In the 1990s when SOEs reform was in full swing, thermal electricity generation technology gradually improved. Projects conforming to the larger size requirement and higher technological standards (such as long-distance power transmission technology) were developed by the central government (Zhang & Heller, 2004). During the Eleventh FYP period, the government closed down inefficient small generators and replaced them with larger units. The generation units smaller than 300 MW accounted for about 53% of China's thermal power generation in 2005, but less than 31% in 2009. Units larger than 600 megawatt accounted for 13% of the thermal power generation in 2005, while it increased to 34% in 2009 (Climate Policy Initiative, 2010, p. 2). Technological advancement and the closure of inefficient older facilities helped the larger power plants to improve their generation efficiency significantly. The AP-2 ordinal value increased steadily and consistently during 30 years of economic reform. China's oil refining capacity also improved. The reform in state oil companies in the late 1990s made these companies more business-oriented. Profit incentive of the business-oriented oil companies as well as projected dramatic increase in petroleum demand brought about a flurry of refinery construction activities (Wang, 1999). Sufficient distillation capacity was available. The ordinal value of AP-3 increased from 3 in 1995 to 6 in 2000 and 10 in 2010.

Since 2000, China's coal mining technologies greatly improved. The *Coal Industry Policy* issued by the NDRC in 2007 implemented several major geological surveying and coal-mining technologies to improve the output and efficiency of the coalmines (NDRC, 2007c). The *National Plan for Medium- to Long-Term Scientific and Technological Development (2006–2020)* ranked efficient coal mining technological development as a key objective (State Council, 2006a). Besides, China made strides in researching for new technologies that can substitute for conventional oil. Coal liquefaction technology drew much attention in the early new century due to China's growing dependence on foreign oil. In August 2004, Shenhua Group, one of China's largest state-owned coal producers, started to build China's first coal liquefaction project in Inner Mongolia. This project began its operation in late 2008, with the capacity to produce one million metric tons of oil products a year (Wang, 2009). The AP-4 ordinal value increased very fast in the first decade of the 2000s, from 3 in 2000 to 10 in both 2005 and 2010.

4.4. Energy Policies of the AC Dimension[14]

All energy consumption can affect the environment, thus every decision on energy consumption and economic growth would carry environmental implications. Efficient use of energy can lower energy consumption and improve the environment and vice versa. Policies that affect the environment regarding energy use are discussed in this section.

4.4.1. Air Pollution Control During the Reform Period

In the 1980s, environmental protection was incorporated as an integral part of economic and social planning. A series of legislations and regulations were adopted to protect the environment. However, economic development topped the government agenda at that time. Effects of these legislations and regulations were very limited (Freeman & Holslag, 2009). For example, in 1982, the State Council issued the *Tentative Provisions on Pollution Charge*, which stipulated that a pollutant discharge fee of 0.04 Yuan would be charged for every 10 m^3 of SO_2 emitted in excess of standards. This policy encouraged enterprises to build

[14]For data source of this section, see Section 3.2 except otherwise specified.

pollution control facilities, but with the continuous increase of the prices of raw materials, the operation costs of the enterprises gradually exceeded the pollution charges. Consequently, most enterprises would rather pay for the discharge fees than to reduce emissions (Yun, 1998).

Along with the economic reform in the 1980s was the fast growth of small enterprises, especially the township and village enterprises (TVEs), which facilitated China's economic development. However, it resulted in environmental pollution because of the TVEs' ignorance of emissions control. In the power sector, for example, various investment sources, easy government approval, and low-cost financing led to the proliferation of less-efficient small thermal power plants.[15] By 1987, 86% of the nation's total generating capacity was made up of plants smaller than 100 megawatt (Blackman & Wu, 1999, p. 698). The small inefficient thermal power plants discharged more energy wastes and caused more serious environmental pollution than the large ones (Ma & He, 2008). Both the AC-1 and AC-2 ordinal values deteriorated in the 1980s. To address this problem, the State Council issued the *Decision of the State Council on further Strengthening the Work of Environmental Protection* in 1990, which required the local authorities to strictly implement the *Environmental Protection Law*[16] and to strengthen the management of polluting and energy-wasting enterprises, especially the small enterprises and TVEs (People's Daily, 1990).

When China was successful in re-invigorating its economy in the early 1990s, it faced a limited supply of high-quality energy resources such as petroleum, natural gas, and electricity. During the mid-1990s, China's domestic oil production could not meet demand. Hydropower development was slow. Nuclear power development was in its infancy. Sustained rapid economic growth would continue to depend on coal, which in turn would worsen environmental problems. Air pollution from the combustion of coal became more severe. CO_2 emissions, SO_2 emissions, and soot emissions increased steadily except for soot emissions which hit the lowest ordinal value in 1995, followed by a rebound in 2000. Correspondingly, the ordinal values of the indicators AC-1, AC-2, and AC-3 decreased steadily and consistently from 1980 to 1995. Therefore, environmental protection became a priority on China's political and policy agenda.

After the United Nations Conference on Environment and Development in 1992, *China's Agenda 21* was developed. This document emphasised the application of renewable energy, clean coal technology, and nuclear power to promote environmental protection. In March 1994, the *Sustainable Energy Programs under Agenda 21* was approved by the State Council. In September 1995, the Fifth Plenary Session

[15]Projects of 50 megawatt capacity or smaller needed the approval of the provincial governments, not the State Development Planning Commission.

[16]China adopted its *Environmental Protection Law* in 1979. The Law was revised and the new *Environmental Protection Law* was promulgated in 1989. The 1989 *Environmental Protection Law* not only authorised the NEPA to set standards for environmental quality, but also allowed the local authorities to have their local standards for the things not covered by the national standards (MacBean, 2007).

of the Fourteenth Party Congress adopted the *Chinese Communist Party Central Committee Suggestions on Formulating the Ninth Five-Year Plan for National Economic and Social Development and the Long-Term Objectives for the Year 2010*. The objective was to realise sustainable economic and social development, which required the economic growth pattern be transformed from extensive to intensive and that improving the economic efficiency be the guiding principle. The government highlighted that sustainable development must be taken as a major strategy. Since then, the government accelerated the construction of a comprehensive regulatory and institutional framework for environmental protection, and strengthened the position of the national environmental agency. In 1998, the State Environmental Protection Administration (SEPA) was created to support government restructuring. On 1 September 2000, the *Air Pollution Prevention Law* took effect.

Specific policies dealing with environmental pollution in the energy sector during the 1990s mainly focused on the control of emissions caused by the coal consumption and production in China's energy structure. Penalties and fines were meted out to the violating enterprises. In the 1980s, as discussed earlier, China attempted to impose fines on enterprises that discharged SO_2 and other pollutants exceeding national standards. But the effects were modest because the polluting enterprises found it cheaper to pay pollutant discharge fees than to install pollution control equipment with clean coal technology. To counter this, the NEPA increased the fee on a trial basis in 1992: the enterprises discharging SO_2 in excess of national standards had to pay 0.2 Yuan per kilogram SO_2 (Ohshita & Ortolano, 2006, p. 81). A further significant progress was made in 1998 when the State Council approved the NEPA's proposal regarding the 'Two Control Zones' to control SO_2 emissions and acid rain. This authorised the collection of emission fines beyond the 1992 trial regions (State Council, 1998). In 2000, the SEPA issued the *Notice Concerning Implementation of the Expanded Pilot SO_2 Discharge Fee Collection* to emphasise the role of the local government to collect the SO_2 emission fines (SEPA, 2000).

Besides imposing fees, the government decommissioned obsolete plants, closed down small thermal power generating units, and monitored thermal power plants' compliance with the regulation to install desulphurisation equipment. In 1997, the State Council and the State Economic and Trade Commission (SETC) required the power plants to close down small inefficient generating units with generating capacity below 50 megawatt. In September 1999, the Fourth Plenary Session of the Fifteenth Party Congress made arrangements to advance the 'strategic reorganization' of the SOEs. To facilitate the reorganisation of SOEs, the government resolutely shut down the 'five types of small-scale industrial enterprises' (*wuxiao qiye* in Chinese), including hundreds of small fossil fuel-fired power plants, coalmines, oil refineries, cement, and glass plants that were polluting the environment and depleting the natural resources. Between 1996 and 2000, around 800 small power plants were shut down. The closure of these plants contributed to reduction of 400,000 tons of SO_2 emissions. In the 1990s, the State Council also required thermal power plants to install desulphurisation equipment for their electricity generating units. The equipment must be designed, built, and put into operation together with the operating of the power-generating units. By the end of 2000, electricity-generating units amounting to 5,000 megawatt of capacity had installed desulphurisation equipment (Chang & Wang, 2010, p. 3360). The TVCMs closure campaign in 1998[17] also had a secondary aim of upgrading the environmental conservation role of the small coal-mining sector.[18] All these measures contributed to the slow-down of the increase of SO_2 emissions from 1995 to 2000.

The policies formulated in the 1990s reflected a shift of focus from 'management by governments' to 'elimination and control of pollutants'. For example, in the 1980s, policies were focused on controlling the discharges by enterprises; in the 1990s, the government focused on the control of the production process itself. In the 1980s, the government paid more attention to control of pollutants emitted by a single enterprise; in the 1990s, the government focused on the centralised control of the total discharge volume[19] rather than an individual enterprise's polluting activity (Matsuno, 2009).

Despite government effort in the 1990s, these policies were still 'declarative and unrealistic', and environmental protection did not appear to be a key issue in the energy sector. The environmental regulations were not coordinated, and different levels of the administration held conflicting interests. The actual implementation did not improve dramatically, because the demand for economic growth exceeded the requirement for environmental protection. This compromised the work of the implementation bureaus at the local level and resulted in widespread non-compliance with the environmental requirements (Economy, 2004; OECD, 2006). A lack of coordination among relevant institutions also accounted for the insufficient implementation of these policies.

Another problem was found in the management of environmental protection at the local level. As the administrative rank of the environmental protection

---

[17]For details, see Section 4.2.1.

[18]It is noteworthy that was no coherent planning in environmental protection. For example, in Shanxi province, hasty closure was carried out by dynamiting the adit (entrance to an underground mine) or shaft, blocking it up with cement, or destroying buildings. The authorities were not concerned about the possible subsidence above the underground mines or the pollution of surface or underground waters (Andrews-Speed, 2004). All of these constitute a threat to the environment. For a long time, the economic criteria served as the key incentive for policymaking in China. In the coal sector, for example, an adequate supply of coal to fuel the economy encouraged the growth of the TVCMs. The TVCMs were known for their poor safety records and negative impact on the environment. During the economic slowdown in the late 1990s, when the large state-owned coalmines were undermined by the fast-growing TVCMs, the central government made up its mind to protect the large state-owned coalmines at all costs. It was not because of the poor safety records or environmental pollution that the government decided to close down the TVCMs, but the desire to rescue its own state mines.

[19]The national FYP started to set national emission control targets from the Ninth FYP, which selected 12 key pollutants and set the upper limit of total emission quantity for each of them, also known as 'Total Load Control' (*Zongliang Kongzhi* in Chinese), which was first introduced in 1994 and legalised in the revised *Air Pollution Prevention and Control Law* in 2000 (Chang & Wang, 2010).

institution was sometimes lower than that of the enterprises under its supervision (Ma & Ortolano, 2000), it had to frequently show 'respect' and defer to the enterprises. This largely resulted from the triangular relations among the local government, the local environmental protection institutions, and the enterprises. The local environmental protection institutions partly depended on the local government for the annual budget and other sources of financing, which were largely collected from the enterprises' taxes. This limited the local institution's authority to impose regulations on the enterprises. Ordinal values of both AC-1 and AC-2 continued to decrease in the 1990s.

The implementation and management of environmental protection continued to prove ineffective in the twenty-first century and this led to the central government's plan to reinforce its pollution control measures. The Tenth FYP planned to reduce the SO_2 emissions in the 'two control areas' by 20% and to reduce emissions of major pollutants by 10% (compared to 2000 figures) in 2005. To provide technical guidance and support to control the SO_2 pollution (caused by burning coal) and encourage the use of washed coal, the SEPA, the SETC, and the Ministry of Science and Technology jointly announced the *Technology Policy on Coal-fired Sulfur Dioxide Emissions Control* in March 2002 (People's Daily, 2002).

However, the SO_2 emissions increased from 19,951,000 tons in 2000 to 25,494,000 tons in 2005, and the soot emissions increased from 11,654,000 tons in 2000 to 11,825,000 tons in 2005. The failure of SO_2 control could be attributed to the several reasons. First, the policies did not indicate implementation requirements in detail. Although the policies encouraged the use of washed coal, they did not stop the related agencies from receiving equipment designed for low-quality coal from the manufacturers of boilers. Besides, the users of washed coal faced increased costs without any obvious gains of efficiency (IEA, 2009). By 2005, only about 21% of coal produced by China's large-scale coal enterprises had been washed (Kong, 2005, p. 47). Second, the Chinese economic development model, which had been planned to be transformed from extensive to intensive production, reversed to be more extensive, which was accompanied by high energy consumption and high emissions of pollutants (Hu & Wang, 2006, p. 11). Third, both economic growth and energy demand exceeded expectations during the Tenth FYP period. Since late 2002, the accelerated growth of heavy and chemical industries (such as iron, steel, and building materials) led to a significant increase in the national coal consumption. The SO_2 emissions from the coal-fired power plants worsened the regional acid rain pollution (Hu, Wang, & Yan, 2006, p. 54). Fourth, the pollution treatment projects progressed very slowly. By 2003, half of the key projects were delayed. Fifth, due to the tight electricity supply, the plan to shut down by 2003 the coal-fired power plants below 50,000 kilowatt failed. Many plants that had already been shut down had to be reopened (People's Daily, 2004).

During the Eleventh FYP period, the obligatory targets of environmental protection were listed and the momentum increased rapidly. The Eleventh FYP for *Preventing and Controlling Acid Rain and SO_2 Emissions* set the target of reducing SO_2 emissions in 2010 by 10% from the 2005 level. In the coal sector, the *Several Opinions of the State Council on Promoting the Sound Development of Coal Industry*, a document issued in 2005, stated that the government would continue to shut down the small coalmines that violated safety requirements, wasted resources, and damaged the environment (People's Daily, 2005b). In the power sector, the SEPA signed obligation agreements in 2006 with six domestic large power producers to enforce SO_2 emission reduction in the Eleventh FYP period. Specific reduction targets and emission reduction methods were clearly stated in these agreements. In addition to the requirements on the large power plants, the local governments also had to shut down small-scale thermal power units with high energy consumption and poor pollution control.

To do so, the State Council issued the *Notice on Some Joint Opinions of NDRC and the Office of the National Energy Leading Group on Accelerating the Closure of Small Thermal Power Generation Units* in January 2007. The Notice specified that the shutdown power plants would receive compensation equivalent to their profits of three years of power generation. The closure went smoothly and significant progress was made towards this aim (IEA, 2009; Policy Information, 2008). Between 2006 and 2008, inefficient thermal power plants, which accounted for a total capacity of 34.21 gigawatts, were shut down (Chang & Wang, 2010, p. 3356). In 2007, all the inefficient small thermal power plants with the capacity of 14.38 gigawatts were shut down even though the initial closure year plan was 10 gigawatts. The closure helped to reduce raw coal consumption by 18.8 million tons, SO_2 emissions by 290 thousand tons, and CO_2 emissions by 37,600 thousand tons (Policy Information, 2008, p. 4).

Besides the specific obligatory targets set by the government, rising investments helped to improve environmental quality. Between 2006 and 2008, the government allocated more than 90 billion Yuan for environmental improvement projects (Chai & Zhang, 2010, p. 4000). In 2010, the government announced at the NPC that ambitious environmental protection initiatives were planned. A funding of 20.7 billion USD would be spent on engineering solutions for environmental problems (Xin & Stone, 2010, p. 1440). During the Eleventh FYP period, China also improved its clean coal technologies including coal gasification, flue gas desulfurisation, and coal liquefaction.[20] The total installed capacity of flue gas desulfurisation technology increased from 53 gigawatt in 2005 to 270 gigawatt in 2007, accounting for over 50% of total installed thermal power capacity (Zhou, 2010, p. 3759). By the end of the Eleventh FYP, both SO_2 emissions and soot emissions were reduced. The SO_2 emissions decreased from 25,494,000 tons in 2005 to 21,851,000 tons in 2010, and soot emissions decreased from 11,825,000 tons in 2005 to 8,291,000 tons in 2010.

[20]The policies encouraging clean coal technologies were only 'directive', not 'mandatory', and they were not always consistent because they frequently came from different government departments. Another problem was that both R&D funding and qualified personnel were inadequate. For example, insufficient R&D of ultra-supercritical units made its core technologies unattainable for the manufacture of power generation equipment. The R&D of circulating fluidised bed combustion technology was also inadequate (IEA, 2009). Similar problems also existed in the application of carbon capture and storage (CCS) technology. The insufficient R&D funding, absence of a national strategy for the CCS utilisation, and the lack of research and experience impeded the CCS implementation in China (Duan, 2010).

4.4.2. Policies on Renewable Energies and Nuclear Power

4.4.2.1. Renewable Energies. With abundant reserves of renewable energy, the Chinese government implemented policies to encourage the development of renewable energy resources beginning in the 1980s. These policies include financial subsidies, favourable taxation, favourable pricing, and supportive industrial and technical policies, reflecting the government's realisation of the need to mitigate the environmental damage caused by using fossil fuels.

During the Sixth FYP, biogas, small hydro generation, and other renewable energies were encouraged in the rural energy sector. For the purpose of energy structure optimisation, the Seventh FYP continued to promote the development and utilisation of solar, wind, geothermal, and other renewable energy resources (NDRC, 1986). In the 1990s, the government's interests in diversifying energy resources and protecting the environment stimulated the development of renewable energy resources. Several energy-related regulations and laws have articles about harnessing renewable energy resources. In 1995, *China's new energy and renewable energy development outline (1996–2010)* was issued to promote a specific target for renewable energy development. In 1996, the *Ninth Five-Year Plan for National Economic and Social Development and the Long-Term Objectives for the Year 2010* was issued. This document pointed out that China should actively develop new energy to improve the energy structure. In addition to the general policy programs, some specific initiatives, laws, and economic incentives were also proposed to promote renewable energy development. *The 1996 Electric Power Law of the People's Republic of China* stated clearly in the general provisions that '[t]he State encourages and supports electricity generation through the use of renewable and clean energy resources' (Article 5). *The Law of the People's Republic of China on Conserving Energy 1998* reaffirmed the strategic role of renewable energy resources in greenhouse gas reduction and environmental improvement: '[t]he State encourages the development and utilization of new and renewable resources of energy' (Article 4).[21] Wind power[22] was the key to successful renewable energy development. Imported wind turbines were exempted from customs duty from 1990 to 1995.[23] Besides, the former Ministry of Electric Power issued the 1994 *Regulation on Management of Grid-connected Wind Farms*. The grid administrative authority was required to allow wind farms to connect to the grid and to share the price difference between wind power price and the average price in the grid. In 1996, the former State Development and Planning Commission (SDPC)

---

[21] *The Law of the People's Republic of China on Conserving Energy* was revised in 2007. The revised version took effect on 1 April 2008.

[22] The development of grid-connected wind power began in the late 1980s. In 1986, two pilot wind farms were built, one in Rongcheng County in Shandong Province and the other in Pingtan County in Fujian Province. Wind farms have been constructed throughout China after the two pilot projects and this led to the rapid increase in the installed capacity of wind in the 1990s (Liu, Gan, & Zhang, 2002).

[23] To develop domestic wind turbine industry, the tariffs were adjusted in 1996 and the actual level was increased.

initiated the *Ride the Wind Program*, which aimed at establishing a high quality wind turbine generator sector in China. This initiative successfully introduced the wind turbine generator technology into China (Xia & Song, 2009). Preferential loans of 900 million Yuan were to be invested in wind turbine installation with a total capacity of 81.6 megawatt. At the same time, subsidies were provided for the diffusion of wind power technology (Liu et al., 2002, p. 758). Another program, the *Brightness Project Implementation Planning*, was established in 1998 to provide electricity in remote northwest areas via several wind and solar power systems (NREL, 2004a). In 1999, the SPC and the Ministry of Science and Technology jointly issued the *Notice on Issues of Further Support for Renewable Energy Development*. It stipulated that preferential loans would be provided to finance renewable energy projects to promote electricity generation.

At the beginning of the new century, the document *Outline of Action for Sustainable Development at the Beginning of the 21st Century* expressed the government resolution to develop renewable and clean energy. The government aimed to reduce the proportion of coal in the primary energy consumption and develop energy-saving stoves and exploit biogas, solar, and wind energy in suitable rural areas to improve the rural energy structure (People's Daily, 2003b). In 2001, the SDPC launched the *Sending Electricity to Townships* (*Song Dian Dao Xiang* in Chinese) program to develop renewable energy supply for more than 1,000 townships. The program, completed in June 2003, installed 200 megawatt from small hydropower and 840 kilowatt from wind power (NREL, 2004b). Using *Song Dian Dao Xiang* as opportunity, China rapidly developed solar photovoltaic and small wind power and hydropower, and promoted decentralised renewable energy technological development in the rural areas. Under the background of improving county environment, China vigorously developed rural biogas, which was enlisted as a national debt project since 2003. The central government invested more than 2.5 billion Yuan per year to develop rural biogas (China Renewable Energy Society, 2009, p. 13). The government subsidies on technological dissemination helped China succeed in developing the rural household biogas. The biogas industry and market were formed. By 2006, 70 million rural residents benefited from the biogas development (Gan & Yu, 2008, p. 533).

But these policies could not stop renewable energy in total electricity generation from declining from 23.4% in 1985 to 16.8% in 2005. Several factors hindered China's renewable energy development. First, the regulatory framework for the renewable energy sector failed to provide clear guidelines on the scope of duties for the renewable energy policymaking. The duties were spread over a variety of institutions including the NDRC, SETC, Ministry of Water Conservation, Ministry of Science and Technology, Ministry of Finance, Ministry of Agriculture, former Ministry of Power, and former Ministry of Forestry (Cherni & Kentish, 2007; Zhang et al., 2009). All of them had sections dealing with renewable energy. Each institution made its policies independently without consulting or coordinating with its counterparts. The lack of consistency and coordination made it difficult to develop renewable energy effectively in the long run.

Second, subsidies for renewable energy were insufficient. China's technical R&D investments in renewable energy were inadequate too. The technique-intensive renewable energy development required a large amount of R&D funding but in China, only a very small proportion of total investment in renewable energy was directed to technical R&D. For a long time, domestic SOEs, which should have been the main investment body, had invested too little in renewable energy development. The investment mainly depended upon government funding, foreign loan and donation, and foreign direct investment. China's investment in the renewable energy R&D amounted to only 0.045% of its total GDP in 2005, which was much lower than that of industrialised countries (Zhang et al., 2009, p. 446).

Third, the government intentionally kept electricity prices low to support economic growth. The delay in the liberalisation of electricity pricing also hindered renewable energy development. The prices of electricity generated by renewable energy were much higher than those of coal-fired electricity. For example, the wind power price was considerably higher than the conventional power price, making it less competitive than conventional power. As the pricing regulation ensured high wind power tariff for developers to generate wind power, they sought the approval of high prices and did not pay attention to cost reduction. Besides, the pricing regulation did not help the local utilities to share the price difference nor purchase power from this clean but costly source. In short, the pricing regulation provided little economic incentives for either wind power developers or grid companies, thus impeding the development of wind energy.

Fourth, the nature of these policies was administrative rather than market based. The administrative measures sometimes hindered renewable energy development in China. For example, the tariff exemption on wind turbine did not create a fair competition environment for domestic wind turbine manufacturing. When the preferential loan program ended, the investment in wind farm construction rapidly shrank and stalled the increase of wind power capacity (Liu et al., 2002).

Fifth, the power-sector reforms did not make the policy framework conducive for the rapid development of renewable energy. China's power sector has been disaggregated both vertically and horizontally, evolving into a 'dual electricity system' with dominant state planning at the core, and decentralised generation and transmission companies at the periphery (Cherni & Kentish, 2007). The government's cautious approach to the liberalisation of the renewable energy industry was met with uncertainty on the part of investors.

The year 2005 was a turning point in renewable energy development. The NDRC decided to implement projects on renewable energy and new energy high-tech industrialisation between 2005 and 2007 to accelerate the process of the industrialisation of renewable energy (People's Daily, 2005a). The then-Vice Chairman of NDRC, Chen Deming, announced the government plan to accelerate renewable energy exploitation. China was thus positioned to develop renewable energy resources on an unprecedented scale (Martinot & Li, 2007). The government began to take substantial effort to create a legal environment for renewable energy development. The *Renewable Energy Law*, which took effect in 2006, highlighted the strategic position of renewable energy in the exploitation and use of energy resources. It provided a coherent framework and legal basis for increasing the renewable energy share in China's electricity system. It was 'a very positive development for the renewable energy industry in China'

(Cherni & Kentish, 2007, p. 3627). For the first time, a renewable energy target was written into the Law. According to the Law, all major power companies in China were expected to create 3% of their energy from renewable resources other than hydropower by 2010 and 8% by 2020 (Cyranoski, 2009, p. 372).

Immediately after the *Renewable Energy Law* took effect, China began to enact several more relevant supporting laws and regulations to develop renewable energy. The State Council department in charge of energy was expected to draw up medium- and long-term goals for the national total renewable energy development and utilisation. The NDRC announced the *Plan on medium- and long-term development of renewable energy resources* in 2007.[24] The Plan, as a comprehensive complement to the *Renewable Energy Law*, quantified the specific development goals of renewable energy resources and stipulated the setting up of a fund to support the renewable energy R&D. It was projected that by 2020, China would have 300 million kilowatts installed capacity of hydropower, 30 million kilowatts of biomass power, 30 million kilowatts of wind power, and 1.8 million kilowatts of solar power (NDRC, 2007b). All these goal specifications guided the development of renewable energy resources in China.

Other laws and regulations were issued to manage the pricing and special capital in renewable energy electricity generation. In 2006, the Ministry of Finance released a fund for renewable energy development. It comprised grants and interest subsidies in power generation, oil alternatives, and construction (Yang, 2006). These policies helped to increase the share of renewable energy out of total electricity generation from 16.8% in 2005 to 19.3% in 2010.

4.4.2.2. Nuclear Power. Despite the early development of indigenous nuclear technology, China did not build nuclear power plants until the 1980s. In September 1987, Prime Minister Zhao Ziyang met the Director-General of the International Atomic Energy Agency and expressed that China was optimistic about the development of nuclear technology in agriculture and industry (People's Daily, 1987). The first Chinese nuclear power plant, Qinshan Nuclear Power Plant in Zhejiang Province, began commercial production in 1993. China's first large commercial nuclear power plant was in utilisation in February 1994, when the Daya Bay Nuclear Power Station Unit 1 started commercial operation (People's Daily, 1994). Since the utilisation of the first large commercial nuclear power plant, the nuclear power growth in China had been slow. In 1999, the first phase of Qinshan Nuclear Power Plant was shut down for about one year for maintenance and repair (Chen & Chen, 2007, p. 2047). As a result, the nuclear share fell from 1.29% in 1995 to 1.24% in 2000.

Due to electricity shortages, nuclear energy was developed faster in the early twenty-first century than before. The second phase of the Qinshan Nuclear Power Plant and the first phase of Ling'ao Nuclear Power Plant were put into operation in 2002; the third phase of Qinshan was running in 2003; and Tianwan Nuclear Power Plant started operating in 2004 (Chen & Chen, 2007, p. 2047). The

---

[24]The NDRC completed the preliminary draft of the Plan in 2005 (People's Daily, 2005d).

operation of new nuclear power plants during the Tenth FYP raised the AC-5 up to 2.12% in 2005, the highest among the years in calculation. One favourable factor was perhaps the willingness of the Chinese public to embrace the role of nuclear power in the country's economic development. The nuclear industry had 'never before been incorporated into national economic planning' (Zhou, 2010, p. 3761). Yet with nuclear expansion, China continued to grapple with the social, technological, and financial challenges to address waste disposal and other safety concerns. Compared to other energy resources, nuclear energy still contributed a relatively small share in the Eleventh FYP period. In 2010, the share of nuclear power in total electricity generation fell to 1.77%.

4.5. Energy Policies of the AF Dimension[25]

Energy pricing had been a long-term problem for the Chinese government as its deregulation process did not run smoothly. Commodity prices were under strict central government control before the 1978 economic reform. During the reform period, state-controlled prices were gradually replaced by market-mediated prices. However, the price reform in energy sectors was sluggish in the 1980s. In the early 1990s, the energy price reform was accelerated. In 1998, the Chinese government took a wide-ranging reform package to limit government intervention in the commercial management of SOEs. This helped to relax the control of pricing across energy sectors. Under China's energy pricing reform, each energy resource received a different treatment and this resulted in substantial differences in price of each energy resource, hence the separate discussion on reforms in following subsections.

4.5.1. Policies on Coal Price

In the coal sector, the market mechanism was introduced in the domestic coal market incrementally since 1979, followed by slow progress in the 1980s. In the mid-1980s, the central government made it clear that energy prices were to increase within approved limits and that a rational energy pricing system would be formed gradually (NDRC, 1985). In 1985, a dual-tier pricing system for energy resources took effect. Under this system, coal was distributed at relatively low state-controlled prices, but firms and individuals could purchase more at negotiated prices in the free market (Perlack & Russell, 1991). In 1989, the government decided to solve the problems arising from the two-tier pricing system and the *jiage chuangguan*.[26] It aimed to first change the coal pricing from 'dual track' to 'single-track', and then gradually abolish the two-tier system (CCP Central Committee, 1989). This helped to progressively liberalise coal pricing and gradually establish the market mechanism in the domestic coal market.

---

[25]For data source of this section, see Section 3.2 except otherwise specified.

[26]See Chapter 5 for a discussion of the problems caused by the two-tier pricing system and the failure of *jiage chuangguan*.

After Deng Xiaoping's 1992 Southern Tour, China entered into a new stage of economic reform. The domestic economy was reinvigorated and soon overheated as energy prices, including coal, electricity, and oil, rocketed to the highest level of increase in history in 1995. The drastic reform package put forward in 1994 accelerated the formation of the market mechanism in China and also pushed price increase in the energy sector.[27] All the indicators AF-1, AF-2, and AF-3 have their highest values (and lowest ordinal values) in 1995, of the seven years in analysis. In the second half of 1992, the pricing of some unified distribution coalmines in the eastern region were liberalised. The coal trading market was established in Shanghai (People's Daily, 1993). In 1993, the central government announced its intention to decontrol the pricing of coal. It stated explicitly that a market-oriented pricing mechanism should be established and energy and raw materials prices should be adjusted accordingly (Li, 1993a; State Council, 1993). On 1 December 1993, Prime Minister Li Peng stated in the national economic work conference that the pricing of the unified distribution coalmines would be liberalised in 1994 (Li, 1993b). Therefore, the unified distribution coalmines were pushed to compete in the market. Coal retail prices began to be deregulated. However, the guiding role of the central government still existed. In 1994, the SPC announced that the coal prices should not rise too rapidly lest the downstream consumers would be seriously affected. In addition, the coal-consuming enterprises were not allowed to raise their own prices to recover rising costs. The coal sold for household use was also controlled according to the State Council pricing policy (State Planning Commission, 1994). Moreover, the subsidised and controlled prices for coal supplied to large power stations indicate that the government still retained direct control over pricing in the key areas of electricity generation (Tu, 2011).

In 2002, after China's economy recovered from the Asian Financial Crisis, energy consumption increased rapidly. The thermal coal demand also grew dramatically. The increased demand, however, did not arouse the thermal coal producers' enthusiasm to increase the coal supply. This was due to its low price supervised by the central government. In order to increase the thermal coal supply, the central government relaxed the pricing controls over thermal coal in 2002. Consequently, the central government no longer directly controlled coal pricing (Peng, 2009), but continued to intervene for a long time. The government issued the 2004 Coal-Electricity Price Linkage Mechanism[28] to lower the financial pressure caused by high coal prices in the power sector. In 2009, the NDRC gave coal enterprises and power plants the right to directly negotiate thermal coal contracts. After that, the government

[27]For the detailed discussion, see Chapter 5.

[28]Since 2002, China's electricity pricing is still almost completely controlled by the government whereas the price of coal, the main raw material for electricity generation, is decided by the market. A sharp increase in the price of coal would create operating difficulties for China's power generation companies. China responded by linking coal and electricity prices. However, the linkage was 'not a free market adjustment'; it was 'regulated and determined periodically by the NDRC to avoid extreme price fluctuations' (Ma & He, 2008, p. 1704).

stopped intervening and the deregulation of coal pricing finally materialised (Tu, 2011). Since 2000, the coal market became more liberalised and mature, resulting in modest AF-1 values in 2005 and 2010, hitting 5 and 6, respectively.

4.5.2. Policies on Electricity Price

Low financing costs and subsidised coal prices kept electricity prices rather low in the early 1980s. The standard nationwide electricity prices in China did not change before the economic reform. With the reform, the Chinese government increased electricity prices to realistic market levels. In 1985, electricity tariffs were increased for the first time throughout the country. The government recognised that the gap between energy supply and demand was largely caused by severe power shortage. In order to increase the supply of power, curb the increase in demand, and increase investment in the power industry, the central government introduced several policies to reform electricity tariffs. In 1985, the State Council issued one of the most important policies to encourage foreign investment in the power industry. By implementing the policy *Encouraging Investment in the Power Industry and Executing Multi-tiers of Electricity Tariffs*, it established a multi-tiered and diversified pricing system (Lam, 2004; Yang & Yu, 1996).

The new local power plants established after 1985 did not get cheaper fuel supplies as only plants built by the central government received such benefits. A new policy compensated the new plants with tariffs based on actual costs via a special dual-track pricing system (Chen, 2010). As a result, these independent power producers (IPPs) did not seek to control cost nor improve efficiency but passed the cost fluctuation onto the generation price. To get a higher price, some IPPs would even exaggerate their costs (Ma & He, 2008). This caused the overall level of electricity generation prices to rise rapidly. In 1987, the Chinese government issued the *Two-cent policy* to increase electricity tariff by two Chinese cents per kilowatt-hour throughout China.[29] The local governments used the revenue to build large and medium power plants (Hang & Tu, 2007; Lam, 2004).

In the early 1990s, the enforcement of relevant pricing policies resulted in highly diversified electricity tariffs. In 1991, the central government issued the *High-in and High-out* policy to prevent the state-owned power enterprises from running into deficit. This policy allowed electricity tariffs to fluctuate subject to the prices of the primary energy and other production materials (Yang & Yu, 1996). In 1993, a *New Plant, New Price* policy was issued to reflect capital costs. The new power plants built after 1992 were allowed to sell power to the provincial power companies at prices that repaid loan capital with interests. With the implementation of the *New Plant, New Price* policy, the prices of electricity generated by the new power plants were significantly higher than those generated by the old plants. Electricity tariffs increased rapidly (Lam, 2004). The AF-3 ordinal value turned out to be the lowest in 1995. In some remote rural areas, electricity tariffs

---

[29]The *Two-cent Policy* lasted from 1987 to 1996. All households and a few electricity-intensive industrial sectors were exempted from this policy.

were illegally imposed.[30] The surcharges were collected to supplement administration funds. The tariff-setting system in China was described as 'extremely complex and heterogeneous'. The electricity tariffs and the rules and regulations for price-setting were so confusing that no one could fully understand how the tariffs were determined (Andrews-Speed, 2004).

The distorted and confusing electricity tariffs in the mid-1990s stimulated the reform of electricity pricing. The 1996 *Electric Power Law of the People's Republic of China* provided the legal basis for China's electricity tariff reform. To simplify the electricity prices and boost investment in the old and new generation plants, a new tariff scheme was implemented in 1997. The scheme was formally issued in *Notice on Regulating Administration of Electricity Prices* in 2001. The new scheme allowed wholesale prices to be individually subject to the cost of a power plant. Based on an average generation cost and a unified internal rate of return on capital during the remaining operation period, the price was actually an operation-period price (for incumbent power plants) or a unified yardstick price (for new plants) (Ma & He, 2008). The new policy improved the AF-3 indicator, with its ordinal value increasing to 7 in 2000.

Since 2002, the electricity reform entered a substantive stage. After the separation of generation interests from grid companies, the reform was formally launched via a tariff formation mechanism to build a competitive market for electricity. In 2003, the State Council issued the *Tariff Reform Plan* (People's Daily, 2003a), which provided the preliminary framework for future pricing reform. In 2005, the NDRC issued three milestone policies for electricity pricing: *NDRC Interim Provision on the Regulation of Whole Electricity Price*, *NDRC Interim Provision on the Regulation of Retail Electricity Price*, and *NDRC Interim Provision on the Regulation of Power Transmission and Distribution Price*. These policies set the new electricity pricing scheme in China's power industry. The new scheme set a structure of two-part prices for electricity in the wholesale market. The two parts were capacity price and system marginal price. The former was set by the NDRC Department of Price while the latter was determined by market competition. This new scheme linked the wholesale electricity price directly to fuel cost. At the early stages of the implementation of the new scheme, the government controlled the retail price. However, the government would allow it to be determined by the market forces later on when the distribution activities are separated from retailing activities. This new scheme was aimed at injecting competition into the wholesale market first and gradually introducing it into the retail market (Pittman & Zhang, 2010). In 2009, electricity producers and wholesale end users were allowed to negotiate prices with each other directly (Betz, 2013, p. 20). These policies, which tried to introduce competition into the power market, continued to improve the AF-3 indicator while its ordinal values remained at the highest level both in 2005 and 2010.

[30]The local governments imposed illegal surcharges on top of the catalogue prices, which made the rural users pay higher tariffs than urban users. In 1999, the illegal electricity surcharges for rural users were abolished to lower tariffs in rural areas.

4.5.3. Policies on Oil Price

Crude oil had been sold at a single and state-controlled price before the economic reform. In 1981, the State Council approved the *Production Lump Sum Policy*, which allowed the over-quota production to be sold at the international oil price. From then on, the domestic oil prices were subject to a two-tier pricing system: quota oil sold at fixed prices and oil in excess of the quota sold at freely negotiated prices (Lin, 2010). From January 1993, the in-plan output from certain oilfields was sold at international prices. In 1993, the government adjusted the quota prices closer to the global prices and expanded the scope of production for the market. The proportion of market-priced refined products increased from about 10% in 1983 to 65% in 1993. From 1988 until 1993, the in-quota prices[31] – the prices set for allocations within the plan – for crude oil were raised from 115 to 300 Yuan/ton for low prices and from 500 to 700 Yuan/ton for high prices (Wang, 1995, p. 630). The AF-2 indicator hit its lowest ordinal value in 1995.

Along with Deng Xiaoping's 1992 Southern Tour and the ongoing reforms to construct a socialist market economy, China's national economy had expanded quickly between 1992 and 1993. However, excessive increases in the prices of basic goods and basic production prices caused the inflation pressure to rise again. The central government regarded the stabilisation of prices to curb inflation as the government's most urgent task (Peng & Chen, 2011b). In the oil sector, the high inflation and overheated economy forced the government to control the prices of oil and refined products again in 1994. In April 1994, the State Council approved the *Opinions on the reform of the crude oil and refined oil circulation system*. The *Opinions* abolished the two-tier pricing system for crude oil and oil products to make way for price-setting by the central government to tackle the disorder in the oil market (Lin, 2010). Between 1994 and 1998, the pricing of crude oil and oil products was under the strict control of the government. Restrictions on oil pricing were imposed to discourage imports and stimulate domestic output. In the second half of the 1990s, the anti-inflation measures took effect. The implementation of the macroeconomic regulations had gradually improved the fiscal and financial situation. The inflation rate fell to 8.3% in 1996 while the GDP grew at satisfactory rates (Dreyer, 2008, p. 156). This created a more favourable environment for the oil pricing reform.

In June 1998, the Chinese government made a revolutionary decision to peg its domestic oil prices to Singapore prices, with a one-month lag built in. Since then, the domestic oil prices had been based on Singapore export prices and were adjusted monthly. This was seen as a significant step to integrate China's oil industry into the world market (Anonymous, 1998; Hang & Tu, 2007). In November 2001, the domestic oil prices were adjusted to peg to the package price (the prices of New York, Rotterdam, and Singapore markets) (Lin, 2010). The market mechanism had begun to play a fundamental role in oil pricing. Compared to the 1990s, the oil market became relatively mature since 2000, and hence stabilised the ordinal value of the indicator AF-2 at 8.

---

[31]There were three different prices in the upstream sector: in-quota low prices, in-quota high prices, and market prices.

The swinging between control and relaxation of oil prices in China shows that frequently the government very passively issued energy policies just to solve the problems whenever and wherever they took place. Similarly, the way the government managed the tensions (whenever there were) was like this: they tried to settle the problem whenever and wherever they met the problem. The government did not have forward-looking energy policies. The reason behind this lies in the argument of the book: no energy policies in China are proactively issued or originally intended to improve energy security.

4.6. Chapter Summary and Further Discussion

China's energy policies have directly affected energy security indicators, making different shapes and areas of grids as presented in Chapter 3. In the process of promulgation and implementation of these energy policies, the challenges are various. The ineffective coordination at the local levels could be one challenge, which is especially prominent when the environmental protection is concerned. On the one hand, the Chinese producers violate environmental regulations to reduce cost of production. On the other hand, it is often to the advantage of local governments to allow the pollution illegally in order to promote faster economic growth of their own regions and the central government cannot control them. Local government officials benefit from higher rates of economic growth as they receive credits for economic development and even bribes from the polluting producers. These factors have hindered the implementation of environmental regulations and worsened or slowed down the improvement of the AC dimension.

Another challenge could be found in the SOEs' increasing independence and their capability to affect the central government's policies. The economic reform has gradually liberalised and decentralised Chinese industry. While energy has remained a strategic sector, there has still been a great shift of power from government to the National Oil Companies (NOCs). For instance, the China National Petroleum Corporation (CNPC) was created from the Ministry of Petroleum Industry and China Petroleum & Chemical Corporation (Sinopec) was established by merging assets from the Ministry of Petroleum Industry and the Ministry of Chemical Industry. The power and influence these ministries had held over the policymaking process were largely transferred to these NOCs.[32]

Since June 1998, China implemented a new and more market-based oil pricing system that improved the NOCs profitability. In addition to the new pricing system, the then-Prime Minister Zhu Rongji deliberately enhanced the financial and administrative autonomy of China's NOCs to prepare them for the listing of their subsidiaries on international stock markets. The price adjustment and the enhanced autonomy of NOCs facilitated the overseas listing of CNPC and Sinopec in 2000. The NOCs lobbied for further progress in liberalisation of oil price setting. In November 2001, the domestic oil prices were adjusted again and the market mechanism has begun to play a fundamental role in oil pricing. All these

[32]For details, see Chapter 5.

factors contributed to profitability increase and financial independence of the NOCs. Greater profitability brought the NOCs greater autonomy from the central government, and greater independence provided them with additional protection against government intervention (Downs, 2006). For example, the NOCs stated that the Energy Leading Group was not a decision-making bureau and it could only give suggestions rather than make decisions. Furthermore, the power of the NOCs (and other energy companies) has been fully demonstrated by their successful lobbying to prevent formation of a ministry-level energy agency. This leaves the government with relatively less capability in pursuing strategic energy objectives (Jiang & Sinton, 2011).

However, the growing conflicts among interest groups are only intervening variables that account for energy policymaking. They are not the key force behind the promulgation and implementation of energy policy in China. It is the macroeconomic reform that makes itself a force so strong that it diminishes all intervening variables. Macroeconomic reform is the key driving force that is behind the energy policy and security formation. The following chapter analyses China's macroeconomic reform and its impact on energy policies.

Chapter 5

The Impact of Economic Reforms on the Energy Sector and Energy Security[1]

The quantitative analysis in Chapter 3 shows that China's energy security was at its best during the Sixth Five-Year Plan (FYP) period (1981–1985) and subsequently deteriorated until 1995. During the Ninth and Tenth FYP periods (1995–2000 and 2001–2005, respectively), the situation improved but fell short of its best record. In the Eleventh FYP period, the situation deteriorated again. In Chapter 4, the author analyses how energy policies have affected China's energy security situation. In this chapter, the author argues that China's energy policies are only reactive to its macroeconomic reform. The macroeconomic reform is a variable so strong that it predominates over all other factors that might function in China's energy policy promulgation and implementation. By analysing the predominance of macroeconomic reform, the author also gives the reasons why China's energy security situation, despite some improvements in the new millennium, fell short of the level of the early reform period. Reasons for the inefficacy of China's energy policies in restoring the situation to that of the initial reform period are also given here.

Amid economic reform, China's energy sector also experienced a series of reforms. China's energy policies, issued and implemented along with economic reform measures, have deeply affected its energy security situation. In other words, it is the economic reform that determines the central government's energy policy decisions which affects the evolution of the energy security situation. Energy policies only passively respond to the economic reform measures and cannot play full function in pursuing energy security of the country. What are the reforms implemented in the energy sector in response to the economic reform? What is the impact of China's energy sector reforms on its energy security situation? Answers to these questions are addressed in detail in this chapter by discussing China's economic reform policies and analysing how the macroeconomic reform compels the reform in energy sector and affects the formulation of energy policies.

[1]The major part of this chapter has been published in *Energy Policy*, Vol. 77, Lixia Yao and Youngho Chang, Shaping China's energy security: The impact of domestic reforms, Pages 131–139, 2015, with permission from Elsevier.

Energy Security in Times of Economic Transition: Lessons from China, 113–150

doi:10.1108/978-1-83982-464-720201006

5.1. Introduction

Before the economic reform, China had a Soviet-style centrally planned economy (often called a 'command economy') which could mobilise resources for rapid economic development. Since the central government during that time desired high growth rates to be on a par with and eventually overtake the developed countries quickly, they favoured heavy industries such as steel and machine building. A large share of the nation's resources was thus channelled to these industries. Consequently, China's traditional economic system was driven by a heavy industry-oriented development strategy (Shirk, 1993). As heavy industries are mostly capital-intensive and China was then a capital-scarce economy, the central government had to 'artificially suppress' the prices of capital, energy, and raw materials in order to lower the capital formation threshold in these heavy industries. The distorted prices of these production factors led to a 'shortage economy', characterised by a combination of planned resource allocation system and dependent micro-institutions (Lin, Cai, & Li, 2003). During this period, China's economic efficiency was low. Energy and transportation infrastructure was neglected and not reflected in annual growth rates. The result was that the nation's economy was severely constrained by energy and transport shortage (Shirk, 1993). The people's livelihoods suffered. The mass living standards were very low.

To revamp China's economy, the central government initiated economic reform in 1978. In the past more than 40 years, China experienced a drastic economic transition with a continuous high rate of GDP growth undergoing various economic reforms. These reforms could be categorised into four phases covering Deng Xiaoping, Jiang Zemin, Hu Jintao, and Xi Jinping administrations, respectively.[2] This chapter explores the first three phases, whereas the next chapter discusses the last phase of Chinese energy policies and energy security against the background of the Belt and Road Initiative.

The first phase of the reform (1978–1992) was a period of unexpected fast economic growth during Deng Xiaoping's administration. This phase of the reform was very experimental and limited. It started in the rural area with the Household Responsibility System (HRS). With its success, the reform was extended to urban industrial sectors in 1984. Since Deng Xiaoping's Southern Tour in 1992, the reform underwent recovery with full range encompassing many aspects. The second phase of the reform aimed at the establishment of a 'socialist market economy', and largely focused on fiscal, financial, and state-owned enterprises (SOEs) sectors. The third phase of the reform was a response to the success of the second phase, which brought urbanisation, social equality, and environmental pollution to the forefront of governmental concerns. The priorities of each reform phases had a direct bearing on the energy policies. At the same time, the characteristics of economic reform through incremental change are reflected in the energy sector, making changes in energy policy incremental as well. Maxims such as 'take one

[2]With regard to the division of reform stages, scholars' views varied according to their categorising coarseness and basis (Lin, 2009b; Ma & Cao, 2002; Tan, 2007). This book divides the reform period in accordance with governmental administration periods to assess their respective policy emphasis.

step and look around before taking another', 'take small steps at the early stage', and 'crossing the river by groping the stones', which appeared frequently in the government official documents in the initial reform period, were actually applied throughout economic reform for more than 30 years. Correspondingly, tried and tested measures were also adopted throughout energy policymaking. As Lin and Tsai (2004) characterised:

> China has adopted an alternative gradual, evolutional approach to the transition since the reform started at the end of 1978. This approach is piecemeal, partial, incremental, often experimental, and especially without large-scale privatization. The Chinese approach is neither guided by a well-founded theory nor followed a predetermined blueprint. (p. 336)

China's approach to economic reform does not have a blueprint. Neither does its energy policies. The reaction and responsiveness make China unable to have coherent energy policies. China's energy security did not improve over the first three phases of economic reform. The following sections explain and analyse economic reforms and their impact on the energy sectors in three phases: Section 5.2 focuses on the first phase of the economic reform, 5.3 the second phase, and 5.4 the third phase, respectively.

5.2. Economic Reform and Energy Sector Reform: The First Phase (1978–1992)

When the Chinese government began its economic reform, it did not have any blueprint. The measures taken were gradual and piecemeal to deal with the most pressing economic problems. The step-by-step approach had four major objectives: to institute a contract responsibility system (CRS) in agricultural sectors, to revive private sectors in urban areas, to delegate greater authority to SOEs, and to reform the irrational price system (Dreyer, 2008). These objectives had all been reflected in the major reform measures in the first phase of the reform. China's economic reform was initiated with the Third Plenary Session of the Eleventh CCP Central Committee, which identified the guideline, principle, and direction of the reform. It pointed out that:

> One of the severe deficiencies in our country's economic management system is the over-concentration of power, and it is necessary to shift it to lower levels under proper leadership so that the local authorities as well as industrial and agricultural enterprises will have greater management authority under the guidance of unified state planning. (Peng & Chen, 2011a, p. 5)

The Session clearly delivered the thought of decentralisation of economic power to the lower levels of the economy, which gave much room for the economic reform at the micro-level. This thought constituted a platform for the policies implemented throughout the initial period of the economic reform. The introduction of HRS, the rise of township and village enterprises (TVEs), and the allowance for 'market' and enterprises to play their dual roles in the national economy – all reflected this thought of decentralisation and the government's reform measures at the micro-level. The delegation of autonomy and profit-sharing to micro-management institutions gave production incentives and resulted in surplus (above-planned) new products/resources, which were allowed to be disposed at the discretion of the micro-management institutions. It follows that a new channel to allocate resources was needed and this led to the emergence of the dual-tier pricing system. The reform at the micro-level had created spillover effects at the macro-level. The following subsections discuss these reform measures and analyse their impact on the energy sector.

5.2.1. The Initial Period (1978–1984): Planned Economy Dominating, Market Regulation Supplemented

5.2.1.1. Adjustment of the Economy. Beginning with the First FYP (1953–1957), China's regional economic development had followed the strategy of balanced development for the interior inland provinces. This strategy greatly undermined economic development. Due to the requirement for the 'Third Front' factories to 'scatter and hide in mountains' (*Fensan, Kaoshan, Yinbi* in Chinese), the connection of production was artificially severed (Peng & Chen, 2011a). This development strategy of pouring investments in the interior regions clearly violated the comparative advantage principle. The growth of the interior regions occurred at the expense of the coastal regions and lowered the overall growth rate of the national economy (Démurger et al., 2002). Therefore, during the initial period of the economic reform, the guiding ideology of China's economic development was to adjust, reform, rectify, and improve the economic order (*tiaozheng, gaige, zhengdun, tigao* in Chinese). In a State Council workshop held in March 1980, Deng Xiaoping stressed that '(we need to) play comparative advantages and circumvent disadvantages, and admit to the problem of imbalance' (Peng & Chen, 2011a, p. 124). The development strategy was thus shifted to an efficiency-based one. The landmark for this strategic shift was the Sixth FYP, which made a significant readjustment of the regional economic development strategy by means of a shift from focusing on balanced development to focusing on macro-economic returns and 'efficiency first with due consideration to fairness' (*Xiaolv Youxian, Jiangu Gongping* in Chinese). Therefore, the regional economic development priority began to move to the light textile industry and technological innovation of the existing textile, mechanics, and electronics industries in the eastern coastal cities. At the same time, energy and raw material bases in the interior areas were also enhanced to fuel the industrial development in the east. The decision to adjust, reform, rectify, and improve the economic order had led to the adjustment of energy industry distribution. As discussed in Chapter 4, the adjustment of coal industry most typically reflected this decision. The coal industry was shifted to the coal-rich areas, especially Shanxi and eastern Inner Mongolia, leading to a great increase in coal output.

5.2.1.2. The Introduction of HRS and the Coal Sector Reform. The economic reform stimulated the development of town and village coalmines (TVCMs), the root of which was the HRS initiative, a reform in the agricultural sector. At the beginning of the reform, nobody knew where the reform would lead to. As discussed, the reforms were characterised by experimentation ('crossing the river by groping the stones'). The first 'stone' was the HRS, whereby farmers were allotted usage rights of the land with contracted production quotas. This allowed them to make operating decisions independently as long as they fulfilled the terms set by the contract with collective organisations. More importantly, the over-quota production could be disposed freely by the households (Hou, 2011). This was also the starting point of the delegation of autonomy. This rural household system reform spurred farmers to be more efficient when farming. This led to high agricultural productivity, which meant that fewer workers were needed by the farming work and thus provided surplus labour for the rural non-agricultural sector.[3]

In the early 1980s, the government issued a new policy towards rural non-agricultural development described as 'leave the land plot but not the countryside; enter the factory but not the city (*Litu bu Lixiang, Jinchang bu Jincheng* in Chinese)'. In other words, the peasants still remained in the countryside but were allowed to participate in non-agricultural activities. This policy made the non-agricultural development in rural area:

> not so much as a way to serve and support agriculture but as a way of generating employment opportunities so that surplus rural labor could be reallocated from cultivation to more productive activities while keeping rural-urban migration to a minimum.[4] (Ho, 1995, p. 361)

The rural household system reform provided outlets for expanding TVEs, which were 'a new force that just came into being spontaneously', as Deng Xiaoping described (Vogel, 2011, p. 445), and shot up quickly. The TVCMs, as one of the major forces of TVEs, began to develop.[5] The policy shift to the rural

[3]In 1978, 'commune enterprises' employed 28.3 million people whereas in 1992, 105.8 million people were employed in TVEs (Vogel, 2011, p. 447).

[4]The responsibility system reform called for persuasive theoretical supporting documents, which gave birth to the document *Several Issues Concerning Current Rural Economic Policies* in January 1983. This document highly appraised the HRS and proposed 'two transitions' (*Liangge Zhuanhua*). One was the transition from subsistence or semi-subsistence economy to larger commodity production, and the other was the transition from traditional agriculture to modern agriculture. This stimulated large-scale commodity production in rural sector. The rural commodity economy became prosperous since then (Peng & Chen, 2011a).

[5]The term 'township and village enterprises' (TVE) first appeared in China's official documents in 1984. The emergence of TVEs has a long history. The predecessors of TVEs were enterprises run by communes and brigades in the late 1950s. Before the reform, their development had experienced ups and downs. The *Decision on Several Issues on Accelerating Agricultural Development* passed in 1978 at the Third Plenary

non-agricultural sector relaxed the TVCMs development throughout the country. First, the reform provided surplus labor for the TVCMs as discussed. Second, the reform stimulated changes in the investment system to provide funding for the TVCMs. The underinvestment in the coal industry before the reform indicated that the investment system must be changed. A successful policy encouraged investment in the coal industry in the early reform period: 'walking on two legs',[6] meaning that the central government actively encouraged the use of social and individual funds to develop the capacity of TVCMs (Compilation Commission, 1999). Third, the reform freed up the pricing system to some extent. The introduction of the two-tier system in the coal sector in 1985 increased incentives of production in the coal industry, particularly the TVCMs. Fourth, following the example of HRS, a 'General Contract Programme' was put into practice in the coal sector in 1985, and this further promoted coal production (Andrews-Speed, 2004; Chen & Chen, 2007). Completely flexible in adapting to market demand, the TVCMs supplemented state coalmines supply significantly: the annual TVCMs output increased at a rate of more than 20% in the early 1980s; by 1996 the coal produced by TVCMs had constituted more than 50% of the country's total output, which finally brought China's long history of coal shortages to an end (Rui, 2005, p. 698).

5.2.1.3. Emergence of the Word 'Market' with Very Cautious Reform Measures. The 1980 government work report stated that the government would change the economic regulation mechanism from single planning to the planning-cum-market combination. From then on, the word 'market' began to appear frequently in China's official documents and was embedded in China's leading ideology of economic reform. At the end of 1981, Prime Minister Zhao Ziyang stressed in the government work report that the basic direction of China's economic reform should adhere to the premise of the socialist planned economy and at the same time allow the market to play a supplementary role.[7] This was the first

---

Session of the Eleventh CCP Central Committee pointed out the need to increase the proportion of revenue of commune and brigade enterprises in the total commune revenues. Agricultural products that would be better processed in rural areas should be processed by these enterprises. This document greatly encouraged the development of these enterprises. In July 1979, the State Council promulgated the *Provisions on Several Issues Regarding the Development of Commune and Brigade Enterprises (Trial)*, which clearly stated that the commune and brigade enterprises could enjoy a low tax or no tax policy. Newly established small iron ores, small coalmines, small power stations, and small cement plants could be exempted from taxes for three years since their start-up. This document brought to these enterprises a historical turning point in their development. During the first half of the 1980s, the commune and brigade enterprises became an important force in national economy. To adapt to the transformation of rural communes into township and village governments, commune and brigade enterprises were renamed as TVEs in 1984 (Peng & Chen, 2011a).

[6]One leg was the state coalmines and the other the TVCMs.

[7]This thought was reiterated by Hu Yaobang as the principle of 'planned economy playing the leading role and market regulation playing the supplementary role' in the *Report of the Twelfth Party Congress* made in September 1982, titled *Creating A New Situation in All Fields of Socialist Modernization* (Peng & Chen, 2011a).

systematic economic reform model created in the 1980s. The Twelfth Party Congress in 1982 stressed that the fundamental issue of economic reform was the dominance of planned economy supplemented by market regulation (Guo & Li, 2009). It could be seen through these statements that at the beginning of the reform, the concept of 'market' had been in the mind of the reformers. However, it was surely not the right timing for China to adopt a free market. Therefore, the word 'supplementary' was always put together with 'market'. The government could afford to let the market simply play a 'supplementary' role. This economic structure determined that most industries and SOEs were still firmly in the hands of the government. The government's major task during that time was to lay a good foundation for further reform rather than drastically reform the nation's economic structure. Reflected in the energy sector, a key sector in the economy, there were no major reforms in the energy enterprises. Although the government emphasised decentralisation, it tightened its control over enterprises of key importance to the national economy at the early stage of the reform. The government work report stated that production of essential goods should be carried out in accordance with the mandatory state plans (People's Daily, 1981). As a consequence, reform did not take place in the state enterprises of the energy sector at the beginning of the reform period. Since energy pricing was largely controlled by the central government, the initial reform period saw low and stable energy prices.

5.2.1.4. Summary. From the initial reform period, macroeconomic reform in China began to function as a predominant force affecting energy policies. The major reform then was the introduction of HRS and delegation of autonomy to micro-levels. This provided opportunities for the TVEs to enter into new lines of business to engage in almost any income-generating activities. Among them were the TVCMs, which have affected China's coal sector throughout the reform period. The adjustment of the economy and the emergence of the concept 'market' prepared the government for subsequent reform measures in both the economy and energy sector. During the early 1980s, relatively abundant energy reserves, sound environment unscathed by the fast economic growth, and low and stable energy prices – three factors made the rhombus (presented in Chapter 3) the largest in 1985, depicting the best energy security situation during the reform period. The macroeconomic reform, from its very beginning, began to show its powerful strength in prompting policies and reforms towards the energy sector.

5.2.2. From Rural to Urban: Further and Faster Reforms until 1989 (1984–1989)

5.2.2.1. Emergence of 'Socialist Planned Commodity Economy' and 'Socialism with Chinese Characteristics'. Success in the rural reform gave the government confidence to extend the reform to the urban area. China's urban reform was mainly focused on improving the performance of SOEs. In May 1984, the State Council issued *Regulations for Further Expanding the Autonomy of State-Owned Enterprises*, which granted enterprises more autonomy and flexibility to participate in the 'market' after meeting their planned targets. The term 'socialism with Chinese characteristics' advocated by Deng Xiaoping granted the SOEs expanded use of market prices under the two-tier pricing system (Vogel, 2011). More decision-making power was devolved to them under the assumption that they would be in a better position to judge what to do. This greatly increased the production incentives for these enterprises. Productivity soared and products variety increased (Dreyer, 2008). In addition to the increase of vigour of SOEs, the urban reform also created new markets and found new sources for raw materials, contributing to the expansion of TVEs and urban collective enterprises (Brandt & Rawski, 2008). The economic contribution of the private sector in urban areas burgeoned.[8] All these prepared China's economy to move towards a market economy. The macroeconomic reform that originated in the rural area spread into the urban. It was such a natural and unstoppable process that it had penetrated into most sectors of the economy before people realised that.

The government grasped the moment to issue official document to give legitimacy to the reform spreading across the country. In October 1984, the Third Plenum of the Twelfth Party Congress approved the *Decision on the Reform of the Economic Structure*, which officially coined the phrase 'to build socialism with Chinese characteristics', paving the way for further market expansion (Peng & Chen, 2011a; Vogel, 2011). To further revamp China's rigid economic structure, the 1984 Decision made it clear that China's economic structure must undergo reform. Affirming the progress of the past six years, it officially sanctioned commodity production and exchange, expanded the reform from the agricultural production sector to the urban industrial sector and proposed the theory of 'socialist planned commodity economy' (Fei & Hou, 1994, Larus, 2005; Peng & Chen, 2011a). It officially gave legitimacy to comprehensive market reform in China and reduced the scope of central planning and at the same time, expanded enterprises' operational autonomy.

Under this background, some of the central government's responsibilities were delegated to sub-national governments. Large- and medium-sized state enterprises were given more autonomy (Fewsmith, 1994; Research Committee of China's Economic Structural Reform, 1987). The delegation of autonomy was reiterated in the 13th Party Congress report in 1987, which pointed out that the 'socialist planned commodity economy' should be an internally unified system of the plan and market: the State regulates the market, while the market leads the enterprises. The reform decision to delegate more autonomy to local governments and enterprises provided a favourable pro-local context for the power sector to launch its first round of reform, diversification of investment at local levels (Chen, 2010).

5.2.2.2. Power Sector Reform. In the mid-1980s, rapid economic growth led to surging demand for electricity. The gap between electricity demand and supply had widened. Prime Minister Zhao Ziyang had mentioned several times in his government work reports that the electricity supply was running low. When the economic reform began in 1979, electricity shortage was about 10 gigawatts of capacity and 40 terawatt-hour of generation. By 1986, the capacity shortage

---

[8]Since the early 1980s, private enterprises have been allowed to operate and develop. In 1982, the 5th National People's Congress stated that the State sector was the centre of economy and the non-State sector was the supplement. This statement gave the non-State sector the legitimacy to be engaged in economic activities (Hou, 2011).

had grown to about 15 gigawatts and the generation shortage was 700 terawatt-hour. (Zhang & Heller, 2004, p. 25) Thanks to the macroeconomic reform that delegated more autonomy to the lower levels, the central government stimulated investments in electricity generation by decentralising investment authority. The local governments, SOEs, and foreign companies were encouraged to finance and have their own power generation facilities. Incentives to diversify financing sources were issued by the State Council in 1985.[9] The document, *Provisional Regulation on Encouraging Fund-raising for Power Plant Construction and Allowing Multiple Electricity Prices,* reflected the theme of the policy: the electricity users and beneficiaries should be those who make investment in the electricity sector. The initiative increased the sources of investments in energy industry. It was estimated that from 1981 to 2001, about 1,107 billion Yuan was invested in new generation and transmission capacity, leading to impressive development of the Chinese electricity industry (Zhang & Heller, 2004, p. 6). As various new sources of capital were attracted, the financial burden on the central government was reduced. The share of the central government investment decreased from 78% in 1985 to 52% in 1988. During this period, around 40% of the newly increased generation capacity was financed by the new investment sources (Lu, 1993, p. 53). This policy was quite effective in terms of removing the financial constraint on China's power industry. It is noteworthy that despite the introduction of new actors and new dynamics in the electricity sector, the first phase of the reform did not significantly 'shift the underlying operations, market rules, corporate governance or regulatory/environmental performance' of the electricity sector (Zhang & Heller, 2004, p. 32).

5.2.2.3. Two-Tier Pricing System. Early economic reform during the late 1970s saw the emergence of a two-tier pricing system. This system consisted of two types of pricing: a government-set price covered by the state plan and a negotiated price for the products above the state quota. In 1985, this system was formally constructed by decontrolling the price of the market portion of industrial goods sold outside the plan (Byrd, 1987). It was a logical outcome of the process of economic reform. It came into being spontaneously along with delegation of autonomy and surplus of products. This system emerged in the energy sector in the early 1980s.

In 1981, to develop the oil industry, the State Council permitted the Ministry of Petroleum Industry to adopt the contract responsibility policy. The selling prices of crude oil produced above the quota were based on international prices. In 1983, in order to increase supply of oil products and funds for oil exploration and development, the State Council permitted local oil products (produced and sold domestically) to be sold at international prices, thus creating two-tier pricing for oil products by phasing out subsidised prices for them.

In the same year, to stimulate coal production, a 25–50% price markup for above-quota production was implemented, thus giving rise to two-tier pricing for coal (Peng & Chen, 2011a; Wright, 1996). Consequently, some were distributed

[9]Before that, the only source of energy investment financing had been the central government.

at market prices, while others were sold at state prices under the control of the planning system. Since 1984, local state mines were allowed to sell coal produced over their quotas at a premium, and all non-state mines were allowed to sell their products at market prices. In 1986, the central state mines were also given similar concessions for their over-quota output (Wright, 1996). The two-tier pricing system was successful in providing sufficient incentive for coal producers to increase production and for coal consumers to hold back consumption. It also fostered the growth of the TVCMs (Zhang, 1992). The two-tier pricing system was established for natural gas sector as well in the late 1980s.[10] The penetration of two-tier pricing system into the energy sector shows how the macroeconomic reform affects energy policies and how the energy sector reacts to the macroeconomic measures.

As an interim measure, the two-tier pricing system was effective, but it also had the unintended result of hoarding and speculation. Speculators bought as much as they could at the state-set price and sold them at a higher negotiated price. These practices caused serious economic inefficiencies. From the point of view of the national economy as a whole, the two-tier system had led to economic chaos and corruption. The enterprises tried to hide their production capacity so that they got lower production quotas from the state.[11] Smuggling also happened. Under this system, the smugglers resold allocated materials and made profits (Wu & Zhao, 1987). The two-tier pricing system was seen by the World Bank as the economic basis of corruption (Zhang, 1992). Officials made profits through the system (*guandao* in Chinese), which contributed to widespread corruption in China at that time. The defects were especially obvious in the energy sector. As a sector of basic raw materials, its prices were set far below their actual production costs, while the products made from them could be sold at much higher negotiated prices. This made the hoarding and speculation activities in the energy sector, particularly the coal sector, very serious. All these led to shortages of energy and other raw materials.

The drawbacks of the two-tier pricing system were more prominent in the late 1980s along with the increase in exports. Trading companies rushed to export severely underpriced energy and other raw materials, and sold them at much higher international prices. The result was a severe shortage of these materials domestically (Dreyer, 2008). In addition to the speculation in the energy sector, low state prices of coal discouraged efficient coal utilisation (Albouy, 1991). The pricing system had to be changed and this led to the government's decision to 'cross the price hurdle'.

5.2.2.4. Price Reform and 'Cross the Price Hurdle' (*jiage chuangguan* in Chinese). Back in September 1982, when Hu Yaobang made the *Report of the Twelfth Party Congress* titled *Creating A New Situation in All Fields of Socialist*

---

[10]Historically, gas prices were set low for the reason of subsidising fertiliser and other industrial production. The low gas prices offered little incentive for the development of natural gas industry.

[11]The state enterprises would surely try to sell the maximum proportion of its output at the market prices and to minimise the quota within the plan set by the state. For example, the state coalmines spent much time in negotiating their obligations under the plan so that they could minimise the portion that circulated within the plan and maximise their returns.

Modernization, it was mentioned that there was a need to reform the pricing system and price management measures 'in a steady manner' (Peng & Chen, 2011a). However, problems caused by the two-tier pricing system left the central government determined to accelerate the price reform. The government believed that too much emphasis on price stability would only cause difficulty in price reform. Since the mid-1980s, the central government frequently expressed its determination to reform the pricing system.[12] The major aim was to readjust prices at the macro-level to more directly reflect demand and supply. With greater pricing flexibility, economic resources could be reallocated to aid enterprises to adapt rapidly to the changing economic conditions (Wright, 1996).

The price reform took place in the mid-1980s. The *Decision on the Reform of the Economic Structure* adopted by the twelfth CCP Central Committee in October 1984 directly propelled the pricing reform to readjust irrational prices and make them subject to the principles of supply–demand forces. The pricing reform was laid out in two steps, as proposed in *Suggestions on Formulating the Seventh Five-Year Plan for National Economic and Social Development* in 1985. First, from 1986 to 1987, stabilising the economy was top priority. Hence, improving indirect regulation on macro-level was emphasised without any drastic pricing reform. This was actually the preparation stage of the pricing reform.

Second, from 1988 until 1990, the indirect macro-regulation and reform of production pricing were to improve. Adhering to 'Suggestions', the government began to mobilise the pricing reform in 1985. It was stated in the *People's Daily* that the pricing system was not reasonable because pricing did not reflect the value of goods, nor did it reflect the relationship between supply and demand. The pricing system must be reformed. The reform which covered all national economy impelled the price reform in the energy sector. In the early 1980s, the energy prices were so low that some prices were only equivalent to a fraction of the international market price. Nevertheless, the costs of the processing enterprises were much higher than those of the products in the international market. This was because the cheap energy put no pressure on the processing enterprises to reduce energy consumption or improve technology. Therefore, China must reform its pricing system to mobilise the energy enterprises to increase production and reduce costs (People's Daily, 1985a). At the same time, the government emphasised that the price increase should remain affordable for processing enterprises (People's Daily, 1985b).

The idea of the reform schedule and measures were good. It was believed that without the reform, it was impossible to create a complete socialist market system that was indispensable for the development of the socialist commodity economy (People's Daily, 1987). Towards the end of the 1980s, the government decided to accelerate the price reform. The government work report on 15 March 1988 indicated that the State Council decided to take comprehensive supporting measures to reform the pricing system. At the same time, accelerated economic growth in the first half of 1988 led to inflated demand for consumption and investment. The government report and the economic situation increased the expectation of inflation.

---

[12]See People's Daily (1985a, 1985b, 1985c, 1985d).

In early August 1988, when the *Preliminary Plan on Price and Wage Reform* approved by Political Bureau of CCP Central Committee was publicised in the media, people misunderstood that the prices would be fully deregulated. This brought about a surge of panic buying across the country that severely hindered the progress of pricing reform (Peng & Chen, 2011a). Making matters worse, on 24 August 1988, the *People's Daily* published an editorial stating that the old price formation mechanism had been a large obstacle of reform and economic development. The price reform 'hurdle' must be crossed. The price reform could not be delayed any more. Otherwise, the price reform would only be more and more difficult (People's Daily, 1988). The editorial exacerbated the people's panic. This situation was the so-called *jiage chuangguan* in 1988. Through the price reform, the government had expected to gradually form a reasonable price system that would reflect the true value of the product and the relationship between supply and demand. However, the price reform in 1988 was interrupted and *jiage chuangguan* failed at last. The overheated Chinese economy exacerbated by the panic buying turned to be out of control in late 1980s. In 1988, the inflation soared from 7% to almost 19%. The crazy high inflation rate and the provoked bank run forced the central government to tighten the economic policy by stringently controlling investments and credits until the end of 1991 (Hussain & Stern, 1991, p. 146).

On 30 August 1988, the 20th executive meeting of the State Council restated 'stabilizing the economy' and highlighted that market-regulating prices of most commodities specified in the price reform plan was a long-term objective. On the same day, the State Council issued the *Urgent Notice on Current Price Work and Stabilizing the Market*. The meeting and the notice curbed the pricing reform (Peng & Chen, 2011a). A series of stringent measures were adopted to restrict spending and control inflation. In late 1988, China began to cut back capital construction to impose control over the pace of economic development. But as the inflation continued to increase, the central government adopted much more stringent measures in 1989 to exert greater control over the economy.

As a result of these tightening measures, China saw a steep economic downturn in the subsequent years (Dreyer, 2008). Inflation was effectively controlled. In 1990, the growth rate was 3.8%, which was a significant decline from 11.3% in 1988. Consumer price index fell from 18.8% in 1988 to 3.1% in 1990 (Vogel, 2011, p. 473). China's economy had entered into a period of adjustment and recovering.

5.2.3. Adjustment and Recovering of the Economy (1989–1992): Combination of Planned Economy and Market Regulation

The relatively depressed economy in the early 1990s offered an ideal opportunity for the central government to rescind certain stringent measures. Though the national economic situation improved, the government was still uncertain how to proceed. Evidence could be found in Jiang Zemin's National Day address in 1989. He stated that an economic system should be created such that the degree, manner, and scope of the combination of planning and market regulation could be adjusted and improved according to the actual situation in China (Guo & Li, 2009). But Jiang did not mention specifics so the government did not know how to adjust the combination. This uncertainty was also reflected by the government's contradictory pronouncements of the need for structural reforms on the one hand and for economic retrenchment on the other hand. This period was described by analysts as a suspended economy in a state of disequilibrium (Dreyer, 2008). Nonetheless, reform tendencies had already been strongly entrenched in the economy and its continued transformation to a market economy cannot be reversed.

During the two years of adjustment, the central government managed to maintain the stability and continuity of the policy of reform and opening up, and introduced macroeconomic measures to expand the range and the extent of market regulation. The *Report on the Ten-Year Plan for National Economic and Social Development and the Draft of Eighth Five-Year Plan* made in March 1991 indicated that the government would continue its exploration on the specific ways to combine planned economy and market regulation. In early 1992, the overall economic situation has improved. Gross National Product (GNP) increased by 7% in 1991 compared to the figure in 1990; the costs of living of urban and rural residents rose by 3.4%; total fixed asset investment growth rate was 18.6%; retail sales growth rate was 13.2%; export growth rate was 15.8%. As the *People's Daily* published, 'China already has the conditions to speed up reforms' (People's Daily, 1992a).

The economic improvement prepared China to speed up reform and marketisation. In early 1992, Deng's southern tour signalled the new period of reforms. In Zhuhai, he reaffirmed that China's development in the past decade proved the efficacy of the principles and policies formulated in the Third Plenary Session of the 11th Party Congress, and he concluded that China must stick to them. He also told China's top decision makers decisively: 'Development is the absolute principle' (*Fazhan caishi yingdaoli* in Chinese) (Peng & Chen, 2011b, p. 7). In his talk with Jiangxi Provincial governors, he re-emphasised the necessity of faster development and said '[w]e should be bolder and more open…If there is an opportunity to leap, just leap' (Peng & Chen, 2011b, p. 7).

Deng Xiaoping's speech during his southern tour thus initiated another tide of reform and opening up. The essence of his speech was fully reflected in the report to the Fourteenth National People's Congress of CCP, delivered by President Jiang Zemin on 12 October 1992. Jiang Zemin stated that the government would accelerate the pace of economic reform and establish the socialist market economic system. To do so, the government should adopt the following measures: transform the operating mechanism of large- and medium-sized SOEs and push them into the market; develop the production market, financial market, and technology, labour, information, and real estate market; reform the revenue-sharing system; and transform the government's role and separate enterprises from government management (People's Daily, 1992b). The report initiated a radical package of reforms in the 1990s, including the SOEs reform, fiscal and financial reform, and government restructuring.[13]

5.2.3.1. Energy Sector during the Adjustment Period. To rectify the economic order and gradually reduce inflation, the Fifth Plenary Session of the Thirteenth CCP Central Committee passed the *Decision on Further Managing the Economic*

[13]All these reforms directly affected the energy sector throughout the 1990s. For details, see Section 5.3.

Environment, Rectifying Economic Order and Deepening Reform in November 1989. One main objective of the Decision was to increase the supply of energy and raw materials. To realise this objective, the central government increased input in basic industries. In early 1990, the State Planning Commission and the State Council Production Commission proposed the *Report on Piloting the Method of 'Two-guarantees' in 234 Key Enterprises.*

The Report identified 234 key enterprises as 'two-guarantee' (*Shuangbao* in Chinese) enterprises. The first guarantee refers to enterprises' operating under unified central planning to pledge to turn over to the country the following products: 323 million tons of raw coal, 136 million tons of crude oil, and 367.1 billion kilowatts-hours of generating capacity. The second guarantee refers to the central and local governments' pledge to equip the enterprises with production necessities such as energy, raw materials, and funding. As a result, the total output of raw coal and electricity increased by 2.5% and 6.2%, respectively, in 1990 (Peng & Chen, 2011a, p. 425). The year 1991 was designated by the State Council as the 'year of product quality, brands, and economic performance' (*Zhiliang, Pinzhong, Xiaoyi Nian* in Chinese). An important measure taken in this year was 'chain debt clearance',[14] which managed to partially solve the enterprises' fund shortage. This helped to accelerate their capital turnover. A large group of key projects in energy and raw materials could be completed and put into operation (Peng & Chen, 2011a).

The relaxed economic environment in the beginning of the 1990s witnessed an acceleration of price reform. The central government began to gradually reduce the price differences caused by the two-tier pricing system. From 7 March 1990, a ceiling price was imposed on coal output that exceeded state-quota; from 10 March 1990, ex-factory prices of domestically produced crude oil and some oil products were increased. Price limit measures were also imposed in several other sectors and industries. All these measures made a big step towards the final elimination of the two-tier pricing system (Peng & Chen, 2011a; Wright, 1996).

In August 1992, the State Bureau of Commodity Prices introduced two major initiatives in the price reform: relaxation of government control over a number of production prices and reducing the scope of prices administered by the government. The State Council approved the removal of the state unified maximum ex-factory prices or fixed prices of crude oil, oil products, and steel above the state plan. In the same year, the newly re-established Ministry of Coal increased the price of state-allocated coal by 20% and this prepared the coal industry for further price deregulation (Wright, 1996, p. 16). During 1993–1994, the two-tier pricing system of coal and crude oil were eliminated. The macroeconomic measures – the adjustment of economy after the failure of 'cross the price hurdle' – created an environment for the final abolishment of the two-tier pricing system. The emergence and elimination of the two-tier pricing system in the energy sector was inseparable from the emergence and elimination of the system throughout the economy. Once again, energy policy was subject to the macroeconomic measures in China.

---

[14]'Chain debts' were actually 'circular debts' involving several enterprises: enterprise A owes enterprise B, which owes enterprise C, while C, in turn, owes enterprise A.

5.3. Economic Reform and Energy Sector Reform: The Second Phase (1993–2002)

The second phase of China's economic reform was a time of rapid economic growth. Following a period of economic retrenchment and slowdown between 1989 and 1991, Deng Xiaoping's 1992 Southern Tour reinvigorated China's economy and reinstated the reform movement. The Fourteenth Party Congress held in October 1992 conducted a comprehensive review of the past economic reform. The Congress affirmed that reform was the only way out for China's economic development, officially endorsed Deng's theory of 'building socialism with Chinese characteristics' (Larus, 2005), and proclaimed that the reform aimed to establish a socialist market economic system. In the next year, Jiang Zemin visited Shanghai, Xi'an, Dalian, and Guangzhou to preside over seminars on regional economic work. During the seminars, he emphasised that the reform of the traditional economic system must be continued to establish the socialist market economy and that reform of the investment system, the fiscal and taxation system, and the financial system should be put forward. The core idea was that establishment of socialist market economy should be accelerated as it was vital to solve current and future problems in economic development (Peng & Chen, 2011b). With this background in mind, the Third Plenary Session of the Fourteenth Party Congress in November 1993 made it clear that 'the construction of this socialistic market economic system is to designate the State with the role of making fundamental resource distribution decisions on the macro level' (Hou, 2011, p. 422). The Session adopted the *Decision of the CCP Central Committee on Certain Issues in Establishing the Socialist Market Economic System*, which explained in detail the socialist market economic system and emphasised that effective measures must be taken to actively and comprehensively promote reform step by step in order to establish the system. It served as a guide for China's economic restructuring in the subsequent years.

Since then, China's historical transformation from 'socialist commodity economy' to 'socialist market economy' has begun. A package of drastic reforms to develop 'socialist market economy' was introduced to legitimatise market competition in China. The package included three categories of reforms: government structure, national fiscal and financial systems, and SOEs. All these reforms had profoundly affected China's energy sector. The following subsections review the major reform measures and discuss their impact on the energy industry.

5.3.1. Government Structure Reform and Its Impacts on Energy Sector

5.3.1.1. Government Restructuring. The transition to market economy required the creation of new organisational structures within the government. Prior to 1982, there were nearly 100 ministries under the State Council. The central government performed institutional restructuring every five years respectively in 1982, 1988, 1993, and 1998. Among them, the 1993 and 1998 reforms had more far-reaching implications on the energy sector. In 1993, several ministries were dissolved including the Ministry of Energy. Since then, China did not have a unified national energy agency (Yu, 2010). The State Economic and Trade Commission (SETC) was re-established to supervise the national economy. The SETC and State Development and Planning Commission (SDPC) were assigned to oversee the energy sector and long-term economic planning. Both eventually became 'the most influential bureaucratic bodies in the energy sector' (Meidan et al., 2009, p. 601).

After the 1993 reform, there were still 40 ministries and institutions left under the jurisdiction of the State Council. China's central government was overstaffed and its central finance was overburdened. The year 1998 saw further government restructuring. A plan for the institutional reform of the State Council was adopted in February 1998 during the Second Plenary Session of the Fifteenth CCP Congress. A major aim of the reform is to establish a government administrative system suitable for the 'socialist market economic system'. During this reform, nine ministries of industry had been removed (Peng & Chen, 2011b). In March 1998, the First Session of the Ninth National People's Congress streamlined the State Council. In the year 2000, another nine professional bureaus under the SETC were revoked (People's Daily, 2001).[15] This shows that the central government has made attempts to move away from direct interference tactics to macroeconomic regulation methods in governing SOEs. This introduced the market mechanism into operations of SOEs and reduced government control. Consequently, the government restructuring has made it imperative to reform the SOEs at the same time.[16]

5.3.1.2. Energy Sector under the Government Restructuring. The government restructuring led to the decentralisation of leadership in various government departments in the energy sector. This led to the declining ability of the central government to effectively manage the energy industry. For example, in the coal sector, the Ministry of Coal Industry was abolished in 1998 as its administrative functions were transferred to the SETC. Business responsibilities were assigned to the newly created State Administration for the Coal Industry, which was abolished in 2001 (Zhu & Cherni, 2009). In March 1998, China's ninth National People's Congress approved the creation of the State Petrochemical Industry Bureau

[15]The abolished nine professional state bureaus are the State Bureau of Internal Trade, the State Administration of Coal Industry, the State Administration of Machinery Industry, the State Administration of Metallurgical Industry, the State Administration of Petroleum and Chemical Industry, the State Administration of Light Industry, the State Administration of Textile Industry, the State Bureau of Building Materials Industry, and the State Administration of Nonferrous Metal Industry (Peng & Chen, 2011b, p. 274; People's Daily, 2001).

[16]The SOEs reform and government restructuring are mutually reinforcing. During the early years of the economic reform, the government had recognised that the planned economy gave the SOEs little incentives for efficient production. In the early 1990s, the government eliminated the transfer of all net revenues from the SOEs to the state to transform them into more commercially oriented enterprises. In 1994, the tax reform allowed the SOEs to retain residual profits. Yet many SOEs' commercial decisions in the late 1990s were still largely under government control despite these reforms. Lack of innovation and continuing losses in many SOEs led the second wave of government restructuring in 1998 to further separate government administration from corporate operations.

(SPIB) along with the abolition of the Ministry of Chemical Industry. The government functions of China's oil companies had been transferred to the newly established SPIB (Young, 1998). This paved way for the subsequent reorganisation of the country's petroleum and petrochemical industry, and gave birth to two large enterprise groups: China National Petroleum Corporation (CNPC) and China Petrochemical Corporation (Sinopec Group) in July 1998 (CNPC, 2012; People's Daily, 2002).[17] Since the beginning of the twenty-first century, respective ministries in charge of coal, petrochemical, and power industries have been abolished. Both the absence of an institution overseeing the whole energy industry and the decentralisation of leadership after the government restructuring severely weakened the already fragmented administration in the individual energy sectors and the bureaucratic energy management apparatus in China. The areas of government-controlled decision-making became fewer.[18]

The result of all the government restructuring was that the old planning system lost most of its effectiveness in energy conservation. In the early reform period, the central government directly invested in energy conservation projects. Energy conservation service centres were established throughout the ministry's systems. As a result of government restructuring, the energy conservation service centres that created channels for increasing the flow of information on energy efficiency technologies, gradually lost their government funding. Some programs were even phased out during the government restructuring. The government's attention to energy conservation had begun to wane. On the other hand, the newly established system expected to promote energy efficiency through market-based instruments had not functioned as intended (Sinton et al. 1998; Zhao, 2001).

There were some mutually offsetting effects within the government restructuring. In addition to the structural change in the coal, oil, and power sectors, the government restructuring in 1998 reflected the central government's increasing concern for environmental protection. The former National Environmental Protection Agency was upgraded to the State Environmental Protection Administration (SEPA). The former Environmental Protection Committee of the State Council was abolished. The environmental administrative restructuring improved environmental administration and reduced the fragmentation of central government policymaking regarding clean coal technology adoption and environmental protection. On the other hand, however, after the Ministry of Coal Industry was abolished, its environmental responsibility was passed to the SEPA and local environmental protection bureaus, which undertook jobs related to environmental protection for all industrial sectors.

[17]As the sole initiator, Sinopec Group incorporated China Petroleum & Chemical Corporation (Sinopec Corp.) on 25 February 2000, according to the Company Law of the People's Republic of China (Sinopec Corp., 2012).

[18]Although the NDRC's Energy Bureau was established in 2003, it did not have the authority or resources to effectively coordinate the energy policies and plans among ministries and energy companies. The National Energy Administration was established in 2008, but it still did not have sufficient clout to impose its will on the energy policymaking or coordination.

The Ministry of Coal Industry, which was once very active in environmental protection in the coal industry and day-to-day administration of environmental matters, stopped carrying out these functions since its abolishment. In other words, though the creation of SEPA did enhance environmental protection in general, less involvement and cooperation from the coal administration led to undesirable environmental protection, particularly in the coal sector (Zhu & Cherni, 2009).

The environmental protection responsibility with regard to the coal sector has been transferred from the Ministry of Coal Industry to the SEPA and local environmental protection bureaus. With the local governments obtaining the environmental responsibility, successful implementation of environmental regulations will be difficult since there are economic benefits by violating the regulations for environment protection. It is very difficult to manage the conflicting interests of the central and the local levels.

In addition, the devolution of power and the ineffectiveness of implementation of environmental regulations particularly in the coal sector once again offer evidence in support of the argument of the study: the energy policies are reactive to the country's macroeconomic reforms. The government restructuring resulted in the devolution of power in the environmental sector and this led to less involvement and cooperation from the coal administration when the Ministry of Coal Industry was abolished. Environmental protection in the coal sector was undesirable in the 1990s.

5.3.2. Fiscal and Financial Reforms and Their Impact on Energy Sector

5.3.2.1. Fiscal Reform and Energy Sector. Before the reform in the end 1970s, China's fiscal system had been dominated by 'unified revenue' and 'unified expenditure'. Under this system that almost no autonomy was in the hands of local governments, it was impossible for them to mobilise local initiatives to increase revenue or control expenditure, and this hindered local economic development. To change the situation, the central government decided to implement a new fiscal system of 'dividing revenue and expenditure between central and local governments and of hierarchical responsibility' (*huafen shouzhi, fenji baogan* in Chinese) (Peng & Chen, 2011a, p. 87). In February 1980, the State Council promulgated the *Notice on Implementing the Fiscal Management System of Dividing Revenue and Expenditure between Central and Local Governments and Hierarchical Responsibility*. This document clearly clarified the range of revenue and expenditure of central and local governments. The system improved the fiscal situation of the country (Peng & Chen, 2011a).

However, this system had given excessive stimulus to local industrialisation while constraining the central government's revenue-raising capability. Gradually, the steady decentralisation of revenue authority reduced fiscal capabilities of the central government. Before the economic reform, financing for social services had been provided by the central government. All revenues had belonged to the central government and all expenditures had been determined by them. Since the Chinese tax system had rested on the local collection of revenues that were then remitted to the central level, as soon as the economic reform started and the mechanism of planned economy began to fall apart, the former revenue system quickly began to erode (Wong, 1992).

The ratio of central government revenue to total government revenue declined from 1985 to 1992. The ratio of fiscal revenues to GDP continued to decline as well (Wong, Heady, & Woo, 1995). The decline in fiscal capacity was accompanied by the underprovided social services and even physical infrastructure investment. In the energy sector, fixed investment in electricity during the 1980s was less than 4% of GDP on average, which was below the rule-of-thumb benchmark of 6% of GDP for successful growth (Naughton, 2008, p. 109). To stem the decline of the revenue/GDP ratio and increase the central government's capability in its macroeconomic management, the State Council issued *Decisions on Implementing Tax-sharing Fiscal Management System* in December 1993, and implemented it in 1994. The 1994 fiscal reform unified the tax division and established central government's own branch tax bureaus at the local level. By this arrangement, the central government collected shared taxes and then allocated a portion to the local governments. This helped to standardise tax rates and simplify tax categories. The central government also had the authority to carry out tax reduction and exemption (Zhang, Niu, & Bartle, 2006).

However, these fiscal reform measures had some side effects on energy conservation. In the 1980s, the government had offered tax allowances to encourage enterprises to invest in energy-saving measures. Due to the simplification of the tax system in the 1994 fiscal reform, many of these tax reductions on energy conservation projects and efficient technology development were removed (Andrews-Speed, 2004), resulting in the decline of the share of energy conservation investment in the total energy supply. Another negative effect was environmental degradation. Local governments implemented the fiscal reform in 1994 by seeking new ways to boost revenues as they were responsible for their own economic growth. Consequently, they often neglected environmental protection in their rush to exceed the energy targets set by the central government. For example, the use of inefficient and highly polluting equipment was often overlooked as long as operations fuelled local economic development (Kong, 2011, p. 55). This made it difficult to achieve environmental improving targets.

5.3.2.2. Financial Reform and Energy Sector. China had been trying to reform its old state-planned financial system in the 1980s, by increasing the autonomy and commercial orientation of the banks to a very limited extent (Breslin, 2003). In order to foster market economy with indirect but effective macroeconomic regulations, the central government decided in 1994 to initiate a new phase of financial reform comprising a new and comprehensive set of financial policies. The most relevant policy to this study was converting old specialised banks into regular commercial banks. (Li & Ma, 1995) This had a direct adverse impact on the energy sector. With the shift of their operational focus from social benefits to economic benefits, banks were reluctant to extend loans for energy conservation projects because they became highly concerned about the borrowers' repayment ability (Zhao, 2001). Consequently, the preferential interest rates offered for energy conservation projects were cancelled.

In the 1980s, a series of energy-saving incentives were implemented to spur energy savings and energy-efficient technologies (Sinton et al., 1998). Among them, two major financing programs for promoting energy-efficient investment were established in the early 1980s. One program was managed by the former SETC which provided interest subsidies to enterprises that would undertake technical renovation for energy conservation. The other program was managed through China Energy Conservation Investment Corporation (CECIC), a government branch in charge of selecting projects for loans and overseeing their progress under the direction of the former SDPC.[19] Under this program, the energy conservation loans were on favourable interests, almost one-third below the prevailing rates at that time (Levine et al., 1992; Lin, 2007). By 1994, however, the preferential interest rate was revoked along with the financial reform. Since 1996, the share of energy conservation investment to the total energy investment has declined in importance (Lin, 2007).[20]

5.3.2.3. Summary. The transition to a market economy entailed the removal of old regulations that had previously stimulated energy conservation. Tax allowance and reductions for energy efficiency improvement were removed. The energy efficiency loans from the government ceased. The commercial banks operated for economic benefits rather than social benefits. CECIC operated more like a private-sector entity rather than a government institution (Levine, 2008). Policies to support energy conservation in China weakened during the turn of the twenty-first century when China was in transition towards a more market-based economy by reforming its economic systems, which removed old regulations, including measures that had stimulated energy conservation. The financial incentives created in the 1980s were important tools in encouraging energy conservation. Sinton et al. (1998) described the discontinuation of these national incentives as '[o]ne of the great ironies of the economic system reforms of the early 1990s' (p. 827). The fiscal and financial reforms in the 1990s show how strong the force of macroeconomic reform is that it dominates the energy sector and deeply affects its development trend.

Nevertheless, the central government's fiscal capacity was invigorated through the tax and financial reform. The financial reform improved the central bank's control of state-owned commercial banks, strengthened the central control over domestic stock markets, and increased the country's foreign reserves (Lardy, 1998; Shih, 2009). These reforms reinforced the central government's leverage over SOEs which struggled with losses and debts, paving the way for SOEs reform.

5.3.3. SOEs Reform and Its Impact on Energy Sector

5.3.3.1. Reform of SOEs. From the early 1980s, the central government began to render some autonomy to the SOEs via the CRS. But it eventually proved to be unsatisfactory since it lacked a standard and transparent contract between the state and the enterprises. Politically well-connected enterprises were able to negotiate a better deal with the government (Hassard, Sheehan, & Morris, 1999).

---

[19]CECIC is a state-owned company that supervised the loans of two billion Yuan for energy-efficiency investment projects, mainly industrial energy-efficiency projects and combined heat and power cogeneration projects (Sinton, Levine, Fridley, Yang, & Lin, 1999). It had been the major channel for the state's program of energy-efficiency investment.

[20]For more discussion on this issue, see Chapter 4, Section 4.3.1 Energy conservation and energy intensity.

CRS was the product of the planned economic system without any clear clarification of property rights, which became the bottleneck of further SOEs reform. At the same time, the Chinese economy became more market oriented and increasingly integrated into the world economy. To sustain fast economic growth, it was necessary to clarify the property rights to fulfil the SOEs reform objectives for innovations and technological advancement, and autonomy of operations.

As the successors of CRS, the Modern Enterprise System (MES) and the Group Company System (GCS) were to be established during the second phase of the economic reform. The aim was to promote the corporatisation of large and medium-sized SOEs and clarify the property rights (Hassard & Sheehan, 1997). This aim was reflected in several government conferences and reports. In March 1991, Li Peng's government work report to the Fourth Session of the Seventh NPC had stressed the focus of the future of economic reform: to further enhance the vitality of the large- and medium-sized SOEs (People's Daily, 1991). In November 1993, the Third Plenary Session of the 14th Party Congress implemented a new round of SOEs reform aimed to remove the SOEs from direct government control and render them more commercially oriented. In March 1997, the State Commission for Economic Restructuring issued the *Key Points of the Implementation of the Economic System Reform in 1997*. This encouraged corporate restructuring by means of leaving most small- and medium-sized SOEs to be merged, sold off, or allowed to go bankrupt, as well as establishing and developing large companies and groups (People's Daily, 1997a).

In March 1998, Prime Minister Li Peng stressed in the government work report that the reform of SOEs should achieve new breakthroughs. In some important and key industries, the establishment of large enterprise groups should be encouraged to enhance their competitiveness in the domestic and foreign markets (People's Daily, 1998). The primary aims of the MES and GCS were to adopt modern business management methods and at the same time, reallocate resources and assets and restructure SOEs in order to reduce their reliance on the government, and also create large internationally competitive companies (Hassard et al., 1999; Hassard, Sheehan, Zhou, Terpstra-Tong, & Morris, 2007). The SOEs reform during the second phase of economic reform could be characterised by 'a mixture of experimentation and pragmatism'. Despite the increased marketisation of SOEs via the reform, the state intervention and ownership was still predominant (Hassard, Morris, Sheehan, & Xiao, 2010, p. 507). The SOEs reform and the MES and GCS initiatives were applied to all state enterprises in the national economy, including those in the energy sector. Although the energy sector was one of the pillar industries identified to remain under tight government control, it underwent reform to adopt more commercial approach in business operations.

SOEs reform in the energy sector created the dominant role of the State Power Corporation of China (SPCC) and the three national oil companies (NOCs). These large enterprise groups, either the SPCC or the NOCs, severely limited the competition in the energy industry. This reflects the government's hesitancy in introducing market forces into the country's energy industry and its fear of the risks of rapid market liberalisation in the energy sector. In short, the gradualist and incremental ('crossing river by feeling stones') approach reflected the government's cautious optimism towards reform in the energy sector.

5.3.3.2. SOEs Reform in the Power Sector. Socialist market economy requires its enterprises to be market oriented. As earlier discussed, the second phase of the reform was characterised by transforming government functions to establish the MES. Enterprises became independent economic entities responsible for their own performance and profits. The multiple sources of investments in the power sector created in the 1980s also required relationship adjustments between government and enterprises, IPPs and power grids, and among IPPs (Ministry of Power Industry, 1995). Under this context, Prime Minister Zhu Rongji formally proposed in 1996 to corporatise the power industry. In January 1997, restructuring in power industry was implemented and the SPCC was established as a state corporation with independent legal status. The assets of the Ministry of Electrical Power (MEP) were transferred to the new SPCC. The business functions of the previous MEP were transferred to SPCC, while its regulatory and administrative functions were passed on to the SETC (Chen, 2010; Ma & He, 2008). This separation of administrative functions from business operations in the power sector was regarded by the central government as a significant step towards a 'socialist market economy' (People's Daily, 1997b). During the second phase of the reform, SPCC and SETC put forward mainly three policy measures for the power sector: the corporatisation of the subsidiaries at the provincial and regional levels; the expansion of nationwide power grids; and the introduction of market competition into power generation.

To corporatise subsidiaries at the provincial and regional levels, the previous provincial power bureaus were converted to power companies and new regional divisions were established. By 2000, all the previous provincial power bureaus and the regional groups came under the management of the SPCC, either as its direct subsidiaries or as its regional divisions. By this way, the SPCC was more vertically integrated. Shortly after the corporatisation, the SPCC argued that to create a competition environment, the power market must be large enough to contain a sufficient number of competitors. To create such a large market for effective competition, well-connected interprovincial grids were compulsory (Gao, 1999). The SPCC hence proposed a project to construct and improve cross-provincial transmissions and distribution networks. The nationwide power grids were thus expanded, which once again reinforced the top-down consolidation of the SPCC.

The reform measures in the power sector led by the SPCC incurred criticism that the so-called 'market reforms' only strengthened the market power of the SPCC and in fact returned the power sector to the centrally planned economy. To introduce real market competition, the SPCC should separate power generation and distribution from power transmission (Liu, 2004). Therefore, another reform measure was advocated by the SPCC to unbundle the generation enterprises from power companies in six provinces (Heilongjiang, Liaoning, Jilin, Shandong, Zhejiang, and Shanghai) to help the generation enterprises compete in an electricity pooling system. But due to their disappointing performance, this reform measure was suspended by the State Council in 2000 (State Council, 2000).[21]

[21]Ma and He (2008) argued that the reason of failure of this reform measure was largely because the separation of electricity generation enterprises from power companies was still constrained by the monopolistic SPCC.

Generally speaking, the second phase of reform aimed at restructuring the electricity sector to increase efficiency and competition. However, the introduction of market mechanisms in this phase proved to be less effective than the first phase of reform which sought to raise capital for expanding power generation. The success was blocked by cautious approach of the SETC and SPCC against their loss of control of electricity. Instead of injecting the market mechanism further into the electricity sector, the SPCC monopolised the sector: shut down small thermal power plants to protect state enterprises, and controlled most of the transmission and distribution (T&D) assets and half of China's generation assets. These moves severely hindered the creation of a competitive electricity market in China (Ma & He, 2008). The momentum of introducing competition forces in the power sector was stalled in the 1990s due to the SOEs reform, which constitutes a strong force dominating the energy sector. The most positive impact of the power-sector reform was this: the state enterprises in the power sector were largely the major force of technological advancement in generation efficiency.

5.3.3.3. SOEs Reform in the Oil Sector. In the first half of the 1990s, as a result of a series of policy stimulus and reforms after Deng Xiaoping's 1992 Southern Tour, shortages arose for many industrial goods, including crude oil and oil products. Due to the shortage economy as well as the fixed prices and restrictions on imports, refineries had no worries about the sales of their products. China's oil sector had to be reformed to inject more competition into the industry. The timing was right when China began its new round of SOEs reform with the aim of establishing the MES and GCS in the mid-1990s. In July 1998, assets and operations of the Chinese oil industry were reconsolidated into three integrated and territorially protected NOCs: CNPC, China Petrochemical Corporation (Sinopec), and China National Offshore Oil Corporation (CNOOC). As 'experimental enterprise groups', CNPC and Sinopec were reorganised along geographical lines. CNPC took over many of Sinopec's refineries and petrochemical plants in northern and western China and retained its own oilfields in these regions. Sinopec took over most of CNPC's oilfields in eastern and southern China and retained its own refineries and petrochemical facilities in these areas. The vertical integration bound together the financial interests of upstream and downstream resources. CNOOC was the largest producer of offshore crude oil and natural gas in China. Since then, an oligopoly was created to ensure profitability of the three NOCs. Through this organisational structure, the resource-dependent relations between upstream and downstream sectors were managed at the intra-firm level, rather than at the level of government planning. This was described as a crucial shift in industrial management 'from administrative to corporate hierarchy in production relations' (Lin, 2008, p. 70). The three NOCs have been empowered to make their own financing and investment decisions. Among the three NOCs, both CNPC and Sinopec accounted for most of the crude oil production, oil-refining capacity, and the natural gas output in China's oil sector. CNOOC, with its operations being primarily offshore, has a marginal role relative to CNPC and Sinopec. With the reorganisation, the central government aimed to transform them into integrated oil and petrochemical conglomerates that can compete with major international producers (Young, 1998).

To summarise, China's oil sector has been dominated by an oligopoly situation since 1998. To facilitate the formation of the oligopoly, mergers and acquisitions had taken place during the restructuring in the oil sector. It is noteworthy that many mergers in China during that time were in effect 'takeovers': 'administrative mergers' with loss-making companies taken over by more powerful firms, under the mediation of the superior authority. The primary aim of the merger was to modernise the loss-making SOEs' management methods and technologies (Nolan & Wang, 1999). For instance, in November 1997, Qilu Petrochemical, a subsidiary of Sinopec, took over two SOEs in Zibo, Shandong Province, namely Zibo Petrochemical and Zibo Chemical Fiber. Prior to the merger, the two Zibo plants had been municipal SOEs on the verge of bankruptcy, with losses amounting to 2.13 billion Yuan and liabilities 3.62 billion Yuan (Huang & Yan, 2000, p. 116). After the merger, Qilu Petrochemical has integrated the upstream and downstream sectors of the petrochemical industry in Zibo and has made itself the largest SOE in the petrochemical sector in Shandong Province. This is just one example of many such mergers during the restructuring that strengthened the oligopoly in the oil and chemical industry.

The integration of upstream and downstream enterprises has two prominent benefits: first, elimination of unnecessary internal competition between oil enterprises in the same area, and attainment of economies of scale; second, advancement of research and development. The second benefit was a result of changes in the size and composition of business portfolios. In the case of Qilu Petrochemical, the upstream and downstream industries in Zibo were unified after the merger. The production capacity of acrylonitrile plant was increased from 25,000 tons per year to 40,000 tons per year and the profits of both companies (Zibo Petrochemical and Zibo Chemical Fiber) soared to 650 million Yuan in 1999 while their unit cost was reduced by 35% and 49%, respectively (Huang & Yan, 2000, pp. 116–117).

The oil giants not only made themselves conglomerates, but also listed stock companies. When CNPC and Sinopec were created, they began restructuring to transform into full-fledged stock companies. Their subsidiaries were separated into production and non-manufacturing companies, with better quality assets included in the production companies and the social welfare responsibilities given to the non-manufacturing companies. By restructuring, the production companies could be more efficient and attractive to more potential investors (Mollet, 1999). With the purpose of domestic and overseas share listing, PetroChina was established by CNPC in November 1999 as a holding company for all of CNPC's domestic exploration, production, and marketing activities (Nielsen, 2000). Sinopec Limited was formed in February 2000 as a joint stock entity under the Sinopec Group (Wu & Fesharaki, 2001).

5.3.3.4. NOCs and Oil Price Liberalisation. China's overheated economy and high inflation in 1993 resulted in high prices of inputs that affected some downstream SOEs (Goldstein, 1993). The government sought to control inflation by reversing the course of oil price reform. Along with the new tax system and the unified foreign exchange system, the government-mandated price guidelines were put forward. In May 1994, prices for both crude oil and refined products were controlled by the government again. Wholesale and retail prices for different regions and cities were also decided by the government. The ex-factory prices of refined oil were set by the government. Products at all gas stations were strictly subject to the government-set prices (People's Daily, 1994). The central government's re-control of prices was seen as a general retreat from reform in the oil sector. This was a sharp reversal from a general trend towards a more open oil market beginning in 1992 (Kahn, 1994). The price control lasted until 1998. At that time, the establishment of the three oil giants sought to upgrade the management system to meet international standards, and for the prices of their products to be consistent with international prices. Coincidently, China's oil imports expanded substantially since the mid-1990s, particularly after the Asian Financial Crisis.[22] In face of the pressure from the NOCs and the increasing dependence on foreign oil imports, China adjusted its domestic oil prices. This price adjustment facilitated the overseas share listing of CNPC and Sinopec in 2000. In November 2001, the domestic oil prices were adjusted to peg to package price, namely, the prices of New York, Rotterdam, and Singapore markets (Lin, 2010). The market mechanism has begun to play a fundamental role in oil pricing.[23]

5.3.3.5. SOEs Reform in the Coal Sector. The decision to establish MES and GCS led to massive changes in the coal sector through consolidations and closures. The state coalmines were transformed into limited liability companies with the state retaining a controlling interest in the companies. For example, as an enterprise under the direct administration of the State Council, Shenhua Group was formed in 1995 by the Shenfu Dongsheng mines, pit mouth power plants, Huanghua coal transport sea port, and the Shenhuang double tracking electrified railway (Peng, 2009, p. 15). This restructuring made Shenhua Group the largest state-owned coal company in China. Its production and sales topped in the country while its fatality rate was significantly lower than the national average. Besides the formation of Shenhua Group, three coking enterprises in Shanxi merged to form the Shanxi Coking Coal Group in 2001. In 2002, Ningxia Coal Group was established by the mines in Ningxia (IEA, 2009). State coalmines still dominated the economy. In 2005, coal mining enterprises that were state-owned or had state-held shares had a design capacity of 1,340.5 million tons per year, which was 59.2% of the national total (Peng, 2009, p. 20).

5.3.3.6. State Coalmines, Coal Pricing, and the Closure of TVCMs. The coal pricing liberalisation took a gradual approach, as China's economic reform.

---

[22]It is noteworthy that the price shocks of regional and global magnitude from 1997 till 1998 created a good opportunity in China's history of price liberalisation. At the regional level, the devalued refined oil products came into China from the neighbouring countries affected by the Asian Financial Crisis in 1997, which resulted in huge losses for Sinopec, China's largest downstream producer. At the global level, the crude oil price collapsed at the end of 1997 and stayed bottom through 1998, which made it fall below the domestic price for the first time in the reform era. Thus, CNPC, China's largest upstream producer, also incurred huge losses when the refineries rushed for cheaper oil imports. Thus, resistance to central government intervention diminished and the central government took major steps to liberalise prices in the oil sector. For more discussion about the forces driving China's industrial organisational and pricing reforms in the 1990s, see Lin (2008).

[23]For details, see Section 4.5.3.

China operated a two-tier coal pricing system before 1994. Under this system, state-owned mines sold coal to SOEs at government-controlled prices that were too low to cover costs. This not only discouraged coal production but also led to serious technology inefficiencies and financial deficits in coal mining companies. More than 90% of state-owned coalmines incurred losses in 1993. Facing this difficulty and on route to establishing a 'socialist market economy', the central government was determined to relax the coal pricing. In 1994, the two-tier pricing system for most of the coal market was abolished and the state-owned mines were allowed to sell part of their coal on the market. The prices charged by the state coalmines were raised to more realistic market levels.[24] With market mechanism being introduced into the coal sector to make it profitable in the long term,[25] the pricing formation of coal grew more mature.

Despite liberalisation, the state coalmines remained very passive towards the reform and did not work out measures for innovation and cost-cutting. The liberalisation of coal prices would not automatically lead to the end of losses of state coalmines. The losses were inherited from historical legacy and could not be eliminated or reduced in the short term (Wright, 1996). In 1996, there were still 72% of the state-owned coalmines losing money (IEA, 1999, p. 51). By 1998, state coalmines incurred a loss of 3.7 billion Yuan, making them the principal loss-maker in China (Rui, 2005, p. 704). The long-term losses of state coalmines, peaked in 1998, prompted the central government to shut down TVCMs nationwide. In the early 1990s, the target of establishing a 'socialist market economy' had stimulated the expansion of TVCMs, and rapid development was evident since 1992. As discussed, during the same period, most state coalmines operated at a loss, but this was not considered a serious problem until the end of the 1990s because the state coalmines did not have to worry about their sales in a market that suffered constant shortages. However, at the end of the 1990s, as surplus emerged, the losses suffered by the state coalmines became prominent (Rui, 2005). In fact, 60% of major state coalmines partially or completely stopped production. Until 1998, the unused production capacity amounted to 90 million tons. In contrast, 51,200 out of a total of 61,000 small coalmines were illegal, with a production capacity

[24]The price of thermal coal was still controlled by the government until 2002. The demand for thermal coal increased rapidly when China's economy recovered from the 1997 Asian Financial Crisis. However, the artificially low prices of thermal coal discouraged the thermal coal producers from increasing supply. To increase thermal coal supply, the central government further relaxed controls over prices of thermal coal. Since 1 January 2002, guidance price for thermal coal has been cancelled. See Chapter 4 for more discussions on this issue.

[25]The process of liberalisation witnessed fierce coal price fluctuation. Since the coal prices began to be decontrolled in 1993, the prices increased quite steeply and the price rise accelerated until the beginning of 1994. Since then, partly as a result of the state effort to control inflation, prices stabilised in 1994. In early 1995, prices rose again quite steeply on a regular basis. It is noteworthy that the coal market had not been totally decontrolled. The government still interfered and adopted control measures when inflation was high, such as in 1994 (Wright, 1996).

of 430 million tons, and 13,000 of the illegal coalmines were located in the fields of the state coalmines (Peng, 2009, p. 19). In addition to the long-term losses, state coalmines also suffered from overstaffing and high welfare expenditure, both legacies of the former state enterprise system. Yet the government could not allow the large numbers of state coalmines to declare bankruptcy, hence the TVCMs became the target for closure.

Since the government rectified the coal business order, coal production decreased at the turn of the twenty-first century. Besides closing down the TVCMs to salvage the state coalmines, the provincial governments took over the SOEs (Zhu & Cherni, 2009).[26] The administration of the unified distribution coalmines bureaus was transferred to the local authorities. Thus, the key state coalmines were decentralised to provincial governments while the central government focused mostly on the administration of coal mining safety and environmental protection.[27]

5.3.4. Western Development Strategy and Its Impacts on Energy Sector

5.3.4.1. China's Regional Disparities and the Western Development Strategy. At the very beginning of the reform, Deng Xiaoping recognised that it was necessary to let some people get rich first before the vast majority shared the wealth. The stepwise development started from the coastal east. The first two decades of the reform witnessed economic development gap between the eastern and western China enlarging. In 1999, after two years' high growth rate and low inflation rate, China's economy plunged into deflation. Both domestic investment and consumption fell sharply in 1999. Under these conditions, the government had to implement a series of macroeconomic policies to boost domestic demand and consumption to stop the flagging economic growth and to narrow down regional disparities. Western Development Strategy was one of these policies.[28] The strategy aimed to balance regional development, boost domestic demand, and develop the domestic market.

---

[26]Shenhua Group was an exception as it was still under the central government's control. The main reason that Shenhua Group has not been transferred to any local government is because it is a vertically integrated enterprise, the operation of which needs approval and coordination from more than four ministries and six provincial governments. Transferring it to the local governments will cause difficulty in coordinating these complex interests (Peng, 2009, p. 19). Another exception was China Coal Energy Company. All the other key state-owned coal enterprises have been supervised by provincial governments (Tu, 2011, p. 5).

[27]The decentralisation of state coalmines to local governments does not mean that the coalmines become independent. The behaviour of the coalmines is strongly influenced by the local governments, which treat them more favourably as a source of local tax revenues to boost the local economy.

[28]Hou (2011) pointed out that the driving force for the 'Development of Western China' strategy was the 1997 Asian Financial Crisis. During the crisis, the Renminbi (RMB) did not depreciate, which caused significant losses in Chinese trade. The economic downturn urged the Chinese government to carry out massive fiscal expansion

The Asian Financial Crisis in 1997 made the policymakers realise that it was unrealistic to drive economic growth by exports in the long term. Therefore, huge investment in infrastructure building made up the core of the Western Development Strategy. In September 1999, the Fourth Plenary Session of the Fifteenth Party Congress formally proposed the Western Development Strategy. Developing Western China's infrastructure became a strategic task for the government in the twenty-first century. In January 2000, a leading group for the Western development was set up by the State Council. Financial, fiscal and taxation support were offered to the West (Peng & Chen, 2011b).

5.3.4.2. Energy Sector under the Western Development Strategy. In the energy sector, two large projects were initiated under the Western Development Strategy: West-East natural gas transmission project (*Xiqi Dongshu* in Chinese) and the West-East electricity transmission project (*Xidian Dongsong* in Chinese). The West-East natural gas transmission project began in 2000, when the government decided to initiate the Qaidam Basin-Xi'ning-Lanzhou gas pipeline. The project was officially started on 4 July 2002. A 2,500 mile natural gas pipeline was completed in August 2004, supplying Eastern China with gas resources from the West. Its annual capacity is about 12 billion cubic meters (Hou, 2011, p. 426). Foreigners had opportunities to invest in the West-East natural gas transmission project. They could hold shares in the project without limits on the shareholding ratio. The equipment imported for the project could be exempted from tariffs and import value-added tax (Peng & Chen, 2011b). The price of natural gas from the West was set by the government, which incorporated market factors. In October 2000, the government began to establish a research group to set the pipeline gas price, which was the key factor affecting the downstream market. On this matter, CNPC and local governments hold different views. The former preferred a higher price of about 1.4 Yuan/m^3, while the latter insisted on 1.2 Yuan/m^3. At last, the State Council set the price at 1.35 Yuan/m^3 (Zeng, 2010, p. 297).

The West-East electricity transmission project started in November 2000. The Project was aimed at transmitting electricity from the resource-rich regions in the West to the regions with high electricity demand in the East (Pittman & Zhang, 2010). It was divided into three areas: the Northern Line, the Central Line, and the Southern Line. Within the Northern Line area, Inner Mongolia and Shaanxi transmitted electricity to the North China power grid; within the Central Line area, Sichuan Province transmitted electricity to the Central China and East China power grid; within the Southern Line area, Guizhou, Yunnan, and Guangxi transmitted electricity to the South China power grid (People's Daily, 2000).

The *Eleventh Five-Year Plan for Western China Development* made it clear that the government would:

> make full use of the western region's advantages such as rich hydropower, coal, oil and gas, in order to adjust the energy structure,

---

to turn the tide. In other words, the massive stimulus package implemented in the form of 'Development of Western China' was a response to the financial crisis.

> and to accelerate the construction of several national energy development bases for hydropower, coal, oil and gas resources and processing bases for major energy and chemical products.

By the end of 2008, the transmission capacity of the Northern, Central, and Southern lines of the West-East electricity transmission project amounted to 25.5, 17.5, and 20.2 gigawatts, respectively (Chen, Li, & Wu, 2010, p. 7108).

5.3.5. A Critical Review of the Economic Reform During the Second Phase and Its Impact on the Energy Sector

Again, the second phase of the reform reflects the force of macroeconomic reform on the energy sector. The Chinese government tried to make the country's economic system more efficient and conducive for a market economy. It restructured the government, reformed its fiscal and financial systems, and the SOEs. The government again was very cautious about its reform measures, strongly evident in the SOEs reform in the energy sector. In spite of that, certain reform measures had mutually offsetting effects.

The formation of SEPA, generally speaking, was conducive to environmental protection and improvement. However, with regard to clean coal technology adoption and environmental protection, the potential benefits of reducing the fragmentation of central government were diluted by other two major reforms in the 1990s, the fiscal reform and the SOEs reform. First, the 1994 fiscal reform redistributed tax revenues between the local and central government. Since the local governments were allowed to keep a large portion of taxes from the enterprises they supervised, they would very carefully scrutinise enterprise investments and their financial performance. They also had a stake in increasing enterprise profits. Thus, investments in clean coal technology were not appealing because they took long time to generate returns. Second, since the SOEs reform forced the SOEs to face hard budget constraints and blocked their credit access (Cao, Qian, & Weingast, 1999), the SOEs were reluctant to invest in pollution controls lest they incur loans and lose net revenues. To sum up, the fiscal and SOEs reforms discouraged both the local governments and the SOEs from investing in clean coal technology and other environmental protection activities that took longer time to yield profits. The task division between the NDRC and the SETC was not clear and this made it difficult for energy policies to be coherent. Deepening economic reform during the second phase left the energy sector stranded between the plan and the market. Both administrative measures and economic incentives proved ineffective.

On the one hand, the government tried to make the SOEs resemble 'modern enterprises' in the developed countries. On the other hand, in the energy sector, the central government was still reluctant to give the oil and power industries considerable market power. It appears to favour the formation of 'conglomerates' of SOEs, such as CNPC and Sinopec in the oil sector or at least maintain the dominant role of SOEs, such as SPCC in the power sector and Shenhua Group in the coal sector. The aim of the reforms was to allow these SOEs, together with other forms of enterprises in the energy sector, to compete with one another in their respective industry. To some extent, the reforms had improved the efficiency of the new SOEs (such as the above-mentioned case of Qilu Petrochemical) and had promoted market competition.

However, this was not free market competition in the real sense. For example, though competition opportunity was provided between CNPC and Sinopec, no further steps were taken to regulate this competition. As long as these SOEs remain in the hands of the government and dominate the economy, it is hard to create a healthy economic structure where all forms of businesses can coexist and flourish and realise true competition.

The liberalisation in the energy sector was also tempered by the government's desire to maintain control over energy prices. This period saw several major initiatives to reform energy pricing. Until 2002, only the coal prices were largely set by market mechanism. The oil prices, albeit explicitly tied to international prices, were still under the supervision of NDRC. In general, energy policies in China still lacked coherence and its energy sector was still far from liberalisation or marketisation. As discussed in Chapter 3, the rhombuses are the smallest during the second phase of reform, which indicates the worst energy security situation of the reform period. The Chinese government believed that China should deepen its economic reform and further liberalise its energy sector.

5.4. Economic Reform and Energy Sector Reform: The Third Phase (2003–2010)

Until 2002, the Chinese government had initially achieved its mission of 'establishing socialist market economy', but it was far from becoming a mature market economy. Chinese market economy during the time was dominated by the SOEs, and over-intervened by the government as well. The economy was dominated by the SOEs in the sense that it was still easier for the SOEs to obtain resources compared to other enterprises. The SOEs were still protected to some extent in the market competition to guarantee their profits. Other enterprises were restricted or shut down in the name of resource-wasting or environmental pollution. The economy was under excessive control by the government in the sense that the government was still very powerful in resource allocation and enterprises' market competition. This economic situation resulted in overconsumption of resources by the SOEs, low efficiency in resource allocation, and government corruption (Zhang, 2003b). Therefore, when Hu administration came into power, the government began to accelerate SOEs reform and economic transformation.

In the energy sector, several challenges were faced by the new administration as well. First, China's economy was surging again after its slowdown during the Asian Financial Crisis. GDP was rising at a rate about 10% annually by 2003. Drastic economic growth enlarged the country's appetite for energy. The increasing rate of energy demand rose from 5% in 2002 to 16% in 2003 (Meidan et al., 2009, p. 608). Energy supply could not keep pace with energy demand. The time of energy surpluses had gone. Second, China's energy intensity rose again after its steady and continuous decline since the beginning of economic reform. Third, coal continued to dominate the country's energy structure while the construction of new coal-fired power plants was accelerating and damaging the environment. In addition to the energy challenges, Hu administration also faced the challenges of enlarging regional and social disparities and worsening corruption.

The challenges need to be addressed comprehensively so as to correct the errors of 'growth at all costs' during the first two decades of reform. Therefore, the third phase is a natural continuation of the second phase but with the aim to address the errors and, according to the Chinese government, to 'perfect' the socialist market economic system. To improve and 'perfect' the system, Hu administration was committed to the policy innovation to address and resolve the negative effects caused by rapid economic development, including the widening gap between rich and poor, environmental degradation, and corruption. The administration realised that, though economic development is of overriding importance, the growth could not be sustainable if the negative effects were not resolved effectively (Zheng, 2011). As a consequence, 'sustainable development' has directed policy orientation in Hu administration, which is more 'social' in terms of the country's economic development. The 'social' can be seen from the administration's slogans include 'Harmonious Society' and 'Scientific Outlook on Development'.[29] Hu administration aims for social equity and balanced growth and hence was careful not to pursue GDP increase at the expense of the social welfare of those left behind (Fewsmith, 2004). The Third Plenary Session of the Sixteenth Party Congress in 2003 made it clear that social development was not simply the pursuit of GDP growth but the holistic and harmonious progress of society.

From then on, the 'Scientific Outlook on Development', which highlighted harmonious and sustainable development, became a priority for the Hu administration and greatly affected the energy sector. First, these slogans indicated that environmental protection attracted more attention of the Hu administration than any of its predecessors. Energy sector, as a major contributor to environmental pollution, was thus directly affected. Second, harmonious and sustainable development needed continuing reforms. At the two conferences (National People's Congress and Chinese People's Political Consultative Conference) held in March 2005, the word 'reform' was frequently used again. Prime Minister Wen Jiabao, in his Government Work Report, proposed to work even harder to promote economic reform. He set out to reform the following: rural sector, SOEs, non-public economic sector, financial sector, fiscal and tax systems and investment system, and the market system (including the pricing reform) (Peng & Chen, 2011b). All these reforms had their respective projections in the energy sector. Therefore, China's energy policy underwent important changes during the third phase of the reform. The following subsections discuss the major reform measures that affected China's energy sector and the corresponding reforms in the energy sector in China.

[29]The concept of 'Scientific Outlook on Development' was first introduced in 2003 and formally endorsed by the 10th National People's Congress in March 2004. The concept was incorporated into the constitution by the Eleventh National People's Congress in March 2008.

5.4.1. Further SOEs Reform

SOEs continued to play a central role in the third phase of the reform process. At the end of 2004, Chinese Vice Prime Minister Huang Ju made it clear that deepening the SOEs reform was the pivot of economic restructuring and that the SOEs reform should be 'accelerated to further do away with obstacles to their healthy development' (Huang, 2004). The urgent task was to cultivate big groups of SOEs to compete in the international market. In 2005, China accelerated the re-distribution of state-owned assets and the regrouping of state-owned firms on the basis of market principles. Until 2010, the SOEs had been more competitive than before, attracting more managerial talents and developing more innovative products and processes. The distinction between the SOEs and private sector companies in China had blurred significantly, and the SOEs began to engage in global partnerships and competition. In general, during the third phase of the economic reform, the SOEs were careful to separate government functions from business operations and be accountable for their own profits and losses (Hassard et al., 2010). Energy sector, with a large share of SOEs, underwent further reforms during this period.

The SDPC was authorised to lead the power sector reform and it continued to introduce market competition into the power sector. The reform was formally launched in 2002 when the State Council issued the *Electric Power Sector Reform Plan* to adopt 'the standard global model of deregulation toward competitive utility markets' (Zhang & Heller, 2004, p. 36). The reform aimed to break the vertical monopoly of the SPCC and introduce competition by means of diversifying the power plants. The SPCC was dismantled into five power generation groups, two power grid companies, and four auxiliary companies. In addition to the vertical separation of the power sector, the SDPC also simultaneously separated the sector horizontally by establishing five regional power grid companies (Chen, 2010; Lam, 2004).[30] Thus, China's power sector was disaggregated both vertically and horizontally. Meanwhile, the State Electricity Regulatory Commission (SERC) became an independent regulatory agency for the sector. Since 2005, the SERC has proposed a series of reform measures to reinforce competition in the power sector (Chen, 2010).[31]

Despite the disaggregation in the power sector and the establishment of the SERC, the competition was *de facto* among the major state power generation enterprises. By the end of 2008, state-owned and state-held share electricity production enterprises accounted for 90% of the total in the country (Tu, 2011,

[30]The five power generation groups are Huaneng, Datang, Huadian, Guodian, and the China Power Investment Group; the two power grid companies are the State Grid Corporation of China and China Southern Power Grid; and the five regional power grid companies are Huabei, Dongbei, Xibei, Huadong, and Huazhong (Chen, 2010). The four auxiliary companies are: Power Generation Consulting (Group) Corporation, Hydropower Engineering Consulting (Group) Corporation, Hydraulic and Hydroelectric Construction (Group) Corporation, and Gezhouba (Group) Corporation (Ma & He, 2008).

[31]NDRC is still the leading regulatory department, hence limiting the SERC's independence.

p. 23). After the *Suggestions on Deepening the Reform of the Electricity Sector in the Eleventh Five-Year Plan* was approved by the State Council in 2006, the State Grid Corporation of China established 30 electricity exchange centres for further electricity market competition. After the establishment of the electricity exchange centres, the power grid companies would be responsible for only power transmission. This separated power transmission from power market transactions, and market mechanisms were further introduced to the power sector. These exchange centres, however, were criticised for failing to introduce changes to the power sector as they were under the direct control of the State Grid Corporation. Electricity T&D were still kept in the hands of the State Grid Corporation (The Beijing News, 2006).

Under the central government's direction of deepening the SOEs reform and establishing big SOE groups, resource consolidation became the overarching policy in the Chinese coal industry during the third phase of the reform. Formation of big groups of SOEs continued in the coal sector. In 2003, more than 10 coalmines were acquired in Shanxi by the Datong Coalmine Group. In 2004, 10 coal companies were consolidated into the Shanxi Coal Group; the Longmei Mining Group was a merger of four state mines in Heilongjiang. In 2005, the state-owned mines in Sichuan province merged into the Sichuan Coal Industry Group. In the same year, three key state-owned mines were consolidated in Anhui. In 2006, the share of national output by the top 10 coal producers in China amounted to 27%, an increase from 14% in 1998 (IEA, 2009, p. 56). The Eleventh FYP for the coal industry planned to continue nurturing large-scale coal mining groups and construct 13 large-scale coal production bases. In 2010, output from these 13 coal bases accounted for 87.5% of the national total (Tu, 2011, p. 12). Since 2002, energy intensive sectors such as the power and steel industries boomed and prompted a powerful rebound of the coal industry. Facing the extraordinary demand for coal, the TVCMs boomed again even though the central government repeatedly gave orders not to blindly re-open the already closed small mines (Zhu & Cherni, 2009). China's coal production is a typical example that reflects how macroeconomic policies predominate over energy policies. The government decision to make full use of comparative advantages of local resources in the early 1980s rationalised coal industry distribution, which greatly stimulated coal production. Since the 1990s, the fluctuation of coal production was deeply affected by the gradual penetration of liberalisation and marketisation. All these explain how strong the force of macroeconomic reform is and how it leads the direction of coal production.

5.4.2. Continuing Marketisation

When the third phase of the economic reform began, the framework of socialist market economic system was still incomplete. Although the planned economic system was not dominant, it still played an important role in many aspects of the national economy. Chinese market economy was still a kind of government-led market economic model in its initial phase of industrialisation and marketisation (Zhang, 2006). To accelerate the process of marketisation in China, the *Decision* of the Third Plenary Session of the Sixteenth Party Congress in 2003 pointed out that the main task was to improve the market economic system. To improve the system, the government revised restrictive policies on the development of non-public economy. Non-public capital was allowed to enter into more industries, as long as the law did not prohibit it. Continued marketisation offered opportunities for the energy sector to intensify competition and liberalise prices.

Since 2005, the government has decided to proceed with the reform of the energy price formation mechanism. It further reduced government intervention in the resource allocation and price formation, and established a market-oriented resource price formation mechanism (People's Daily, 2005c). In the coal sector, testing reforms to fundamentally transform the coal market began in Shanxi in 2007. A major aim was to create an open coal market in 2008, where demand matched supply and all transactions were market based. Foreign investors were allowed to enter China's coal sector after 2008 (Betz, 2013). Also in 2007, NDRC ceased hosting coal-ordering conferences which began in the 1960s for allocating coal resources in China. Government has been much less involved in coal pricing intervention since then (IEA, 2009, p. 58). In December 2009, NDRC issued the *Guidelines Regarding Improving the Linkage Amongst Coal Production, Transport, and Demand.* It specified that the thermal coal contracts should be directly and independently negotiated between the power plants and coal companies without government intervention (Tu, 2011, p. 15). Coal pricing and allocation were fundamentally changed from the government-set or government-indicative system to the market-regulated system. Another prominent impact of further marketisation was that the increasingly market-oriented coal sector weakened the central government's control over coal production. For example, the actual national coal production amounted to 3,240 million tons in 2010,[32] exceeding 25% of the output target of 2,600 million tons set by the NDRC in its Eleventh FYP for the coal industry.

In the power sector, a series of electricity pricing regulations have been issued since 2002, including *Electric Power Sector Reform Plan* in 2002, *Scheme of the Reform of Electricity Prices* in 2003, *Coal-Electricity Price Linkage Mechanism* in 2004,[33] and *Procedures for Implementation of the Reform of Electricity Prices* in 2005. In the regions where competitive wholesale market was not created, the operation-period prices and yardstick prices formulated in 1997 were still in use. In the regions that practiced the competitive wholesale transaction, the price incorporates two components: capacity price and volume price. The former was determined by the government according to the average cost of all generation units whereas the latter was determined by the competitive market (Ma & He, 2008). Nevertheless, since electricity industry is a basic industry affecting many downstream industries and millions of households, the government is very cautious with the increase in electricity prices, making the price hike very difficult. In general, the electricity price is still regulated by the central government. A competitive electricity market in the real sense has not been established yet. Therefore, China's coal and power sector experiences unbalanced development. The coal sector is already subject to market regulation; the power sector is still largely controlled by the government, despite the introduction of market competition.

---

[32]See Section 3.2.1.

[33]The Coal-Electricity Price Linkage Mechanism was less frequently used in subsequent years due to political pressure to keep the electricity prices low.

The unbalanced development of reforms in the coal and power sectors resulted in coal price volatility in China. The coexistence of a competitive coal market and a regulated power market created tension between the power and coal sectors. Under the pressure of rising domestic coal prices, the power companies entered international markets to purchase coal and this reinforced their negotiating power in the domestic coal market. As a result, coal prices were more volatile when the power enterprises entered and exited the international market erratically (Peng, 2009).

Despite the introduction of market competition in the energy sector, Hu administration tried to reassert control over the energy sector with increased administrative means to tighten state control over the energy industry. In March 2003, the government established the Energy Bureau under the NDRC to centralise control over the energy sector and formulate and implement energy policy in a more overarching way (Meidan et al., 2009). From 2003 to 2004, China suffered widespread power shortages, which contributed to a substantial increase in oil demand and imports as diesel generators were run to maintain power. In 2004, blackouts troubled most of China's provinces. Net imports of crude oil grew by almost 50%. The power shortages and surge in oil demand and imports stimulated change in China's energy-sector management. Dissatisfied by the poor energy governance in China, the central government set up the Energy Leading Group (ELG) in 2005, headed by Prime Minster Wen Jiabao (Downs, 2006). The ELG serves as the steering committee for the central government to reinforce its control over the energy sector. Obviously, the formation of ELG was an extemporaneous decision resulted from the energy crisis of 2003–2004 and the leadership's dissatisfaction with China's energy policymaking apparatus. China did not have a forward-looking plan to establish an institute to oversee the whole energy sector, and it still falls short of an authoritative and independent ministerial-level agency to govern the energy sector of the country. This once again shows that the government very passively issued energy policies just to solve the problems whenever and wherever they took place.

The approach that the Chinese government tried to settle the problem whenever and wherever they met the problem inevitably resulted in contradictory policies and actions towards the energy sector. Driven by the macroeconomic reforms, market competition continued to grow in the energy sector. At the same time, the government continued to intervene in the energy sector as it was regarded as the key sector of strategic importance in the national economy. This is exactly the story: on the one hand, the government cannot stop the force of macroeconomic reform once it is initiated; on the other hand, the government, whenever it deem suitable, tries to maintain their control over the strategic sector of energy. The government is frequently put in an afflicting position where it struggles to balance between deepening market reform and steady-state control. This also explains why China does not have coherent energy policies.

5.4.3. Increasing Attention to Environmental Protection

China's economic development during the first two decades of economic reform had emphasised the growth of heavy industry, much of which was energy-intensive and environmentally damaging. What made things worse was the government's disregard for its own environmental regulations in its haste to secure economic growth. When Hu administration came into power, the level of pollution in China continued to worsen. Greenhouse gas emissions abatement became an increasingly important policy concern for the Hu administration. In 2004, after consultation with local and foreign energy experts, the Development Research Center of the State Council announced its *National Energy Strategy and Policy Report*. This report specified the sustainable use of energy as the key national priority. Examples of measures specified in the report include constraining demand for fossil fuels; establishing economic incentives to save energy; encouraging the use of clean coal technology; and implementing stricter energy efficiency and environmental standards (Miller, 2006; Sinton, Stern, Aden, & Levine, 2005). This report reflected the Chinese government's new conscientiousness on energy security.

As the central government understood that China needed to curb its spiking carbon emissions, it developed an increasingly comprehensive and proactive policy to control CO_2 emissions. Since the Tenth FYP (2001–2005), China had gravely fallen far behind its pollution and energy reduction targets: China's global CO_2 emissions soared to nearly 20% in 2005. Environmental concerns were highlighted in energy security policies of China's Eleventh FYP (2006–2010), hence setting the goal of cutting national energy intensity by 20% from 2005 to 2010. This target can be translated into an annual reduction of more than 1.5 billion tons of CO_2 by 2010 (Lin, Zhou, Levine, & Fridley, 2008, p. 954).

The NDRC issued *China's National Climate Change Programme* in 2007. The Programme specified energy-related policies and measures to mitigate climate change by reducing CO_2 emissions. These measures include: proper development of hydropower; active promotion of nuclear power development; expediting technology progress in thermal power generation; vigorous development of coal-bed methane and coal-mine methane industry; promotion of bio-energy development and support for the development and utilisation of renewable energy including wind, solar, geothermal, and tidal energy (NDRC, 2007c). China was the first developing country that had published a national strategy to combat climate change. In the same year, President Hu Jintao highlighted this report at the Seventeenth National Congress of the Communist Party of China:

> The development pattern will be significantly transformed. We will quadruple the per capita GDP of the year 2000 by 2020 through optimizing the economic structure and improving economic returns while reducing consumption of resources and protecting the environment. (Hu, 2007)

As directed by the Program and the government's determination, ambitious goals were set to attain renewable energy development for long-term energy security purposes. Since 2006, China had invested more than 10 billion USD annually in renewable energy resources (Karl, Han, & Olsson, 2009, p. 128).

5.5. China's Economic Reform and Energy Security: A Chapter Conclusion

China, always cautious about its economic reform, had been guided by the philosophy of 'crossing the river by feeling the stones' throughout its more than four decades of reform. At the beginning of the reform, the government did not know which direction to take. It was then imperative to address the irrational distribution of industries left behind by the previous administration. The government adjusted the economy, including the energy industry, by relocating it according to the principle of 'comparative advantage'. The redistribution fostered the fast development of energy industry in subsequent years.

One major policy introduced in the beginning reform era was HRS, which promoted the fast growth of TVEs, including the TVCMs. Their development has both positive and negative effects on the energy sector. The key advantage was the fast increase of coal production, while the disadvantages were mainly wasted resources and environmental pollution. In addition to the introduction of HRS and the growth of TVCMs in the coal sector, the electricity sector during Deng administration had also undergone some degree of reform after its opening to foreign and private investors. The two-tier pricing system resulted in government-set and market-regulated prices in the coal sector. The failure of price reform in 1989 led to the readjustment of the national economy, including the energy sector. From the very beginning of the reform, it is obvious that all the energy sector reforms and policies were merely passive responses (reactions) to the overall macroeconomic reforms. This characteristic is evident during the Jiang and Hu administrations as well.

During Jiang administration, four major reforms directly affected the energy sector: government restructuring, fiscal reform, financial reform, and SOEs reform. As a result, the energy sector reformed its institutions, its SOEs, and changed its energy conservation performance. During Hu administration, reform priorities were adjusted to address deepening market reform and environmental protection issues. Along with this trend, China's energy SOEs experienced further reforms and extended pollution control. Throughout the reform period, energy policies showed no coherence, such as the policies swinging between control and relaxation of oil prices, stimulation and discouragement of TVCMs development, and the establishment and elimination of government mechanism to conserve energy. The non-coherence is exactly the 'by-product' of the macroeconomic reform. Every time there is energy policy change or reverse, there must be some major macroeconomic reform measure taking place in advance.

To summarise, China's energy policies did not originate from energy security concerns and were not intended to improve the energy security situation. They have always been passively reactive and responsive to the country's macroeconomic reform. Therefore, it is impossible for China to have a coherent energy policy or energy strategy targeted to enhance the country's energy security. In other words, China's energy policies are constrained by its reform. The macroeconomic reform is such a strong force that it diminishes other factors that might also affect the energy sector and dominates the energy sector policies. Just as a bird cannot fly out of its cage, China's energy policy cannot escape from the limitations of macroeconomic reform. The data indicate that China's energy security has improved to some extent since 1995 but has not attained the high level of 1985. Future prospects may seem brighter than in what we saw in 1985, but the improvement is still subject to the macroeconomic policies and cannot jump out of the confines of economic reform.

Chapter 6

Belt and Road Initiative and China's Energy Security: Can China be More Energy Secured?

Chapter 5 intensively discussed China's energy policies across the Deng Xiaoping, Jiang Zemin, and Hu Jintao administrations from domestic point of view. This chapter shifts from the domestic to the international view with a discussion of China's energy policies of Xi Jinping Administration through the lens of the flagship project 'Belt and Road Initiative' (BRI). In 2013, Chinese President Xi Jinping proposed the building of the New Silk Road Economic Belt and the 21st Century Maritime Silk Road – collectively called the BRI. Energy plays an important role in China's BRI. On the one hand, using BRI to build energy infrastructure, China will be able to source oil, gas, and electricity from the energy-rich countries nearby. On the other hand, the BRI has provided opportunities for the Chinese companies to acquire more energy resources abroad. Huge Chinese investments have been devoted to energy projects within and across countries alongside the 'Belt' and the 'Road'. By reviewing the BRI investment projects and by analysing the barriers of the projects implementation, this chapter attempts to look into China's energy security from the international relations view so as to explore whether the BRI contributes to enhancing China's energy security or not.

6.1. Introduction

Since 2000, Chinese government's 'going out' policy has enabled the Chinese energy companies to gain support from the central government in signing long-term supply deals, building transnational pipelines, and obtaining the necessary political back-up for their investments in risky countries in Central Asia, Middle East, Southeast Asia, and elsewhere. In 2013, after Chinese President Xi Jinping came into power, the central government proposed the BRI. The aim of BRI, as communicated by the Chinese government, is to increase connectivity, enhance trade flows, and spur long-term economic growth. It is supposed that BRI and the China-led investment and infrastructure construction, together with relevant policy arrangement such as reduced tariffs, would bring about a seamless Eurasian continent by railways and sea lanes.

Energy Security in Times of Economic Transition: Lessons from China, 151–160

doi:10.1108/978-1-83982-464-720201007

As one of BRI's crucial pillars, energy plays an important role in China's BRI and energy security is an important part of it. Huge Chinese investments have been devoted to it within and across countries alongside the 'Belt' and the 'Road'. Using BRI to build energy infrastructure, China will be able to source oil, gas, and electricity from the energy-rich countries nearby. China has the goal to secure its energy security through these energy-related projects.

Ideally, the BRI is conducive to enhancing energy security. On the one hand, with the aim to connect China with countries alongside the Belt and the Road through oil and gas pipelines, ports, and other transportation infrastructure, the BRI can bring foreign energy resources to China with lower logistic costs. On the other hand, as the world's largest energy consumer, China has every reason to secure sufficient energy supplies in order to sustain its economic development, and the BRI has provided more opportunities for the Chinese companies to acquire energy resources overseas. With this said, this chapter reviews the BRI projects alongside the 'Belt' and the 'Road' that aim to be contributable to enhancing China's energy security. These projects include investment in the energy sector to increase energy supply, investment in the interconnectivity infrastructure to ease energy accessibility, and construction of a broader economic corridor to facilitate energy trading and energy transportation. They are reviewed by location in specific sub-regions.

6.2. BRI Projects in the World's Energy Sector

6.2.1. Central Asia

The BRI aims to connect Asia to Europe with the construction of railways, roads, and other infrastructure across countries in the Central Asia. The most significant part of BRI is with various key fossil fuel providers across the Gulf and Central Asia. In the energy sector, the BRI projects in Central Asia would allow China to lock in energy supply from the Central Asian energy-exporting countries. Through BRI, Chinese companies have been actively involved in the extraction of energy resources and in the creation of energy pipelines for trading and transmitting these resources into China.

The energy-rich Kazakhstan, Turkmenistan, and Uzbekistan have been prioritised in the energy projects. Kazakhstan and Turkmenistan are expected to continue and even increase their supply of oil and natural gas to China (Jaborov, 2018). At the time of writing this book, China has two large projects of energy sector investment in Central Asia. One is a crude oil pipeline from Kazakhstan, one of China's most important energy suppliers. Exporting 10 million tons of crude oil to China annually, this oil pipeline is expected to deliver 20 million tons annually by 2020. CNPC the Kazakhstan's state energy company KazMunayGas take equal shares in the pipeline, though some reports suggest that CNPC paid for 85% of the total cost (Jiang & Sinton, 2011, p. 31). The other large project is the Central Asia–China gas pipeline, involving Kazakhstan, Turkmenistan, and Uzbekistan. The gas pipeline is expected to deliver 85 billion cubic metres (bcm) of gas annually by 2020 (Jochec & Kyzy, 2018, p. 71).

As one of China's most important energy suppliers, Kazakhstan is a key transit partner for natural gas from Turkmenistan eastward to the Xinjiang Province of China. It has also sought to leverage its growing partnership with China under BRI to boost economic development. The scale of projects invested by Chinese is spectacular. In the energy sector, China controls up to 30% of all oil extraction in Kazakhstan as of April 2016, according to the then managing director for economics and finance of KazMunayGas (Toleukhanova, 2016).

Yet many challenges exist for smooth and successful implementation of BRI and the energy projects in the Central Asia as well. First, many countries in Central Asia are fraught with investment risks such as terrorist threat and political instability. A typical challenge in Kazakhstan is that China's investment fuels social anxiety among the local community, which in turn stimulates the anti-China rhetoric. A qualitative sampling of the views of Kazakh people reveals that the public opinion tends to be anti-Chinese in general (Clarke, 2014). A protest rolling through Kazakh cities took place in September 2019. The protestors against the government's pronouncement to allow the Chinese to set up more than 50 factories in Kazakhstan worried that the Chinese projects would deepen Kazakhstan's economic dependence on China. They were also concerned about the use of imported Chinese labour and that Kazakhstan would not be able to repay related loans (The Economist, 2019).

Another uncertainty is with Turkmenistan, which is currently China's biggest gas imports supplier. China is the main customer for Turkmen gas. An annual 30–40 bcm of gas is supplied from Turkmen gas fields to China through the Central Asia–China pipeline (Karagianni, 2019). Turkmenistan's giant gas field, South Elotan, produces 25 bcm of gas per year, almost all of which is sent to China, which financed a huge share of the gas field project with direct loan and control of the field's development with Chinese subcontractors (Krashakov, 2014). Given China has been the sole foreign importer of Turkmen gas since Russia halted gas imports from Turkmenistan in 2016, Turkmenistan is under the pressure that its gas trade is dominated by China. To address this issue, the country has been trying to diversify its gas exports, and it is successful to some extent. For the first time since 2016, Turkmenistan resumed gas exports to Russia in April 2019 (Forbes, 2019). This is a good start for gas exports diversification. In other words, Turkmenistan has been trying not to be increasingly dependent on China. For China, only time will tell if Turkmenistan is a reliable supplier of gas.

Second, out of commercial feasibility concerns, Chinese energy companies are more disciplined in making deals. Since 2000, successful acquisitions allowed China's national oil companies (NOCs) to expand their overseas equity oil shares, particularly in some Central Asian countries. Yet evidence shows that the equity oil from Kazakhstan, for example, is not all shipped back to China through the new pipeline from Kazakhstan to China. The CNPC subsidiaries evaluate whether it would be profitable to sell the oil back to China and decide how the CNPC's share of production from its holdings in Kazakhstan are marketed. In some cases, when selling to other players can be more profitable, the Chinese equity oil is transported via some segment of the Kazakhstan–China pipeline and sold on the international market. Representatives from PetroChina also confirmed that decisions on whether to ship the equity oil back to China or to sell it on the international market were purely based on the prevailing market prices (Jiang & Sinton, 2011). Therefore, the pipeline does not necessarily guarantee adequacy of energy supply.

Furthermore, the value of transactions made by Chinese NOCs was much less than the previous years, with an amount of less than $10 billion in total during 2014–2016 (Chen, 2018). A reason that perhaps explains this is that, in 2012, the State-owned Assets Supervision and Administration Commission of the State Council issued a document on *Measures for the Supervision and Administration of Overseas Investments by Central Enterprises*, which indicates that the central enterprises should be responsible for their investment projects. This suggests that the state enterprises are more commercially driven when business decisions are being made. Further, even highly risk-tolerant Chinese investors find it difficult to make investment in Central Asia with its unpredictable, random, and generally high corruption-related barriers imposed by the host countries, such as the heavy bureaucracy involved in obtaining mining permits and unclear and constantly changing tax regulations. The BRI can only succeed in Central Asia when such barriers to investment are removed (Kurbanov, 2018).

6.2.2. South Asia

The flagship project and also one of the key components of China's BRI in South Asia is the China-Pakistan Economic Corridor (CPEC). Through CPEC the Chinese government wants to achieve four main tasks: expand the Gwadar port on Pakistan's southern coast, build power plants, construct roads and railways, and set up special economic zones (Sender & Stacey , 2017).

Among these infrastructures, the Gwadar port is of key importance to China. China has been over reliant on the Malacca Strait as its major oil transit chokepoint. The Gwadar port for ships transporting energy resources and other goods from the Persian Gulf and Africa allows China to reduce its dependencies on longer sea routes through the Indian Ocean and the Malacca Strait. This is because the Indian Ocean port Gwadar links directly to western and southern China overland, which can give China direct access to the Indian Ocean, allowing ships carrying oil from Persian Gulf to bypass Malacca Strait and shortening the existing routes by thousands of kilometres. This can successfully help China to avoid the so-called 'Malacca Dilemma'. The Malacca issue and fears of disruption in China's oil supply motivated China to construct the CPEC, since the risk of interrupted oil supply routes has always been considered as a great risk to its energy security. With Gwadar, China can link its landlocked western region to the Indian Ocean, and CPEC can provide China with an energy corridor, through which the oil from the Middle East can reach China through railroads and pipelines (Yamada & Palma, 2018).

In one sentence, the CPEC with its future railways, highways, and pipelines can transport the shipped goods via a shorter land route from Gwadar to China. In the energy sector, particularly, the Frontier Works Organisation (FWO), an engineering company of Pakistan, in cooperation with foreign investors, wanted to build a crude oil pipeline from Gwadar of Pakistan to Kashgar in China. The FWO had requested the Petroleum Division of the Ministry of Energy in Pakistan to sign a Memorandum of Understanding (MOU) of agreement to assure the investors that the Pakistan government would not take over the planned investment (Bhutta, 2018). As a result, an agreement for the Gwadar–Kashgar Cross-Country Crude Oil Pipeline Project was signed between the government of Pakistan and the FWO in May 2018. This suggestive pipeline of approximately 3,000 km from Gwadar to Kashgar is supposed to effectively diversify the transmission routes of China's imported oil. As Gwadar is near the Persian Gulf and close to the Strait of Hormuz, this oil pipeline can give China quicker access to the Middle East countries, from which China meets about half of its oil demand. The transmission capacity is expected to be one million barrels per day (FWO, 2018).

However, the business environment in Pakistan is poor. The World Bank's report 'Doing Business 2020' shows that Pakistan's ease of doing business score is 61.0 in 2020, ranking 108th of 190 economies (World Bank, 2020, p. 4). The lower ranking means that doing business in Pakistan faces a variety of challenges such as the investment, trade, and operations risks.

First of all, the CPEC is vulnerable to terrorist attack in Pakistan. Some places along the CPEC have been flashpoints for decades. For example, the India and Pakistan have fought two wars and a limited conflict over Kashmir. In October 2014, a border incident involved firing of shells from both sides resulted in a reported five Indian and four Pakistani civilian casualties (BBC, 2014). Such conflict can threaten projects under the CPEC economic corridor. Up to writing of this book, totally 45 projects, including 20 energy projects, are under construction or planned to be started along the CPEC. These projects are mainly distributed in Punjab, Sindh, Cape, and Baluchistan provinces, which accommodate more than 80% of all CPEC projects. However, terrorist attacks in these provinces are also top in Pakistan (Liu, 2018). There have a few warnings of possible terrorist attacks on the CPEC installations, such as bridges at Karakoram Highway and other important points on the CPEC route (Nagri, 2018).

According to the report 'Global Terrorism Index 2019' (GTI) issued by the Institute for Economics and Peace, the impact of terrorism fell for the fifth consecutive year in Pakistan in 2018. With an index (GTI) of 7.889, Pakistan ranks fifth among the countries that are most vulnerable to terrorist attacks in the world. Pakistan continued to be one of the least peaceful countries and terrorism remains a major threat in the country. Particularly, '[l]inks among terrorist groups are especially prevalent across conflict-prone borders, like those separating Pakistan from India and Afghanistan' (IEP, 2019, p. 23). This also suggests the instability and insecurity of South Asia and Middle East.

In addition, as an important part of BRI, the continuous advancement of CPEC across a huge geospatial space may motivate relevant countries to actively participate in geopolitical games. This may activate geopolitical contradictions and may cause the relevant geopolitical parties to rebound or counteract (Zhou, 2016). For example, India expresses strong opposition to CPEC. India believes that the CPEC is a political tool for China to intervene in the India–Pakistan dispute over Kashmir, and the Gwadar port project aims to expand China's influence in the Indian Ocean. India's defence report in 2017 states that the CPEC crosses the Pakistan occupied Kashmir region and that it violates India's territorial sovereignty (Liu, 2017). All these factors can create obstacles to BRI, thereby weakening its positive role in China's energy security.

6.2.3. Middle East

Energy security remains China's primary reason for engagement in the Middle East. Since the end of the Cold War, China's foreign policies in the Middle East have been primarily driven by searching for overseas investment opportunities and seeking energy security (Kennedy, 2010). Since BRI was proposed, China's foreign policies towards the Middle East have been more proactive and energy cooperation is the highlight of the cooperation under BRI between China and the Middle East. Accordingly, China has been expanding its ability to project power throughout the region, and seeking new avenues for energy and investment with its partners in the region. The data show that oil and gas projects currently in development in the Middle East account for 68.1 billion USD, which is led by China and other countries (Murray, 2019).

As the world's largest oil importer, China receives more than half of its total crude oil imports from the Middle East and the dependency on the Middle East oil is growing. Through various investments across the Gulf, the Chinese companies have been primarily interested in securing their own access to oil and gas in the Middle East. China's closest ally in the Middle East is Saudi Arabia. By playing a leading role in the Gulf Cooperation Council, Saudi Arabia has tremendous influence in the Middle East. Therefore, China cannot afford to miscalculate the China–Saudi relationship. The Chinese government considers the relationship with Saudi as a 'comprehensive strategic partnership'. Saudi is the world's largest crude oil exporter and China is Saudi's largest oil export destination country.

In November 2019, Saudi Arabia's state oil company Saudi Aramco officially announced its plan to go public. Just before the initial public offering (IPO) announcement, China was considering acquiring a major stake in the company. Chinese state-owned companies were in talks to invest 5–10 billion USD in the IPO. China's involvement in Aramco is fraught with its own complex geopolitical calculations. The Aramco IPO gives China an opportunity to gain a foothold at the centre of the global oil industry (Dana, 2019). In the non-fossil fuel sector, Chinese companies are also involved in Saudi's plans to build 16 nuclear power plants worthy of 100 billion USD (Williams, 2012).

Besides Saudi Arabia, China has also continued building a strong relationship with other Middle East countries such as Iran. China's increasingly proactive foreign policy towards the Middle East also includes the multifaceted relations with Iran, which has the world's fourth largest reserves of crude oil and the world's second-largest reserves of natural gas. With its rich oil and gas resources, Iran is important for China. The transit role Iran can play in the infrastructure plans of BRI is also important in the sense that it connects the Eurasian continent. In the meantime, China is central to Iran's long-term energy exploration and development strategy. Chinese NOCs have made substantial investments in Iran since 2009 and have a significant presence in the country. Sinopec and energy trader Zhuhai Zhenrong Company jointly extracted about 500,000 barrels per day of crude oil from Iran in 2016 (Zambelis, 2016, p. 10).

Under such circumstances and with Iran's role in China's effort to revive the ancient Silk Road, Chinese President Xi Jinping visited Iran in January 2016 after his visit to another Middle Eastern country Saudi Arabia. Xi's visit to Iran enhanced the consensus to build economic ties worth up to 600 billion USD. Cooperation on peaceful nuclear energy is a centrepiece in the consensus (Ghoshal, 2016). Xi's visit also saw the signing of agreements to further cooperate on oil and gas production. During the trip, both Xi Jinping and the Iranian President Hassan Rouhani highly praised the long Sino-Iranian friendship.

In one sentence, China is expected to remain reliant on the Middle Eastern oil and gas for much of its energy. Meanwhile, as stable and continuous political and foreign policies are the minimum condition for economic cooperation, the politically fragile Middle East region can put challenges and risks to the Chinese engagement in the energy sector in the Middle East. For example, the previously mentioned Sino-Iranian relations are not without hurdles. Iran had terminated its $2.5 billion contract with CNPC to develop the Azadegan oil field (Faucon, 2014) and another project at the South Pars gas field after CNPC failed to start work on the project. Since the United States withdrew from the nuclear accord in May 2018 and re-imposed sanctions on Iran's oil industry, CNPC abandoned the South Pars gas field project (CNA, 2019), a decision regarded by observers to appease the United States.

Further, China has become a hostage of the increasing Saudi-Iranian rivalry in recent years. Regarding such rivalry, China still insists the principle of non-interference. However, tension between the principle of non-interference and the need to protect overseas investments will increase. China's considerable overseas investments particularly in the Middle East surely relate to its security interests. An ever-expanding economic influence means a greater need to protect Chinese facilities and strategic lines of communication. China may want to protect such facilities and lines of communication with its own military, yet this would then be up to the United States and other powers to decide whether or not to accept such increasing Chinese preponderance (Jong et al., 2017).

In addition, the change of political power and the turmoil of the political situation in the Middle East countries have deteriorated the economic situation, which not only makes it difficult for these countries to participate in the BRI construction advocated by China, but also affects the route selection of the Silk Road through the Arab region (Tian, 2016). Iraq's situation well illustrates this. In 2018, China and Iraq have signed an MOU about construction of a 300,000 barrels per day oil refinery and petrochemicals facility in southern Iraq. In 2019, after Iraq announced it had formed a committee on potential BRI projects, China and Iraq signed an investment agreement valued 10 billion USD, which shows a significant increase in China's role in Iraq (Tollast & Al-Maleki, 2019). According to the International Energy Agency, 80% of Iraqi oil will go to China by 2035 (Chaziza, 2016, p. 27). However, Iraq's ongoing struggle for stability still hinders further consolidation of China–Iraq relations. In 2019, a wave of angry anti-government protests swept across much of Iraq, leaving more than 100 dead and thousands wounded (Calabrese, 2019).

Besides the political risk, the security risk is also prominent. Terrorism threatens the implementation of BRI as well. Therefore, anti-terrorism in this region is of particular importance to China. The Islamic State, the jihadist group better known as ISIS, had declared that their territories running from Iraq and Syria towards North Africa, across the Middle East and into Muslim countries verging onto Russia (Mackay, 2014). The active region of the ISIS almost overlapped a large part of BRI countries, which posed severe threat to Chinese projects in these countries. Although Iraq's prime minister declared a final victory over Islamic State in December 2017, cost of doing business may still be high due to unexpected reasons. Although the Islamic State lost its last territory in Syria and tens of thousands of its remaining members were in jail in 2019, thousands of Islamic State and other terrorist prisoners will be released in the coming years, and it is possible that the Islamic State re-emerge (Mironova, 2019). Given the Middle East remains the largest source of China's crude oil and China has increasing energy interests in this region, the terrorist activities remain a threat to China's energy security. They may jeopardise China's heavy investments in the oil industry in the Middle East and disrupt the regular supply of oil as well.

6.2.4. Southeast Asia

The expansion of Chinese investment in Southeast Asia's energy sector under BRI is mainly focused in the hydropower and coal-fired power sectors where Chinese companies have already been engaged in for years. Hydropower basically concentrates in Myanmar, Laos, and Cambodia while the coal-fired power mainly in Indonesia and Vietnam. Yet the political risk in this region is prominent when these power plant projects are being conducted. The case of Myitsone Dam in Myanmar illustrates that political risk can be a major issue for BRI projects in Southeast Asia.

The Myitsone Dam project, the first dam planned to be developed by the State Power Investment Corporation (SPIC), was supposed to be the largest hydropower plant in Myanmar. Most of the power generation would be transmitted to the China Southern Power Grid through the Yunnan Power Grid. However, it was halted in 2011 by Myanmar's former military government with democratic transition and huge pressures from the local community, which criticised the dam's social and environmental impact on them (Shi & Yao, 2019). Strikingly, SPIC only learned about the suspension of the dam project from local television news, and the SPIC has not got any compensation for the government's breach of the contract (Liao, 2019).

In the coal-fired power sector, China has become the world's largest overseas investor of coal power plants. According to a review of public documents by the *New York Times*, Chinese companies have finished, begun building, or formally announced plans to build at least 92 coal-fired power plants in 27 countries since 2010 (Forsythe, 2015). The major destination of the Chinese investments is Indonesia, the region's largest market, where Chinese companies have maintained operations in coalmines in various parts of the country. The major reason for Chinese heavy investments in Indonesia's coal-fired power plants is Indonesia's domestic policy. Indonesian President Joko Widodo introduced an ambitious power generation plan to provide 35,000 megawatts of additional capacity by 2019, of which coal-fired power plants will account for about 55% (Yao, Andrews-Speed, & Mohammad, 2018). In Vietnam, Chinese companies have also been invited to build coal-fired power plants. Vietnam used to purchase electricity from China; now Hanoi's commitment to macroeconomic reforms has led Vietnam to invite Chinese companies to build power plants in the country (Ng, 2017). Chinese companies have built more than a dozen coal-fired plants in Vietnam since 2010. One major reason for the investment of Chinese companies is that, as Erica Downs explained, '[t]here is just so much excess capacity in power generation equipment, so if they're not building it in China, they want to build it abroad' (Forsythe, 2015).

Although coal will remain China's most reliable resource to guarantee base-load stability and energy supply security, Chinese companies overseas' investment in coal-fired power plants is a commercially driven behaviour with little contribution to China's energy supply security. Further, with sustained political risks in Southeast Asia, Chinese investment in this region may encounter problems or even suspension. The commercially driven Chinese investment can be good for the host countries and the Chinese companies, yet it contributes little to the energy security of China.

6.3. Conclusion

BRI is considered a vehicle to interconnect open markets, to promote political stability and security, and to restore Chinese spheres of influence in the Eurasian landmass and beyond. Against this background, Chinese investments in the energy sector alongside BRI countries are changing energy supply patterns and this may have profound impacts on regional political and economic relations in Central Asia, South Asia, Middle East, and Southeast Asia. However, there are huge economic, political, and security challenges for the BRI. China's BRI have to cope with these mounting challenges and problems. Therefore, whether BRI can enhance China's energy security remains to be seen.

First, the 'Belt' and the 'Road' pass through many geopolitically fragile areas, with armed conflicts and religious disputes. The outbreak of any conflicts in the region alongside the 'Belt' and the 'Road' may disrupt the BRI projects and threaten the safety of the relevant personnel. Countries in Central Asia and the Middle East are fraught with investment risks stemming from war, terrorist threat, and political instability. The Middle East countries, particularly, have entered a more turbulent period since the 'Arab Spring'. The investments in infrastructure in this area are endangered in a variety of specific challenges. In South Asia, the CPEC is vulnerable to terrorist attack. In Southeast Asia, Myanmar's cancellation of the Myitsone Dam project clouds China's BRI projects.

Second, even without considering the investment risks, the contribution of some overseas energy investments to China's energy security may be limited.

The Chinese NOCs investments in global upstream assets have and will continue to contribute significantly to expanding global oil and gas supplies, yet a significant proportion of the overseas equity production of the NOCs is sold into the market rather than sent back to China. The NOCs still depend on the international market to purchase most of the oil imported to China. Further, pipelines cannot guarantee energy security either. China will still have to depend on seaborne trades, including those through the Strait of Malacca, to bring in most of its imported oil. Given China's growing reliance on foreign oil and gas imports, it is still necessary for China to make efforts to safeguard the sea lanes of communication.

China will encounter more challenges in pushing forward the BRI, which may undermine BRI's function in enhancing China's energy security. Chinese energy companies will be even more cautious and disciplined to make overseas investment. Taking into account the economic, policy, safety, political, and other challenges, it remains to be seen whether and how the BRI will improve China's energy security.

Chapter 7

Conclusion

This book establishes the Macro Economy-Driven Energy Security Mechanism and answers the following three broadly defined energy security and policy questions: How has China's energy security situation evolved? What is the impact of China's energy policies on the energy security situation? Why has China not improved its energy security during the first three decades of economic reform? After that, this book also looks into China's energy policies under the Belt and Road Initiative (BRI) from the international perspective.

To answer the 'how' question, a quantitative framework is constructed to evaluate energy security in China. The framework explains that China's energy security situation has not improved during its first three decades of economic reform. To answer the 'what' question, the direct impact of China's energy policies on its energy security situation over the three decades is examined, and the evolution of energy policies and the energy security situation in China is explained. To answer the 'why' question, the impetus behind the evolution of energy policies and the energy security situation in China is explored. The key reason is that China's energy policies are not intentional policies derived from an early blueprint. Rather, the policies are a passive reaction to overall economic reform and transition. Reform acts as a constraint on energy policies. The reform measures *per se*, as Deng Xiaoping described, were 'crossing the river by groping for stones'. That is to say China's reform has been undertaken slowly, one step at a time. Constrained by the incremental approach of macroeconomic reform, the energy policies, like a mirror, precisely reflect every change in China's macroeconomic policies. Under this condition, the evolution of energy policies, being incremental as well, was subject to macroeconomic reform in China. This made it impossible for China to develop coherent and creative energy policies to improve its energy security. That explains why energy security in China did not improve.

To explain the causality between macroeconomic reform and the evolution of China's energy security, this study establishes the Macro Economy-Driven Energy Security Mechanism, which integrates both quantitative and qualitative methodologies to address the evolution of energy security in China and explain how macroeconomic reform drives such evolution. This mechanism consists of two parts. The first part reflects the qualitative methodology adopted by this study. It shows that macroeconomic reforms drive/constrain energy policies and that the energy policies directly affect the four dimensions of energy security. The second

Energy Security in Times of Economic Transition: Lessons from China, 161–170

doi:10.1108/978-1-83982-464-720201008

part reflects the quantitative methodology this study uses to quantify energy security in China. Through quantification, the figures of each of the four energy security dimensions can be calculated such that whether energy security situation, constructed by the four dimensions, improved or deteriorated can be concluded. Incorporating the two parts, the Macro Economy-Driven Energy Security Mechanism exactly indicates how macroeconomic reforms, as the key and major driving force, via their function in energy policies, impacted on each of the four dimensions and finally framed the energy security situation.

Applying the Macro Economy-Driven Energy Security Mechanism, this study examines all the major macroeconomic reform measures over three decades in China. It finds that all the reforms have their reflection in energy sector and affect the promulgation and implementation of energy policies. For example, in the 1980s, the central government's decision to rectify the economic disorder led to the adjustment of energy industry distribution. Production efficiency of the coal industry was greatly increased. The Household Responsibility System (HRS) made an outlet for the fast development of town and village enterprises, among them were the town and village coalmines that greatly contributed to coal production in China. The two-tier pricing system made the in-quota and above-quota coal and oil prices that lasted for nearly one decade. In the 1990s, the state-owned enterprises (SOEs) reform led to the shutdown of town and village coalmines. The SOEs reform also created several large state enterprises in the oil and electricity sectors, which hindered the marketisation in these industries. The government restructuring in the 1990s revoked institutions that had been favourable for encouragement of energy efficiency. Since 2000, further marketisation in the economy led to a completely free coal market. To put it simply, every economic reform measure has its reflection in the energy sector and finally frames energy security situation.

The identification of the causality between China's macroeconomic reforms and the evolution of China's energy security has its implications especially for future policymaking. Understanding that China's energy policies are constrained by its macroeconomic reform, the Chinese government could endeavour to have some 'proactive' energy policies to improve energy security. For example, experiences in the 1980s show that administrative measures are more efficient for energy conservation. The government can promulgate favourable tax policies for saving energy. In the coal sector, township and village coalmines that had greatly contributed to China's coal supply should continue to be encouraged. Considering the bad performance of environmental protection in the coal sector after the Ministry of Coal Industry was revoked due to government restructuring in the 1990s, the environmental administrations and other supervising institutions should coordinate to guarantee that these township and village coalmines protect the environment during coal mining. In the electricity sector, the measures to encourage various sources of investment in the 1980s are good examples for the current administration to refer to. The government should continue the variety of investment sources, instead of merely relying on several large state enterprises for investment. In the oil sector, the oligopoly situation does not induce competition efficiently. Although it is not possible to fundamentally liberalise the sector at the moment, further marketisation and competition could be introduced by allowing more foreign and private investors to enter the sector, and thus breaking the oligopoly. In fact, the current administration under President Xi Jinping has been working on the measures to attract new investment sources such as private capitals to enter the energy market. This is an example in point that illustrates the importance of this book in terms of its policy implications. The following subsections reiterate the contributions of this book.

7.1. Contribution of the Book: The Quantitative Methodology

This study establishes a quantitative framework based on a comprehensive concept of energy security to examine China's situation. The framework incorporates 20 indicators that best quantify the evolution of energy security in China. It consists of two tiers. The first tier, the 4-As framework, is common for all countries. The second tier, the 20 indicators quantifying energy security in China, is country specific and contingent on data availability. In this sense, the framework is both universal and country specific. It could do more than evaluate China's energy policy and security, and could be generalised to evaluate the energy policy and energy security of any country by using expanded and/or modified indicators. As long as the key indicators for a country are identified under the framework, the energy security situation of that country could be evaluated. Therefore, the framework is very flexible, expandable, and user-friendly. Future research could be done for the application of the quantitative framework on other countries.

The concept of energy security has evolved over time. In the beginning, it focused on adequate and reliable energy supplies – particularly oil supply – in the narrow sense. In the broad sense, the energy security issue covers various energy resources. Reasonable and stable oil/energy prices are also considered a key component of energy security. To sum up, energy security incorporates three elements: reliability, adequacy, and reasonable price. It is the availability of a stable and reliable energy supply at all times, in sufficient quantities, and at reasonable and affordable prices. These three elements cover several different dimensions of energy security such as economics, technology, and environment. In terms of the economic dimension, energy security means a sufficient supply of energy resources and affordability by energy consumers. In terms of the technological dimension, energy security requires efficient use of energy not only by sound management of energy use but also by technological innovation. In terms of the environmental dimension, energy security requires sustainable energy development, which means that an energy secure country is able to guarantee the availability of energy resources in a sustainable manner. To better understand the essence of energy security, scholars have been trying to add new components and/or dimensions. Beyond the qualitative description of energy security, quantitative indicators have been designed and frameworks incorporating these indicators have been established to quantify energy security, thus making the evaluation and interpretation of energy security more effective.

Based on the existing concepts, indicators, and frameworks of energy security, this book constructs a quantitative instrument – the 4-As evaluation framework (availability, applicability, acceptability, and affordability) – to assess China's

well as the gradual restructuring of institutions to facilitate economic reform and marketisation. From then on, macroeconomic reform began to play a key role in energy policy promulgation and implementation, and it became the key variable in energy security evolution in China. Two major measures were undertaken in the initial period. First, the government granted partial managerial autonomy to the micro units in the agricultural sector by the HRS. The withdrawn incentives were reinstated and local and private initiatives were encouraged. The HRS spurred rapid growth of TVEs. The entry of rural industries increased competition in the industrial sector. The protected industrial sector was thus effectively opened to new entrants, including township and village coalmines. These coalmines greatly contributed to the coal supply and directly affected coal production in China.

At the same time, a dual-tier pricing system was introduced to allow the resources to be increasingly allocated by the micro units. This system had both a traditional plan and a market channel for resource allocation. During Deng's administration, this system offered valuable flexibility by allowing SOEs to transact and cooperate with other firms (Naughton, 1999). It constructed favourable conditions for pricing reform in the energy sector at the time. Any production of coal (by state mines) and oil above the quota set by the government could be sold at a higher market price. Price deregulation had begun to promote the exploration and exploitation of energy resources and improve profitability in the energy industry. Marketisation was, very cautiously and primitively, introduced in China's energy sector.

During Deng's administration, as the reform progress was very cautious and slow, few reforms were carried out in the state sector except for policies stimulating investment in the power industry. State coalmines and oil companies largely kept their status quo. The then macroeconomic situation and related reform measures determined that energy policies mainly focused on encouraging energy supply and partially decontrolling energy prices. The energy policy formulation, given the reform background, reflected the characteristics of China's economic reform: reforms were aimed at increasing incentives and autonomy at the micro-level and expanding market forces and increasing efficiency in resource allocation. The emergence of TVEs was especially prominent. These enterprises drew on labour released from farming by the introduction of the HRS and resources available in the market via the dual-tier pricing system. Correspondingly, the energy sector during this period could be characterised by two major measures. One was the emergence of township and village coalmines, which improved the productivity of the energy industry. The other was the introduction of the unique system of dual-tier pricing, which liberalised the above-quota coal and oil prices to a limited extent.

Following Deng Xiaoping's Southern Tour in 1992, China's economy experienced unprecedented rapid development. Jiang's administration saw drastic reform measures in the Chinese economy. Having recognised the numerous basic deficiencies in the economy, the central government launched comprehensive reforms in 1994 in every major sector in the national economy. From 1994 to 1998, broad reforms in the Chinese economy continued and a series of milestone reforms transformed every aspect of the Chinese economy, including government restructuring, fiscal reform, banking reform, and SOEs reform. In rapid succession, most of the remnants of central planning were abolished and price controls were relaxed. In the second half of the 1990s, the Chinese economy was characterised by a mixture of the old system, which had lost most of its effectiveness, and an emerging market economy that did not function as intended. The reform measures and the relevant macroeconomic situation had a deep impact on the energy sector. Again, China's macroeconomic reform worked as the predominant force directing its energy security evolution. The predominance was reflected mainly in three points.

First, the economic reform weakened the top-down vertical authority of the state government. Jiang's administration witnessed considerable downsizing of central government personnel, institutional structure, and dedicated funding. The wave of institutional reorganisation in 1998 abolished most of the economic ministries and consolidated the planning agencies. China began to move towards a regulatory state suited to a functioning market economy (Yang, 2004). The institutional reorganisation also reshuffled the energy sector. The irreversible shift from a planned economy to a market economy necessitated a shift in the authority over the energy sector from ministries to SOEs. The removal of the government from enterprise work made the business of controlling energy production the responsibility of the emerging independent corporate actors. The government's responsibility was mainly to identify emerging trends and forecast future trends in China's energy situation (Cunningham, 2007).

Second, the fiscal reform had mixed effects on energy policies and the energy security situation. On the one hand, national revenues recovered under the new fiscal system. The central government was able to direct incremental resources to lagging regions to balance regional disparities, such as the initiation of the Western Development Strategy. On the other hand, direct government financing for energy conservation projects was abolished even though continued and active government involvement is crucial for energy conservation. This discouraged the development of energy conservation activities by the enterprises. Since the late 1990s, the decreasing rate of energy intensity has slowed down. In 2005, the energy intensity even increased.

Third, the reform measure during Jiang's administration that had the most far-reaching impact on the energy sector was the reform of SOEs. Although the Deng administration witnessed booming business and fast economic growth, China's economy had deep-seated internal problems. Jiang's administration began to subject SOEs to substantial market disciplines. The government's reform of SOEs created newly empowered corporate actors. The operation of SOEs became more like a business than an administrative institution and they developed an increasingly commercial orientation. In the energy industry, the central government developed restructuring plans for SOEs in the oil, electricity, and coal sectors by creating several rival state-run corporations, which were injected with modern competition. The reform gave these SOEs greater autonomy and improved efficiency. Their market-oriented business behaviour increased sharply. Standard international practices were stimulated in the energy sector along with the expansion of SOEs reform.

In addition, the 1994 reforms in finance and taxation spurred the reform of the energy pricing system. It was generally approved that energy prices should be set by the market. At the same time, the newly established energy corporations required the energy pricing mechanism to be reformed to comply with international standards and practices. The deregulation of coal and oil prices was accelerated in the early 1990s and, when the market track was well on the way, pricing underwent further liberalisation. Energy pricing reform has gained momentum since 1996. To put it simply, energy policies under the Jiang administration underwent substantial changes across the government institutions, state industries, and national economy amid the creation and restructuring of companies, abolishment of ministries, and reformation of pricing systems for energy resources. The strength of macroeconomic reform was reflected in every change in China's energy sector.

In contrast, Hu's administration aimed at overcoming widespread criticisms and social tensions left behind by the economic transition during the Jiang administration. Its macro-policy package was largely a continuation of that of the Jiang administration, but with enhanced policies to deal with the economic and social challenges left by Jiang administration. The enhancement was reflected in three aspects: deeper reforms of SOEs, continued marketisation, and increased attention to environmental protection. Correspondingly, China's energy policies during the Hu administration emphasised continuing marketisation and environmental improvement.

First, the Hu administration tried to induce the market mechanism into the energy sector. To some extent, its efforts succeeded. On the one hand, it is true that the market force had been injected into the energy sector with an open coal market, an increasingly competitive electricity market, and an oil market subject to international oil prices. On the other hand, the competition was largely among state enterprises. The state-owned large-scale coal groups contributed an increasing share of the national coal output, along with government efforts to shut down the town and village coalmines. Despite the disaggregation, the reform in the electricity sector was actually resource reallocation and the competition was *de facto* among the major state enterprises. The oil sector was indeed dominated by the three state oil companies. Although the coal price was regulated by the market and the oil price was pegged to international price indices, they remained under the supervision of the National Development and Reform Commission. The electricity price was still strictly regulated by the central government. A competitive electricity market in the real sense had not yet been established. Changes in energy prices were modest with only regular small adjustments during Hu's administration.

Second, during the Hu administration the environmental issue became a priority on the government's agenda. The environmental regulation framework was a kind of 'command and control' system. The Ministry of Environmental Protection of the People's Republic of China issued regulations. Inspectors were sent to check on the implementation processes and fines were imposed on violators. The problem was that the regulations were not consistent across firms. Large state enterprises received much attention whereas the regulation of small-scale firms, particularly TVEs, was often neglected. This was partly due to officials overlooking pollution caused by firms that local economies were dependent on for jobs and tax revenue (Roumasset,

Burnett, & Wang, 2008). Therefore, although the environment largely improved during the Hu administration, the improvement was not consistent over the years.

To sum up, the Macro Economy-Driven Energy Security Mechanism was in effect throughout the three administrations. Macroeconomic reform in China was such a strong force that no other factor that might impact energy security evolution could prevail against it. China's energy policies and energy security evolution were strictly constrained by its macroeconomic reform measures. Their passive reaction to China's macroeconomic reform meant that specific policies or programs were formulated independently under each macroeconomic reform measure. China's economic reform and energy policies do not have a worked-out plan. They cannot be put into a unified framework and strategy, and this determines that China does not and cannot have coherent energy policies. China's energy security changed very passively as it was subject to the reform imposed by the central government. Energy policies have directly affected the country's energy security evolution, but energy policies *per se* are not the key drivers of energy development nor are they the fundamental forces framing the energy security status. Rather, it is the Chinese economic reform that frames the energy security situation. The energy policies that had been favourable to energy security improvement, such as policies that encouraged the development of town and village coalmines and the enhancement of energy efficiency, could not be sustained under the macroeconomic reform measures.

The tide of Chinese macroeconomic reform is irreversible. Once initiated, it works like water rushing out of a floodgate with great energy. It started with the micro-management institution reform giving autonomy to micro-management units, as reflected by the introduction of HRS and the emergence of TVEs. In the energy sector, town and village coalmines began to contribute an increasing share of China's coal production. The micro-level reform promoted production incentives and created additional resources. These profits were allocated to sectors that had been suppressed under the pre-reform system. In this way, economic growth was accelerated and the whole society benefited from the profit sharing. This was reflected by the SOEs reform and pricing reform. Along with the deepening of the reform, the conflicts between the reformed micro-management units and the macro-policy environment became obvious. In the early 1990s, China's fiscal system, financial system, and government structure were no longer compatible with the situation of the reformed micro-level. Since benefits already given to the micro-level could not be taken back, the conflicts required the reform to be extended to the macro-level. That is to say, the incremental process called for a compatible macro-policy environment. The gradualist reform, beginning with the micro-level and non-public sector of the economy, spilled over to the macro-policy environment, which was reflected by the reform package in 1994. The Jiang administration witnessed drastic reform at the macro-level, which once again deeply affected the energy sector in China. At the same time, reform at the micro-level, which was focused on SOEs, continued. China's energy sector was greatly affected by SOE reforms taking place in the coal, oil, and electricity industries. During the Hu administration, marketisation continued to deepen. Correspondingly, the energy sector continued its reform and adjustment, including its SOEs and prices.

Blackman, A., & Wu, X. (1999, November 1). Foreign direct investment in china's power sector: Trends, benefits and barriers. *Energy Policy*, *27*(12), 695–711.

Blanchard, D. I. (2005, March 7). Equity capital investment in China's energy efficiency sector. *3 Country Energy Efficiency*. Retrieved from http://3countryee.org/public/EquityInvestmentEEChina.pdf. Accessed on June 7, 2012.

Bo, Y. (1958, February 3). *Report on draft of 1958 national economic plan*. The Central People's Government of the People's Republic of China. Retrieved from http://www.gov.cn/test/2006-02/23/content_208767.htm. Accessed on June 23, 2011.

Bohi, D. R., & Toman, M. A. (1996). *The economics of energy security*. Boston, MA: Kluwer Academic Publishers.

Boonekamp, P. G. (2002). *Energy and emission indicators: International inventory and assessment*. The Netherlands: Energy research Centre of the Netherlands (ECN).

Brandt, L., & Rawski, T. G. (2008). China's great economic transformation. In L. Brandt & T. G. Rawski (Eds.), *China's great economic transformation* (pp. 1–26). Cambridge and New York, NY: Cambridge University Press.

Brandt, L., Rawski, T. G., & Sutton, J. (2008). China's industrial development. In L. Brandt & T. G. Rawski (Eds.), *China's great economic transformation* (pp. 569–632). Cambridge and New York, NY: Cambridge University Press.

Breslin, S. (2003, April). Paradigm shifts and time-lags? The politics of financial reform in the People's Republic of China. *Asian Business & Management*, *2*(1), 143–166.

Byrd, W. A. (1987). The impact of the two-tier plan/market system in Chinese industry. *Journal of Comparative Economics*, *11*(3), 295–308.

Byrne, J., Shen, B., & Li, X. (1996). The challenge of sustainability: Balancing China's energy, economic and environmental goals. *Energy Policy*, *24*(5), 455–462.

Cao, Y., Qian, Y., & Weingast, B. R. (1999). From federalism, Chinese style to privatization, Chinese style. *Economics of Transition*, *7*(1), 103–131.

CASS. (1996). *Selected economic archives of the PRC (Zhonghua renmin gongheguo jingji dangan ziliao xuanbian), industry volume: 1949–1952*. Beijing: China Logistics Publishing House.

CASS. (1998). *Selected economic archives of the PRC (Zhonghua renmin gongheguo jingji dangan ziliao xuanbian), industry volume: 1953–1957*. Beijing: China Price Publishing House.

CCP Central Committee. (1989, November 9). Decisions of CCP Central Committee on further rectification and reform (summary). *Xinhua Net*. Retrieved from http://news.xinhuanet.com/ziliao/2005-02/23/content_2608571.htm. Accessed on August 23, 2011.

CCP Central Committee's Literature Research Center. (1993a). PRC's first Five-Year plan of national economic development (Zhonghua Renmin Gongheguo Fazhan Guomin Jingji de Diyige Wunian Jihua). In C. C. Center (Eds.), *Selected important documents since the country foundation* (Vol. VI, pp. 405–568). Beijing: Central Literature Publishing House.

CCP Central Committee's Literature Research Center. (1993b). Report by national planning commission on the implementation of national economic plan in 1953 and several problems of national economic plan in 1954 (Guojia jihua Weiyuanhui Guanyu 1953 Niandu Guomin Jingji Jihua Zhixing de Jiben Qingkuang). In C. C. Center (Eds.), *Selected important documents since the country foundation* (Vol. V, pp. 347–367). Beijing: Central Literature Publishing House.

CCP Central Committee's Literature Research Center. (1995). Opinions of national planning commission on the second Five-Year plan (Guojia Jihua Weiyuanhui Dangzu Guanyu Dierge Wunian Jihua de Yijian). In C. C. Center (Ed.), *Selected important documents since the country foundation* (Vol. XI, pp. 431–438). Beijing: Central Literature Publishing House.

CCP Central Committee's Literature Research Center. (1997). Report by national planning commission on the arrangements for construction plan in 1961. In C. C. Center (Eds.), *Selected important documents since the country foundation* (Vol. XIV, pp. 257–273). Beijing: Central Literature Publishing House.

CCP Central Committee's Literature Research Center. (1998). Report outline on the arrangement of the third Five-Year plan (Draft). In C. C. Center (Eds.), *Selected important documents since the country foundation* (Vol. XX, pp. 359–444). Beijing: Central Literature Publishing House.

Chai, Q., & Zhang, X. (2010). Technologies and policies for the transition to a sustainable energy system in china. *Energy*, *35*, 3995–4002.

Chang, J. (2010, May). *Study on evaluation system of energy security and policy in our country*. Ph.D. Dissertation. China University of Geosciences, Beijing, China.

Chang, Y., & Lee, J. L. (2008). Electricity market deregulation and energy security: Study of the UK and Singapore electricity markets. *International Journal of Global Energy Issues*, *29*(1/2), 109–132.

Chang, Y., & Yong, J. (2007). Differing perspectives of major oil firms on future energy developments: An illustrative framework. *Energy Policy*, *35*, 5466–5480.

Chang, Y.-C., & Wang, N. (2010). Environmental regulations and emissions trading in China. *Energy Policy*, *38*(7), 3356–3364.

Chaziza, M. (2016). China's Middle East policy: The ISIS factor. *Middle East Policy*, *23*(1), 25–33.

Chen, G., & Chen, B. (2007). Resource analysis of the Chinese society 1980–2002 based on energy—Part 1: Fossil fuels and energy minerals. *Energy Policy*, *35*, 2038–2050.

Chen, L. (2010, July). Playing the market reform card: The changing patterns of political struggle in China's electric power sector. *The China Journal*, *64*, 69–95.

Chen, S. (2018, April 19). Is the belt and road initiative set to enhance China's energy security? *Aisa Dialoguei*. Retrieved from https://theasiadialogue.com/2018/04/19/is-the-belt-and-road-initiative-set-to-enhance-chinas-energy-security/. Accessed on January 10, 2020.

Chen, W., Li, H., & Wu, Z. (2010, November). Western China energy development and west to east energy transfer: Application of the western China sustainable energy development model. *Energy Policy*, *38*(11), 7106–7120.

Chen, W., & Xu, R. (2010). Clean coal technology development in China. *Energy Policy*, *38*, 2123–2130.

Chen, Y. (1992). 1952 objectives and tasks of financial work (1952nian caijing gongzuo de fangzhen he renwu). In C. C. Center (Eds.), *Selected important documents since the country foundation* (Vol. III, pp. 41–47). Beijing: Central Party Literature Press.

Chen, Y. (1993). Report on the first Five-Year plan (Guanyu Diyige Wunian Jihua de Huibao). In C. C. Center (Eds.), *Selected important documents since the country foundation* (Vol. V, pp. 335–346). Beijing: Central Literature Publishing House.

Cheng, H.-S. (1999). A midcourse assessment of China's economic reform. In O. Schell & D. Shambaugh (Eds.), *The China reader: The reform era* (pp. 311–321). New York, NY: Vintage Books.

Cheng, J. Y. (2008). A Chinese view of China's energy security. *Journal of Contemporary China*, *17*(55), 297–317.

Cherni, J. A., & Kentish, J. (2007, July). Renewable energy policy and electricity market reforms in China. *Energy Policy*, *35*(7), 3616–3629.

Chester, L. (2008, November 5–7). The (default) strategy determining the security of Australia's energy supply. *Second international association for energy economics (IAEE) Asian conference: Energy security and economic development under environmental constraints in the Asia-Pacific region*. Retrieved from http://www.business.curtin.edu.au/files/Chester_L_2008.pdf. Accessed on October 7, 2011.

Chester, L. (2010). Conceptualising energy security and making explicit its polysemic nature. *Energy Policy*, *38*(2), 887–895.

Chi, A. (2005). An important economic measure in the early days of new China: A series of conferences on specialized trades under the guidance of CHEN Yun. *Contemporary China History Studies*, *12*(4), 39–49.

Chi, C. (2011). *Studies on China's energy security monitoring and early warning (in Chinese)*. Shanghai: Shanghai Jiao Tong University Press.

Chi, C., & Li, Y. (2004, July). Factors affecting appraising energy security and measurement indicator system (in Chinese). *Journal of Harbin Institute of Technology (Social Sciences Edition)*, *6*(4), 80–84.

China Renewable Energy Society. (2009). *China's new energy and renewable energy yearbook 2009*. Beijing: China Renewable Energy Society.

China's Energy Development Strategy and Policy Research Group. (2004). *China's energy development strategy and policy research (Zhongguo Nengyuan Fazhan Zhanlue Yu Zhengce Yanjiu)*. Beijing: Economic Science Press.

China's Energy Research Institute. (1982). *Research report on China's energy policy (Zhongguo Nengyuan Zhengce Yanjiu Baogao)*. Beijing: China's Energy Research Institute.

Chinese Academy of Social Sciences (CASS). (2005, December 31). Understanding China's energy policy: Economic growth and energy use, fuel diversity, energy/carbon intensity, and international cooperation. *HM Treasury*. Retrieved from http://webarchive.nationalarchives.gov.uk/+/http://www.hm-treasury.gov.uk/media/B/B/Climate_Change_CASS_final_report.pdf. Accessed on July 22, 2011.

Clarke, M. (2014). Kazakh responses to the rise of China: Between elite bandwagoning and societal ambivalence? In E. Kavalski (Eds.), *Asian thought on China's changing international relations* (pp. 141–172). London: Palgrave Macmillan UK.

Climate Policy Initiative. (2010). *Review of low carbon development in China: 2010 report*. Beijing: Climate Policy Initiative at Tsinghua.

Clingendael International Energy Programme. (2004). *Study on energy supply security and geopolitics, report prepared for DG TREN*. The Hague: Clingendael International Energy Programme.

CNA. (2019, October 6). Iran says China's CNPC pulls out of gas project. *Channel NewsAsia*. Retrieved from https://www.channelnewsasia.com/news/business/iran-says-china-s-cnpc-pulls-out-of-gas-project-11974344. Accessed on November 7, 2019.

CNA Military Advisory Board. (2007). *National security and the threat of climate change*. Alexandria, VA: The CNA Corporation.

CNPC. (2012). History of CNPC. *China National Petroleum Corporation*. Retrieved from http://www.cnpc.com.cn/CNPC/gsjs/fzlc/. Accessed on January 19, 2012.

Cohen-Tanugi, D. (2010, October). Putting it into perspective: China's carbon intensity target. *Natural Resources Defense Council*. Retrieved from http://china.nrdc.org/files/china_nrdc_org/Chinas%20Carbon%20Intensity%20Target%20in%20Perspective.pdf. Accessed on August 17, 2011.

Compilation Commission. (1999). *History records of China's coal, comprehensive volume (Zhongguo Meitan Zhi, Zonghe Juan)*. Beijing: China Coal Industry Publishing House.

Cong, S., & Zhang, X. (1999). *Economic history of New China (1949-1998)*. Shanghai: Shanghai University of Finance & Economics Press Co., Ltd.

Congress of the United States. (1979). Western technology in the People's Republic of China. In C. o. States (Eds.), *Technology and east-west trade* (pp. 245–283). Washington, DC: Congress of the United States.

Cox, G. W., & McCubbins, M. D. (2001). The institutional determinants of economic policy outcomes. In S. Haggard & M. D. McCubbins (Eds.), *Presidents, parliaments, and policy* (pp. 21–63). Cambridge and New York, NY: Cambridge University Press.

Crabbe, D. (2003). Oil and gas. In G. Boyle, B. Everett, & J. Ramage (Eds.), *Energy systems and sustainability: Power for a sustainable future* (pp. 225–291). Oxford: Oxford University Press.

Cunningham, E. A. (2007, March). *China's energy governance: Perception and reality. The audit of conventional wisdom.* Cambridge, MA: MIT Center for International Studies.

Cyranoski, D. (2009). Beijing's windy bet. *Nature*, *457*, 372–374.

Dana, J. (2019, November 19). China's growing interest in Saudi Aramco is part of a long game. *EURACTIV*. Retrieved from https://www.euractiv.com/section/energy/opinion/chinas-growing-interest-in-saudi-aramco-is-part-of-a-long-game/. Accessed on January 13, 2020.

DBERR. (2007). *Expected energy unserved: A quantitative measure of security of supply, URN 07/1522*. London: Department for Business, Enterprise and Regulatory Reform.

Démurger, S., Sachs, J. D., Woo, W. T., Bao, S., Chang, G., & Mellinger, A. (2002, April). *Geography, economic policy, and regional development in China*. NBER Working Paper No. 8897. National Bureau of Economic Research, Cambridge, MA, USA.

Department for Communities and Local Government. (2009, January). Multi-criteria analysis: A manual. Department for Communities and Local Government, London.

Dooley, J. J. (1998, June). Unintended consequences: Energy R&D in a deregulated energy market. *Energy Policy*, *26*(7), 547–555.

Doriana, J. P., Franssen, H. T., & Simbeck, D. R. (2006). Global challenges in energy. *Energy Policy*, *34*(15), 1984–1991.

Downs, E. (2000). *China's quest for energy security*. Santa Monica, CA: RAND.

Downs, E. (2006). *The Brookings foreign policy studies energy security series: China*. Washington, DC: The Brookings Institution.

Downs, E. (2010). Who's afraid of China's oil companies? In C. Pascual & J. Elkind (Eds.), *Energy security: Economics, politics, strategies, and implications* (pp. 73–102). Washington, DC: Brookings Institution Press.

Dreyer, J. T. (2008). *China's political system: Modernization and tradition (6th ed.)*. New York, NY: Pearson Education, Inc.

DSD. (1998). Measuring changes in consumption and production patterns. *United Nations Commission on Sustainable Development*. Retrieved from http://www.un.org/documents/ecosoc/cn17/1998/background/ecn171998-mccpp59text.htm. Accessed on September 7, 2010.

Duan, H. (2010). The public perspective of carbon capture and storage for CO2 emission reductions in China. *Energy Policy*, *38*, 5281–5289.

Duncan, J. S. (1966, June). The developing economy. *Bulletin of the Atomic Scientists*, *22*(6), 84–87.

Economy, E. C. (2004). *The river runs black: The environmental challenge to China's future*. Ithaca, NY: Cornell University Press.

Eder, T. S., & Mardell, J. (2018, September 18). The BRI in Pakistan: China's flagship economic corridor. *Mercator Institute for China Studies*. Retrieved from https://www.merics.org/en/bri-tracker/the-bri-in-pakistan. Accessed on November 4, 2019.

Editorial Board of 'Contemporary China'. (1988). *Contemporary China's coal industry (Dangdai Zhongguo de Meitan Gongye)*. Beijing: China Social Sciences Press.

EIA. (2011). Glossary. *U.S. Energy Information Administration*. Retrieved from http://www.eia.gov/tools/glossary/index.cfm?id=G#gen_cap. Accessed on August 12, 2011.

European Commission. (2000, November 29). Green paper-towards a European strategy for the security of energy supply. *EUROPA*. Retrieved from http://eur-lex.europa.eu/smartapi/cgi/sga_doc?smartapi!celexplus!prod!DocNumber&lg=en&type_doc=COMfinal&an_doc=2000&nu_doc=769. Accessed on October 6, 2011.

European Commission. (2001). *Towards a European strategy for the security of energy supply*. Brussels: European Commission.

Evera, S. v. (1997). *Guide to methods for students of political science*. New York, NY: Cornell University Press.

Fairbank, J. K., & Goldman, M. (1998). *China: A new history (Enlarged Edition)*. Cambridge, MA: The Belknap Press of Harvard University Press.

Faucon, B. (2014, April 29). Iran cancels $2.5 Billion contract with Chinese oil company. *The Wall Street Journal*. Retrieved from https://www.wsj.com/articles/iran-cancels-2-5-billion-deal-with-chinese-oil-company-1398760835. Accessed on November 7, 2019.

Fei, J., & Hou, J. (1994). The comprehensive economic reform of the PRC (1978). In S-c. Leng (Ed.), *Reform and development in Deng's China, Volume IV, the miller center series on Asian political leadership* (pp. 19–64). New York, NY: University Press of America.

Fewsmith, J. (1994). *Dilemmas of reform in China: Political conflict and economic debate*. Armonk, NY: M.E. Sharpe.

Fewsmith, J. (2004, July 30). Promoting the scientific development concept. *China Leadership Monitor*. Retrieved from http://www.hoover.org/publications/china-leadership-monitor/article/6226. Accessed on June 4, 2012.

Feygin, M., & Satkin, R. (2004). The oil reserves-to-production ratio and its proper interpretation. *Natural Resources Research*, *13*(1), 57–60.

Finon, D. (1994). From energy security to environmental protection: Understanding swings in the energy policy pendulum. *Energy Studies Review*, *6*(1), 1–15.

Fisher-Vanden, K., Jefferson, G. H., Liu, H., & Tao, Q. (2004, March). What is driving China's decline in energy intensity? *Resource and Energy Economics*, *26*(1), 77–97.

Forbes, A. (2019, June 10). Turkmenistan sees light at the end of the tunnel. *Petroleum Economist*. Retrieved from https://www.petroleum-economist.com/articles/upstream/exploration-production/2019/turkmenistan-sees-light-at-the-end-of-the-tunnel. Accessed on November 6, 2019.

Forsythe, M. (2015, December 11). China's emissions pledges are undercut by boom in coal projects abroad. *New York Times*. Retrieved from https://www.nytimes.com/2015/12/12/world/asia/chinas-emissions-pledges-are-undercut-by-boom-in-coal-projects-abroad.html. Accessed on January 10, 2020.

Freeman, D., & Holslag, J. (2009). Climate change, China and the EU: Different policies, same end? *Asia Paper*, *4*, 1–32.

Fried, E. R., & Trezise, P. H. (1993). *Oil security: Retrospect and prospect*. Washington, DC: Brookings Institution Press.

FWO. (2018, May 29). Signing of agreement for Gwadar – Kashgar cross country crude oil pipeline project. *Frontier Works Organization*. Retrieved from https://www.fwo.com.pk/news-info/latest-news/569-29-may-2018-signing-of-agreement-for-gwadar-kashgar-cross-country-crude-oil-pipeline-project. Accessed on September 18, 2019.

Gallagher, K. S., Holdren, J. P., & Sagar, A. D. (2006). Energy-technology innovation. *Annual Review of Environment and Resources*, *31*, 193–237.

Gan, L., & Yu, J. (2008). Bioenergy transition in rural China: Policy options and co-benefits. *Energy Policy*, *36*, 531–540.

Gao, Y. (1999). Speech on the meeting of national grid planning (in Chinese). *Electric Power*, *32*(1), 1–2.

Ghoshal, D. (2016, July 7). China pivots to the Middle East and Iran. *YaleGlobal Online*. Retrieved from https://yaleglobal.yale.edu/content/china-pivots-middle-east-and-iran. Accessed on November 18, 2019.

Goldstein, C. (1993). Energy: Lost privileges. *Far Eastern Economic Review*, *156*(30), 50–51.

Goode, J. (1980). Energy policy. In D. S. Bell (Eds.), *Labour into the eighties* (pp. 62–74). London: Croom Helm Ltd.

Greene, D. L. (2010, April). Measuring energy security: Can the United States achieve oil independence? *Energy Policy*, *38*(4), 1614–1621.

Guo, A., & Li, Y. (2009). On China's reform from the theory of institutional change. *Reformation & Strategy*, *25*(4), 15–18.

Gupta, E. (2008). Oil vulnerability index of oil-importing countries. *Energy Policy*, *36*(3), 1195–1211.

Hang, L., & Tu, M. (2007). The impacts of energy prices on energy intensity: Evidence from China. *Energy Policy*, *35*(5), 2978–2988.

Hartwick, J. M., & Olewiler, N. D. (1998). *The economics of natural resource use* (2nd ed.). Reading: Addison-Wesley Educational Publishers, Inc.

Hassard, J., Morris, J., Sheehan, J., & Xiao, Y. (2010). China's state-owned enterprises: Economic reform and organizational restructuring. *Journal of Organizational Change Management*, *23*(5), 500–516.

Hassard, J., & Sheehan, J. (1997). Enterprise reform and the role of the state: The case of the capital iron and steel works, Beijing. In A. Bugra & B. Usdiken (Eds.), *State, market and organizational form* (pp. 73–103). Berlin: De Gruyter.

Hassard, J., Sheehan, J., & Morris, J. (1999). Enterprise reform in post-Deng China. *International Studies of Management & Organization*, *29*(3), 54–83.

Hassard, J., Sheehan, J., Zhou, M., Terpstra-Tong, J., & Morris, J. (2007). *China's state enterprise reform: From Marx to the market*. London: Routledge.

He, K., Huo, H., & Zhang, Q. (2002). Urban air pollution in China: Current status, characteristics, and progress. *Annual Review of Energy and the Environment*, *27*(1), 397–431.

He, X., Sheng, C., & Wang, F. (2011, June). Strategic choice and suggestions for the situation evaluation of China's energy security. *Natural Resource Economics of China* (6), 13–16.

HELIO International. (2005/2006). *Sustainable energy watch*. Paris: HELIO International.

Herring, H. (2006). Energy efficiency—A critical view. *Energy*, *31*(1), 10–20.

Herzog, T. (2007, April 27). China's carbon intensity target. *World Resources Institute*. Retrieved from http://www.wri.org/stories/2007/04/chinas-carbon-intensity-target. Accessed on August 17, 2011.

Heymann, E. (2006, February 28). Environmental sector China: From major building site to growth market. *Deutsche Bank Research*. Retrieved from http://www.dbresearch.de/PROD/DBR_INTERNET_DE-PROD/PROD0000000000196788.pdf. Accessed on August 16, 2011.

Ho, S. P. (1995). Rural non-agricultural development in post-reform China: Growth, development patterns, and issues. *Pacific Affairs*, *68*(3), 360–391.

Holz, C. A., & Lin, Y.-m. (2001). Pitfalls of China's industrial statistics: Inconsistencies and specification problems. *The China Review*, *1*(1), 29–71.

Hotelling, H. (1931). The economics of exhaustible resources. *The Journal of Political Economy*, *39*(2), 137–175.

Hou, J. (2011). Economic reform of China: Cause and effects. *The Social Science Journal*, *48*(3), 419–434.

Hu, A., & Wang, Y. (2006). How China creates a new situation, and goes up to a new level: Evaluation of the Tenth FYP period (in Chinese). *Review of Economic Research*, *1968*(8), 2–30.

Hu, A., Wang, Y., & Yan, Y. (2006). Evaluation report of the implementation of the tenth Five-Year Plan. *Review of Economic Research*, *1962*(2), 40–55.

Hu, J. (2007, October 15). Hu Jintao's report at 17th party congress. *China Daily Online*. Retrieved from http://www.chinadaily.com.cn/china/2007-10/25/content_6204667.htm. Accessed on September 21, 2011.

Hu, X., & Jiang, K. (2007). Environmental issues and their impact on Chinese energy use. In P. Drysdale, K. Jiang, & D. Meagher (Eds.), *China and East Asian energy:*

Prospects and issues (pp. 66–93). Canberra: Australia-Japan Research Centre, The Australian National University.

Huang, J. (2004, December 13). China to accelerate state-owned enterprise reform - Vice-Premier Huang Ju. *BBC Monitoring Asia Pacific*. London: BBC Worldwide Limited.

Huang, X., & Yan, J. (2000). Save the disadvantaged company, strengthen the advantaged company (in Chinese). *Shandong Social Science*, *3*, 115–118.

Huang, Z., Chen, H., Yip, A., Ng, G., Guo, F., Chen, Z.-K., & Roco, M. C. (2003). Longitudinal patent analysis for nanoscale science and engineering: Country, institution and technology field. *Journal of Nanoparticle Research*, *5*(3-4), 333–363.

Hussain, A., & Stern, N. (1991, April 1). Effective demand, enterprise reforms and public finance in China. *Economic Policy*, *6*(1), 141–186.

IAEA. (2005). *Energy indicators for sustainable development: Guidelines and methodologies*. Vienna: IAEA.

IEA. (1997a). *Indicators of energy use and efficiency: Understanding the link between energy and human activity*. Paris: OECD/IEA.

IEA. (1997b.) *The link between energy and human activity*. Paris: OECD/IEA.

IEA. (1999). *Coal in the energy supply of China. Report of the coal industry advisory board, Asia committee*. Paris: OECD/IEA.

IEA. (2006). *China's power sector reforms: Where to next?* Paris: OECD/IEA.

IEA. (2007a). *World energy outlook 2007: China and India insights*. Paris: OECD/IEA.

IEA. (2007b). *Energy security and climate policy: Assessing interactions*. Paris: OECD/IEA.

IEA. (2009a). *Cleaner coal in China*. Paris: OECD/IEA.

IEA. (2009b). *Towards a more energy efficient future: Applying indicators to enhance energy policy*. Paris: OECD/IEA.

IEP. (2019, November). Global terrorism index 2019. *Institute for Economics & Peace*. Retrieved from http://visionofhumanity.org/app/uploads/2019/11/GTI-2019web.pdf. Accessed on February 13, 2020.

International Atomic Energy Agency, International Energy Agency. (2001). Indicators for sustainable energy development. Report presented at the Ninth Session of the Commission on Sustainable Development, 16-27 April 2001, New York, NY, USA.

Jaborov, S. (2018). Chinese loans in central Asia: Development assistance or "Predatory Lending"? In M. Laruelle (Ed.), *China's belt and road initiative and its impact in central Asia* (pp. 34–40). Washington, DC: The George Washington University.

Jakobson, L., & Zha, D. (2006). China and the worldwide search for oil security. *Asia-Pacific Review*, *13*(2), 60–73.

Jansen, J. C., & Seebregts, A. J. (2010). Long-term energy services security: What is it and how can it be measured and valued? *Energy Policy*, *38*, 1654–1664.

Jansen, J. C., van Arkel, W. G., & Boots, M. G. (2004). *Designing indicators of long-term energy supply security*. Petten: Energy Research Centre of the Netherlands.

Jiang, J., & Sinton, J. (2011). *Overseas investments by Chinese national oil companies: Assessing the drivers and impacts*. Paris: OECD/IEA.

Jiang, Z. (2006). *Selected works of Jiang Zemin: Volume 2 (Jiang Zemin Wenxuan: di er juan)*. Beijing: People's Publishing House.

Jochec, M., & Kyzy, J. J. (2018). China's BRI investments, risks, and opportunities in Kazakhstan and Kyrgyzstan. In M. Laruelle (Ed.), *China's belt and road initiative and its impact in central Asia* (pp. 67–76). Washington, DC: The George Washington University.

Johnstone, N., Hascic, I., & Popp, D. (2010). Renewable energy policies and technological innovation: Evidence based on patent counts. *Environmental and Resource Economics*, *45*(1), 133–155.

Jong, S. d., Oosterveld, W. T., Roelen, M., Klacansky, K., Sileikaite, A., & Siebenga, R. (2017). *A road to riches or a road to ruin? The geo-economic implications of China's new silk road*. The Hague: The Hague Centre for Strategic Studies.

Kahn, J. (1994). China tightens controls on oil industry—Foreign firms are worried as Beijing takes steps to limit import level. *Wall Street Journal (Eastern edition), A11*.

Karagianni, M. (2019, February 20). Turkmenistan looks to gas expansion. *Petroleum Economist*. Retrieved from https://www.petroleum-economist.com/articles/politics-economics/middle-east/2019/turkmenistan-looks-to-gas-expansion. Accessed on September 13, 2019.

Karl, H., Han, G., & Olsson, M. (2009). China's climate- and energy-security dilemma: Shaping a new path of economic growth. *Journal of Current Chinese Affairs*, *38*(3), 119–134.

Keirstead, J. (2007). Selecting sustainability indicators for urban energy systems. *International conference on whole life urban sustainability and its assessment*, Glasgow, Scotland.

Kemmler, A., & Spreng, D. (2007). Energy indicators for tracking sustainability in developing countries. *Energy Policy*, *35*(4), 2466–2480.

Kennedy, A. B. (2010). China's new energy-security debate. *Survival*, *52*, 137–158.

Klare, M. T. (2003). The new geopolitics. *Monthly Review*, *5*(3), 51–56.

Klare, M. T. (2004). *Blood and oil: The dangers and consequences of America's growing petroleum dependency*. New York, NY: Henry Holt and Company, LLC.

Klare, M. T. (2007, Spring/Summer). The futile pursuit of "Energy Security" by military force. *Brown Journal of World Affairs*, *13*(2), 139–153.

Kleber, D. (2009, June 18). The US Department of Defense: Valuing energy security. *Journal of Energy Security*. Retrieved from http://www.ensec.org/index.php?option=com_content&view=article&id=196:the-us-department-of-defense-valuing-energy-security&catid=96:content&Itemid=345. Accessed on October 10, 2011.

Kong, B. (2005). *An anatomy of China's energy insecurity and its strategies*. Springfield: National Technical Information Service.

Kong, B. (2011, September). Governing China's energy in the context of global governance. *Global Policy*, *2*(s1), 51–65.

Krashakov, A. (2014, April 9). Perspectives of trans-Caspian project: Business view. *Azernews*. Retrieved from https://www.azernews.az/analysis/65786.html. Accessed on November 5, 2019.

Kruyt, B., van Vuuren, D. P., de Vries, H. M., & Groenenberg, H. (2009). Indicators for energy security. *Energy Policy*, *37*(6), 2166–2181.

Kurbanov, S. (2018). The importance of anticorruption, trade, and investment climate reforms in Central Asia in the BRI context. In M. Laruelle (Ed.), *China's belt and road initiative and its impact in central Asia* (pp. 86–96). Washington, DC: The George Washington University.

Lam, P.-L. (2004, February). Pricing of electricity in China. *Energy*, *29*(2), 287–300.

Lardy, N. R. (1998). *China's unfinished revolution*. Washington, DC: Brookings Institution Press.

Larus, E. F. (2005). *Economic reform in China, 1979-2003: The marketization of labor and state enterprises*. New York, NY: The Edwin Mellen Press.

Lawrence, G. (1997). Indicators for sustainable development. In F. Dodds (Ed.), *The way forward: Beyond agenda 21* (pp. 179–189). London: Earthscan.

LBNL. (2008). *China energy databook 7.0*. Berkeley, CA: Lawrence Berkeley National Laboratory.

Lee, F., & Sorenson, O. (2001). Technology as a complex adaptive system: Evidence from patent data. *Research Policy*, *30*(7), 1019–1039.

Lent, J., & Conklin, J. (2007). *Developing key energy indicators*. Washington, DC: Energy Information Administration.

Levine, M. D. (2008, December 9). Energy efficiency in China: Glorious history, uncertain future. *AIP Conference Proceedings*, *1044*(1), 15–27.

Levine, M. D., Liu, F., & Sinton, J. E. (1992). China's energy system: Historical evolution, current issues, and prospects. *Annual Review of Energy and the Environment, 17*, 405–435.

Lewis, J. I., & Wiser, R. H. (2007). Fostering a renewable energy technology industry: An international comparison of wind industry policy support mechanisms. *Energy Policy, 35*(3), 1844–1857.

Li, D. (1984). *Brief history of new China power industry (Xinzhongguo Dianli Gongye Fazhan Shilue)*. Beijing: Enterprise Management Press.

Li, F. (1992). Conclusions of the first national industrial conference. In T. P. Committee (Eds.), *Selected important documents since the country foundation (Jianguo Yilai Zhongyao Wenxian Xuanbian)* (Vol. II, pp. 303–321). Beijing: Central Literature Publishing House.

Li, F. (1993). Report on the first Five-Year plan of national economic development (*Guanyu Fazhan Guomin Jingji de Diyige Wunian Jihua de Baogao*). In C. C. Center (Eds.), *Selected important documents since the country foundation* (Vol. VI, pp. 288–361). Beijing: Central Literature Publishing House.

Li, F. (1997). Report on the adjustment and implementation of the last two years of the second Five-Year plan. In T. P. Committee (Eds.), *Selected important documents since the country foundation (Jianguo Yilai Zhongyao Wenxian Xuanbian)* (Vol. XVI, pp. 477–521). Beijing: Central Literature Publishing House.

Li, P. (1993a, March 15). 1993 government work report. *The Chinese Central Government's Official Web Portal*. Retrieved from http://www.gov.cn/test/2006-02/16/content_200926.htm. Accessed on August 24, 2011.

Li, P. (1993b, December 1). Accelerate the establishment of a socialist market economic system, and maintain a sustained, rapid and healthy development of national economy. *Xinhua Net*. Retrieved from http://news.xinhuanet.com/ziliao/2005-03/17/content_2709709.htm. Accessed on August 24, 2011.

Li, X., & Ma, Y. (1995, March). Fiscal decentralisation, financial reform and macroeconomic control in China: The implications for European Monetary Union.

Liao, J. (2019). A good neighbor of bad governance? China's energy and mining development in Southeast Asia. *Journal of Contemporary China, 28*(118), 575–591.

Lin, B. (2010). *2010 China energy development report (2010 Zhongguo Nengyuan Fazhan Baogao)*. Beijing: Tsinghua University Press.

Lin, J. (2007). Energy conservation investments: A comparison between China and the US. *Energy Policy, 35*(2), 916–924.

Lin, J. (2009a). Theoretical analysis of relationship between energy prices changes and economic security (Nengyuan Jiage Biandong Yu Jingji Anquan Guxi De Lilun Fenxi). In J. Lin (Ed.), *Energy prices changes and economic security (Nengyuan Jiage Biandong Yu Jingji Anquan)* (pp. 33–74). Shanghai: Shanghai University of Finance & Economics Press.

Lin, C. (2009b, April). The socialist market economy: Step forward or backward for China? *Science & Society, 73*(2), 228–235.

Lin, J., Cai, F., & Li, Z. (2003). *The China miracle: Development strategy and economic reform*. Hong Kong: The Chinese University Press.

Lin, J., Zhou, N., Levine, M., & Fridley, D. (2008, March). Taking out 1 billion tons of CO2: The magic of China's 11th Five-Year Plan? *Energy Policy, 36*(3), 954–970.

Lin, J. Y., & Tsai, Y. (2004). Reform and development in China: A new institutional economics perspective. *Seoul Journal of Economics, 17*(3), 335–381.

Lin, K.-C. (2008, July). Macroeconomic disequilibria and enterprise reform: Restructuring the Chinese oil and petrochemical industries in the 1990s. *China Journal, 60*(60), 49–79.

Lin, X., & Polenske, K. R. (1995). Input-output anatomy of China's energy use changes in the 1980s. *Economic Systems Research, 7*, 67–84.

Liu, J. (2004, July 13). Thoughts on the institutional problems of electricity shortage (in Chinese). *Economic Information Daily.*

Liu, L., Shen, L., Gao, T., & Liu, X. (2012). Evaluation and spatial-temporal evolution of energy security in China. *Acta Geographica Sinica, 67*(12), 1634–1644.

Liu, W.-Q., Gan, L., & Zhang, X.-L. (2002). Cost-competitive incentives for wind energy development in China: Institutional dynamics and policy changes. *Energy Policy, 30*, 753–765.

Liu, Z. (1995). *A study of China's overall pattern of productivity (Zhongguo Shengchanli Zongti Buju Yanjiu)*. Beijing: China Price Publishing House.

Liu, Y. (2017). India's understanding and response to China-Pakistan Economic Corridor (in Chinese). *International Study Reference, 9*, 23–28.

Liu, Q. (2018). South Asia terrorism and overseas interest protection along the Belt and Road (in Chinese). *Indian Ocean Economic and Political Review, 5*, 55–78.

Liu, Z., Sinton, E. J., Yang, F., Levine, M. D., & Ting, M. K. (1994). *Industrial sector energy conservation programs in the People's Repulbic of China during the seventh five-year plan (1986–1990)*. Beijing: Energy Research Institute, State Planning Commission.

Locatelli, C. (1989). China's energy policy: Energy and economic development. *Energy Studies Review, 1*(2), 144–158.

Loschel, A., Moslener, U., & Rubbelke, D. T. (2010). Indicators of energy security in industrialised countries. *Energy Policy, 38*, 1665–1671.

Lu, Y. (1993). *Fueling one billion: An insider's story of Chinese energy policy development.* Washington, DC: Washington Institute Press.

Ma, C. (1988). A preliminary analysis of China's energy structure as related to its energy policy. *Studies in Science of Science, 3*, 50–59.

Ma, C., & He, L. (2008). From state monopoly to renewable portfolio: Restructuring China's electric utility. *Energy Policy, 36*, 1697–1711.

Ma, K., & Cao, Y. (2002). *Transformation from planned to socialist market economic system (in Chinese)*. Beijing: People's Publishing House.

Ma, X., & Ortolano, L. (2000). *Environmental regulation in China: Institutions, enforcement, and compliance*. Lanham, MD: Rowman & Littlefield Publishers.

MacBean, A. (2007). China's environment: Problems and policies. *The World Economy, 30*(2), 292–307.

Mackay, D. (2014, June 30). ISIS militants in Iraq proclaim new Islamic state and pose threat to 'all countries'. *Mirror*. Retrieved from https://www.mirror.co.uk/news/world-news/isis-militants-iraq-proclaim-new-3790221. Accessed on September 23, 2019.

MacIntyre, A. J. (2003). *The power of institutions: Political architecture and governance.* Ithaca, NY: Cornell University Press.

Margolis, R. M., & Kammen, D. M. (1999, July 30). Underinvestment: The energy technology and R&D policy challenge. *Science, 285*(5428), 690–692.

Martinot, E., & Li, J. (2007). *Powering China's development: The role of renewable energy (Worldwatch Special Report)*. Washington, DC: Worldwatch Institute.

Matsuno, H. (2009, March 1). *China's environmental policy: Its effectiveness and suggested approaches for Japanese companies*. NRI Papers No. 140. Nomura Research Institute, Tokyo, Japan.

McGowan, F. (1996). Energy policy. In H. Kassim & A. Menon (Eds.), *The European Union and national industrial policy* (pp. 132–153). London: Routledge.

Meidan, M., Andrews-Speed, P., & Ma, X. (2009). Shaping China's energy policy: Actors and processes. *Journal of Contemporary China, 18*(61), 591–616.

Mielnik, O., & Goldemberg, J. (1999). The evolution of the "carbonization index" in developing countries. *Energy Policy, 27*(5), 307–308.

Miller, L. R. (2006). In search of China's energy authority. *Far Eastern Economic Review, 169*(1), 38–42.

Pan, K., Pu, J., & Xiang, T. (2002). The research of coal market concentration degree in China. *Management World, 12*, 77–88.

Pearce, D. W., & Atkinson, G. D. (1993, October). Capital theory and the measurement of sustainable development: An indicator of "weak" sustainability. *Ecological Economics, 8*(2), 103–108.

Peng, S., & Chen, L. (2011a). *Reforming China: Major events (1978–1991)*. Singapore: Enrich Professional Publishing (S) Private Limited.

Peng, S., & Chen, L. (2011b). *Reforming China: Major events (1992–2004)*. Singapore: Enrich Professional Publishing (S) Private Limited.

Peng, W. (2009, August). *The evolution of China's coal institutions*. Program on Energy and Sustainable Development (PESD) Working Paper #86. Freeman Spogli Institute for International Studies, Stanford, CA, U.S.

People's Daily. (1980, January 26). State economic commission required various departments to take effective measures to drastically drive down the level of energy consumption. *People's Daily*.

People's Daily. (1981, December 2). Zhao Ziyang talked about the basic direction of China's economic reform. Allow the market to play its role under the premise of the planned economy. *People's Daily*.

People's Daily. (1985a, January 8). Actively and safely reform the pricing system. *People's Daily*.

People's Daily. (1985b, March 31). Tian Jiyun talked about the guiding ideology of the pricing reform. *People's Daily*.

People's Daily. (1985c, March 31). Tian Jiyun talked about the need to reform the current pricing system; Price reform is key to the success of the entire economic system reform. *People's Daily*.

People's Daily. (1985d, April 13). In the press conference held by the General Office of the state council, secretary of the State Price Bureau talked about the price reform in 1985. *People's Daily*.

People's Daily. (1987a, March 27). Premier Zhao talked about the price reform and utilization of foreign investment in the fifth session of the sixth national people's congress. *People's Daily*.

People's Daily. (1987b, May 16). Li Peng talked about the development strategy of China's coal industry. *People's Daily*.

People's Daily. (1987c, September 8). Zhao Ziyang, when meeting with the Director General of the International Atomic Energy Agency, said China's nuclear industry would be perfectly safe. *People's Daily*.

People's Daily. (1988, August 24). Price and wage reform are overall deep reforms. *People's Daily*.

People's Daily. (1989, February 3). Why China's energy supply is so tight? *People's Daily*.

People's Daily. (1990, December 19). Decision of the state council on further strengthening the work of environmental protection. *People's Daily*.

People's Daily. (1991, May 25). Further deepen the reform and invigorate large and medium-sized enterprises. *People's Daily*.

People's Daily. (1992a, March 12). China already has the conditions to speed up reforms. *People's Daily*.

People's Daily. (1992b, October 21). Report to the fourteenth national people's congress of CCP. *People's Daily*.

People's Daily. (1993, January 10). Demand for energy will continue to flourish. *People's Daily*.

People's Daily. (1994a, February 7). Daya Bay nuclear power station unit 1 has started commercial operation. *People's Daily*.

People's Daily. (1994b, June 18). Reform of crude oil and refined products circulation system is carried out smoothly. *People's Daily*.

People's Daily. (1997a, March 28). The state commission for economic restructuring recently introduced 'the key points of the implementation of the economic system reform in 1997. *People's Daily*.

People's Daily. (1997b, January 18). The SPCC has been established. *People's Daily*.

People's Daily. (1998, March 7). The reform of state-owned enterprises should achieve new breakthroughs. *People's Daily*.

People's Daily. (1999, September 27). The decision of the CCP central committee on major issues of the state-owned enterprise reform and development. *People's Daily*.

People's Daily. (2000, November 9). West-East electricity transmission project started. *People's Daily*.

People's Daily. (2001a, February 12). Structure adjustment of power industry: To explore the growth potential and to achieve industrial upgrading. *People's Daily*.

People's Daily. (2001b, February 20). Major reform has been carried out on the state economic and trade commission and its subordinate bureaus. *People's Daily*.

People's Daily. (2002a, February 19). Look at oil after restructuring. *People's Daily*.

People's Daily. (2002b, March 20). Strengthen flue gas desulfurization, encourage clean energy, China strictly control the coal-fired sulfur dioxide emissions. *People's Daily*.

People's Daily. (2003a, September 11). NDRC initiated tariff reform. *People's Daily*.

People's Daily. (2003b, July 25). Outline of action for sustainable development in the beginning of the 21st century. *People's Daily*.

People's Daily. (2004a). China to speed up nuclear power construction. *People's Daily Online*. Retrieved from http://english.people.com.cn/200409/02/print20040902_155614.html. Accessed on August 8, 2011.

People's Daily. (2004b, April 23). Rapid economic growth, lagging-behind pollution treatment capability. *People's Daily*.

People's Daily. (2005a, March 25). The NDRC decided to accelerate the process of industrialization of renewable energy. *People's Daily*.

People's Daily. (2005b, July 23). Several opinions of the state council on promoting the healthy development of coal industry. *People's Daily*.

People's Daily. (2005c, October 29). Zeng Peiyan attended the resource price reform conference and emphasized to promptly improve resource price formation mechanism and vigorously promote economic growth mode transformation. *People's Daily*.

People's Daily. (2005d, November 8). China's plan on medium- and long-term development of renewable energy resources has been preliminarily completed. *People's Daily*.

People's Daily. (2006, January 16). Break the 'one size fits all' price and develop renewable energy. *People's Daily*.

Perlack, R. D., & Russell, M. (1991). Energy and environmental policy in China. *Annual Review of Energy and the Environment, 16*, 205–233.

Pittman, R., & Zhang, V. (2010). Electricity restructuring in China: How competitive will generation markets be? *The Singapore Economic Review*, *55*(2), 377–400.

Policy Information. (2008). The 2007 nation-wide closure of small thermal power plants were completed above quota (in Chinese). *Energy of China*, *30*(1), 4.

Price, L., Wang, X., & Jiang, Y. (2010, November). The challenge of reducing energy consumption of the Top-1000 largest industrial enterprises in China. *Energy Policy*, *38*(11), 6485–6498.

Prontera, A. (2009). Energy policy: Concepts, actors, instruments and recent developments. *World Political Science Review*, *5*(1), 1–30.

Purhonen, M. (2005). Dimensions of energy security. *3rd EAPC/PfP workshop on critical infrastructure protection and civil emergency planning*, Zurich.

Research Committee of China's Economic Structural Reform. (1987). *Dialogue on reform and opening up policies*. Beijing: Economic Science Publishing House.

Rothschild, E. (1995). What is security? *Daedalus*, *124*(3), 53–98.

Roumasset, J., Burnett, K., & Wang, H. (2008). Environmental resources and economic growth. In L. Brandt & T. G. Rawski (Eds.), *China's great economic transformation* (pp. 250–285). Cambridge and New York, NY: Cambridge University Press.

Rui, H. (2005). Development, transition and globalization in China's coal industry. *Development and Change*, *36*(4), 691–710.

Scheepers, M., Seebregts, A., de Jong, J., & Maters, H. (2006). *EU standards for energy security of supply, ECN-C-06-039/CIEP*. The Hague: ECN/Clingendael International Energy Programme.

Schipper, L., & Haas, R. (1997, June). The political relevance of energy and CO2 indicators–An introduction. *Energy Policy*, *25*(7), 639–649.

Schipper, L., Unander, F., & Marie-Lilliu, C. (2000). *The IEA energy indicators effort: Increading the understanding of the energy/emissions link*. Paris: IEA.

Sender, H., & Stacey, K. (2017, May 18). China takes 'project of the century' to Pakistan. *Financial Times*. Retrieved from https://www.ft.com/content/05979e18-2fe4-11e7-9555-23ef563ecf9a. November 4, 2019.

SEPA. (2000, March 30). *Notice concerning implementation of the expanded pilot SO2 discharge fee collection. SEPA [2000] 75*. Beijing: SEPA.

SETC. (2000). *Chinese industry in fifty years: The new China's industry chronicle. Part IX (in Chinese)*. Beijing: China Economic Publishing House.

Shaffer, B. (2009). *Energy politics*. Philadelphia, PA: University of Pennsylvania Press.

Shao, D. (1999). China's petroleum and petrochemical group reorganization from the perspective of industrial organization theory (in Chinese). *International Petroleum Economics*, *5*, 25–28.

Shen, L. (1988). *History of China's petroleum industry (Zhongguo Shiyou Gongye Fazhanshi)*. Beijing: Petroleum Industry Press.

Shi, D. (2005). Market reform and energy secure in China energy industry (in Chinese). *Natural Gas Economy*, *200*(01), 8–12.

Shi, D. (2008). Review and evaluation of thirty years' reform and opening up in energy industry (in Chinese). *Energy of China*, *30*(6), 5–12.

Shi, L. (1996). *Causes and transformation of China's industrial structure (Zhongguo Chanye Jiegou Chengyin yu Zhuanhuan)*. Shanghai: Fudan University Press.

Shi, Q. (1995). *Market economy and the measures for coal development*. Beijing: China Price Publishing House.

Shi, X. (2009, September). The prospects for coal: Global experience and implications for energy policy. *Economic Research Institute for ASEAN and East Asia*. Retrieved from http://www.eria.org/pdf/ERIA-DP-2009-19.pdf. August 16, 2011.

Shi, X., & Yao, L. (2019). Prospect of China's energy investment in Southeast Asia under the belt and road initiative: A sense of ownership perspective. *Energy Strategy Reviews*, *25*, 56–64.

Shi, Z. (2011, May). *Assessment and management of China's energy security based on analytic hierarchy process (AHP)*. Master dissertation, Nanjing University, Nanjing, China.

Shih, V. C. (2009). *Factions and finance in China: Elite conflict and inflation*. Cambridge: Cambridge University Press.

Shirk, S. L. (1993). *The political logic of economic reform in China*. Berkeley, CA: University of California Press.

Shu, X. (2010). U.S.'s oil strategy for Middle East and China's energy security (in Chinese). *West Asia and Africa* (2), 5–10.

Simpson, A. (2007, April). The environment-energy security nexus: Critical analysis of an energy 'love triangle' in Southeast Asia. *Third World Quarterly*, *28*(3), 539–554.

Sinopec Corp. (2012). About Sinopec. *Sinopec Corp*. Retrieved from http://english.sinopec.com/about_sinopec/our_company/20100328/8532.shtml. Accessed on January 19, 2012.

Sinton, J. E., & Fridley, D. G. (2000). What goes up: Recent trends in China's energy consumption. *Energy Policy*, *28*(10), 671–687.

Sinton, J. E., & Levine, M. D. (1994, March). Changing energy intensity in Chinese industry: The relative importance of structural shift and intensity change. *Energy Policy*, *22*(3), 239–255.

Sinton, J. E., Levine, M. D., Fridley, D., Yang, F., & Lin, J. (1999, December 6). Status report on energy efficiency policy and programs in China. *Lawrence Berkeley National Laboratory Report*. Retrieved from http://china.lbl.gov/sites/china.lbl.gov/files/Report.Dec1999.pdf. Accessed on September 5, 2011.

Sinton, J. E., Levine, M. D., & Wang, Q. (1998, September). Energy efficiency in China: Accomplishments and challenges. *Energy Policy*, *26*(11), 813–829.

Sinton, J. E., Stern, R. E., Aden, N. T., & Levine, M. D. (2005). *Evaluation of China's energy strategy options*. Berkeley, CA: Lawrence Berkeley National Laboratory.

Sloan, G., & Gray, C. S. (1999). Why geopolitics? In C. S. Gray & G. Sloan (Eds.), *Geopolitics, geography and strategy* (pp. 1–11). Abingdon: Frank Cass Publishers.

Smil, V. (1981). Energy development in China: The need for a coherent policy. *Energy Policy*, *9*(2), 113–126.

Smil, V. (2010). *Energy transitions: History, requirements, prospects*. Santa Barbara, CA: Praeger.

Sovacool, B. K. (2008, September). The problem with the 'Portfolio Approach' in American energy policy. *Policy Sciences*, *41*(3), 245–261.

Sovacool, B. K., & Brown, M. A. (2010). Competing dimensions of energy security: An international perspective. *Annual Review of Environment and Resources*, *35*, 77–108.

Sovacool, B. K., & Mukherjee, I. (2011). Conceptualizing and measuring energy security: A synthesized approach. *Energy*, *36*(8), 5343–5355.

Sovacool, B. K., Mukherjee, I., Drupady, I. M., & D'Agostino, A. L. (2011). Evaluating energy security performance from 1990 to 2010 for eighteen countries. *Energy*, *36*(10), 5846–5853.

Stacey, K. (2018, July 31). Pakistan's pivot to coal to boost energy gets critics fired up. *Financial Times*. Retrieved from https://www.ft.com/content/5cd07544-7960-11e8-af48-190d103e32a4. Accessed on November 25, 2019.

Stacey, K., & Sender, H. (2017, April 30). Glimmer of light in Pakistan's blackout crisis. *Financial Times*. Retrieved from Https://Www.Ft.Com/Content/12643508-2b0b-11e7-9ec8-168383da43b7. Accessed on November 19, 2019.

State Council. (1986a, January 12). *Regulations regarding energy conservation management*. State Council: Beijing.

State Council. (1986b, July 4). *State council decisions regarding problems in strengthening management of industrial enterprises' management*. Beijing: State Council.

State Council. (1987, March 30). *Several regulations regarding further strengthening electricity savings*. Beijing: State Council.

State Council. (1989, March 4). The notice of the State Council's approval of the elements issued by the state reform committee about the 1989 economic reform. *Xinhua Net*. Retrieved from http://news.xinhuanet.com/ziliao/2005-02/25/content_2618968.htm. Accessed on August 23, 2011.

State Council. (1993, March 8). The notice of the State Council's approval of the elements issued by the state reform committee about the 1993 economic reform. *Xinhua Net*. Retrieved from http://news.xinhuanet.com/ziliao/2005-03/18/content_2713741.htm. Accessed on August 24, 2011.

State Council. (1994, March 25). Outline of state industry policies for the 1990s. *pkulaw.cn*. Retrieved from http://en.pkulaw.cn/display.aspx?cgid=9530&lib=law. Accessed on July 19, 2011.

Woodard, K. (1980). *The international energy relations of China*. Stanford, CA: Stanford University Press.

World Bank Group. (2005, December 5). Energy security issues. *World Bank*. Retrieved from http://siteresources.worldbank.org/INTRUSSIANFEDERATION/Resources/Energy_Security_eng.pdf. Accessed on September 29, 2011.

World Commission on Environment and Development. (1987). *Our common future*. New York, NY: United Nations.

World Economic Forum. (2006, Spring). The new energy security paradigm. *World Economic Forum*. Retrieved from https://members.weforum.org/pdf/Energy.pdf. Accessed on October 6, 2011.

World Energy Council. (2010). *2010 survey of energy resources*. London: World Energy Council.

Wright, T. (1996, August). *Price reform in the Chinese coal industry*. Working Paper No. 66. Asia Research Centre, Murdoch University, Perth, Australia.

Wu, H. T., Pineau, P.-O., & Caporossi, G. (2010). Efficiency evolution of coal-fired electricity generation in China, 1999-2007. *International Journal of Energy Sector Management*, *4*(3), 316–336.

Wu, J., & Zhao, R. (1987). The dual pricing system in China's industry. *Journal of Comparative Economics*, *11*(3), 309–318.

Wu, K., & Fesharaki, F. (2001, February 19). China's refining sector challenges: Surging demand, rising imports of sour crudes, new business models. *Oil & Gas Journal*, *99*(8), 66–70.

Xia, C., & Song, Z. (2009). Wind energy in China: Current scenario and future perspectives. *Renewable and Sustainable Energy Reviews*, *13*(8), 1966–1974.

Xin, H., & Stone, R. (2010, March 19). 2010 budget. China amasses war chest to confront its environmental nightmares. *Science*, *327*(5972), 1440–1441.

Yamada, G., & Palma, S. (2018, March 28). Is China's belt and road working? A progress report from eight countries. *Nikkei Asian Review*. Retrieved from https://asia.nikkei.com/Spotlight/Cover-Story/Is-China-s-Belt-and-Road-working-A-progress-report-from-eight-countries. Accessed on November 22, 2019.

Yang, D. L. (2004). *Remaking the Chinese Leviathan: Market transition and the politics of governance in China*. Stanford, CA: Stanford University Press.

Yang, J. (2006, October 30). China speeds up renewable energy development. *Renewable Energy World*. Retrieved from http://www.renewableenergyworld.com/rea/news/article/2006/10/china-speeds-up-renewable-energy-development-46409. Accessed on October 20, 2012.

Yang, K., & Dong, Y. (2000). On historical change and present policy orientation of Chinese industrial construction (in Chinese). *Journal of Lanzhou University (Social Sciences)*, *28*(2), 5–11.

Yang, M. (2008). China's energy efficiency target 2010. *Energy Policy*, *36*(2), 561–570.

Yang, M., & Yu, X. (1996). China's power management. *Energy Policy*, *24*(8), 735–757.

Yao, L., Andrews-Speed, P., & Mohammad, Z. (2018, May 10). *China-Indonesia coal relationship: A new phase under the belt & road initiative*. ESI Policy Brief 23. Singapore: Energy Studies Institute.

Yeh, E. T., & Lewis, J. I. (2004, Fall). State power and the logic of reform in China's electricity sector. *Pacific Affairs*, *77*(3), 437–465.

Yergin, D. (1988). Energy security in the 1990s. *Foreign Affairs*, *67*(1), 110–132.

Yergin, D. (1991). *The prize: The epic quest for oil, money & power*. New York, NY: Simon & Schuster Inc.

Young, I. (1998, August 26–September 2). Petchem restructuring creates two new giants. *Chemical Week*, *160*(32), 34–37.

Yu, X. (2010). An overview of legislative and institutional approaches to China's energy development. *Energy Policy*, *38*, 2161–2167.

Yun, P. (1998). *The pollution charge system in China: An economic incentive?* Singapore: Economy and Environment Program for Southeast Asia.

Zambelis, C. (2016, March 10). China and Iran expand relations after sanctions' end. *China Brief*, *16*(5). Washington, DC: The Jamestown Foundation.

Zeng, P. (2010). *Review of western development decision-making (Xibu Dakaifa Juece Huigu)*. Beijing: Chinese Communist Party History Publishing House.

Zha, D. (2010b, March). *Oiling the wheels of foreign policy? Energy security and China's international relations*. Asia Security Initiative Policy Series. Singapore: Centre for Non-Traditional Security Studies, RSIS, NTU.

Zhang, C., & Heller, T. C. (2004, January). *Reform of the Chinese electric power market: Economics and institutions*. Working Paper #3 (Revised). Stanford University, Stanford, CA, USA.

Zhang, G. (2004, June 3). Voices from the regions. *Renewables*. Retrieved from http://www.renewables2004.de/pdf/Plenary_Session_A_Guobao.pdf. Accessed on October 20, 2012.

Zhang, H., & Liu, G. (2005). Initial study on China's oil security evaluation index system. *International Petroleum Economics*, *13*(5), 44–48.

Zhang, M., Niu, M., & Bartle, J. R. (2006). Assessing China's 1994 fiscal reforms: An intermdeiate report/comments on "Assessing China's 1994 fiscal reforms: An intermediate report". *Journal of Public Budgeting, Accounting & Financial Management*, *18*(4), 453–479.

Zhang, P., Yang, Y., Shi, J., Zheng, Y., Wang, L., & Li, X. (2009). Opportunities and challenges for renewable energy policy in China. *Renewable and Sustainable Energy Reviews*, *13*(2), 439–449.

Zhang, S. (2007). China's energy security and assessment (in Chinese). *China Population, Resources and Environment*, *17*(6), 101–104.

Zhang, W. (2003a). China's energy security and policy choices (in Chinese). *World Economics and Politics* (5), 11–16.

Zhang, W. (2003b). Chinese economy in the new time (II) (in Chinese). *Review of Economic Research*, *1674*(2), 2–10.

Zhang, W. (1998). U.S. oil geostrategy and the regional security in Tibet and Xinjiang (in Chinese). *Strategy and Management*, *2*, 100–104.

Zhang, Y. (2006, June). China's economic reform model in the later period of economic transformation (in Chinese). *Academic Monthly*, *38*(6), 79–84.

Zhang, Z. (1992). *The reform of China's production material prices (Zhongguo shengchan ziliao jiage gaige)*. Beijing: Economic Science Press.

Zhang, Z. (2010, September). Is it fair to treat China as a Christmas tree to hang everybody's complaints? Putting its own energy saving into perspective. *Energy Economics*, *32*(Suppl. 1), S47–S56.

Zhao, J. (2001, November). *Reform of China's energy institutions and policies: Historical evolution and current challenges*. BCSIA Discussion paper 2001-20, Energy Technology Innovation Project. Kennedy School of Government, Harvard University, Cambridge, MA, USA.

Zhao, X. (2010). *The study of industrialization thought and developing strategy in China (Zhongguo Gongyehua Sixiang ji Fazhan Zhanlue Yanjiu)*. Shanghai: Shanghai University of Finance & Economics Press Co., Ltd.

Zhao, X., Ma, C., & Hong, D. (2010). Why did China's energy intensity increase during 1998—2006: Decomposition and policy analysis. *Energy Policy*, *38*(3), 379–1388.

Zheng, F. (1995). To implement the two documents, and to rectify TVCMs in accordance with the law (in Chinese). *Energy of China*, *2*, 15–17.

Zheng, Y. (2011). Back to Deng Xiaoping? (*Huidao Deng Xiaoping?*). In Y. Zheng (Ed.), *The reform and its enemies* (pp. 18–21). Hangzhou: Zhejiang People's Publishing House.

Zhou, D. (2006). *Research on the energy strategy for building a moderately well off society (Quanmian Jianshe Xiaokang Shehui de Nengyuan Zhanlue Yanjiu)*. Beijing: China Planning Press.

Zhou, Y. (2010, July). Why is China going nuclear? *Energy Policy*, *38*(7), 3755–3762.

Zhu, S., & Cherni, J. A. (2009). Coal mining in China: Policy and environment under market reform. *International Journal of Energy Sector Management*, *3*(1), 9–28.

Zou, Y. (2007). Analysis of influencing factors of the national security of energy supply (in Chinese). *Neijiang Technology*, *12*, 67–68.

Zou, Y. (2009). *China energy security measurement (in Chinese)*. Nanchang: Jiangxi People's Publishing House.

Zweig, D., & Bi, J. (2005). China's global hunt for energy. *Foreign Affairs*, *84*(5), 25–38.

Index

Acceptability (AC)
data, 57
indicators, 49–52
Adequacy, 19, 34
Administrative Measures for the Coal Production License, 85
Affordability (AF), 20
data, 57–58
indicators, 52–53
Aggregated energy security indicators, 34–36
Air pollutant emissions, 49
Air pollution control during reform period, 96–101
Air Pollution Prevention Law, 98
Analytic Hierarchical Process (AHP), 7, 27
Analytical robustness, 41
Applicability (AP)
data, 55–57
indicators, 44–48
4-As evolution, 59
AC trend, 69–71
AF trend, 71–72
AP trend, 68–69
AV trend, 66–67
Asian Financial Crisis, 140
Availability, 20
Availability indicators (AV)
data, 54–55
indicators, 42–44
Availability of resource, applicability of technology, acceptability by society framework (3-A framework), 22–23, 31
Availability of resources, applicability of technologies, acceptability by society, affordability of prices framework (4-As framework), 11–12
Average thermal efficiency of power plants, 47

Belt and Road Initiative (BRI), 5, 10, 151–152, 161
projects in world's energy sector, 152–158
BP Statistical Review of World Energy, 54
Brightness Program and Ride the Wind Program, 70
Brightness Project Implementation Planning, 103

Carbon
factor, 51*n*14
intensity, 50*n*12
Carbon capture and storage technology (CCS technology), 101*n*21
Carbonisation index (*see* Carbon factor)
Central Asia, BRI projects in, 152–154
CFC-Free Energy-Efficient Refrigerator Project, 93
China Energy Conservation Investment Corporation (CECIC), 132
China Energy Statistical Yearbook, 54
China National Offshore Oil Corporation (CNOOC), 135
China National Petroleum Corporation (CNPC), 129, 152

Gezhouba project, 81
Global Terrorism Index (GTI), 155
Globalisation, 2
Government restructuring, 127–128
  energy sector under, 128–130
Great Leap Forward Period, 77
  adjustment of investments in energy industry, 79
  of coal industry, 77–78
  on energy industry, 79
  energy policies in, 77
  of power and oil industries, 78–79
Gross generation efficiency of fossil fuel-fired power plants, 46–47
Group Company System (GCS), 133

HELIO International, 33*n*13
High-in policy, 108
High-out policy, 108
Household Responsibility System (HRS), 12, 114, 117–118, 162
'Hydropower-based' development approach, 78

Imbalance index, 62–63
Import dependence ratio, 43
Independent energy security measurement systems, 36
  CC index, 37
  DSR model, 37–38
  S/D index, 36
Independent power producers (IPPs), 108
Indicators for Sustainable Energy Development (ISED), 37–38
Indicators identification, 32–38
Indirect indicators, 41
Initial public offering (IPO), 156
International Atomic Energy Agency (IAEA), 37
International Energy Agency (IEA), 15, 33*n*10
Investment, 76

Johannesburg Plan of Implementation, 45

Kazakhstan, 153
Kuomintang government (KMT government), 76

Law of the People's Republic of China on the Coal Industry, 86
Lawrence Berkeley National Laboratory (LBNL), 54
Long-term energy security, 19

Macro economy-driven energy security mechanism, 12, 14–15, 161–162, 169 (*see also* Independent energy security measurement systems)
Management Regulations of Township and Village Coalmines, 85
Market, 5, 118–119
  reforms, 134
Marketisation, 145–147
Measurability, 41
Medium and Long-term Renewable Energy Development Plan, 90
Middle East, BRI projects in, 156–158
Middle East Oil Import Dependency (MEOID), 35–36
Military factor, 37
Ministry of Coal Industry, 78, 85, 129–130
Ministry of Electrical Power (MEP), 134
Ministry of Fuel Industry, 75
Mitigation Assessment (MA), 37
Modern Enterprise System (MES), 133
Multi-fossil-fuels approach, 35

National Bureau of Statistics (NBS), 47
National Development and Reform Commission (NDRC), 71, 93, 141
National Economic Commission, 91

National Environmental Protection Agency (NEPA), 95, 129
National oil companies (NOCs), 133, 153
and oil price liberalisation, 136–137
National People's Congress (NPC), 84
National Plan for Medium-to Long-Term Scientific and Technological Development, 96
Natural gas
development in China, 88
reserve-to-consumption ratio, 44
Net Energy Import Dependency (NEID), 35–36
Net Oil Import Dependency (NOID), 35–36
New Plant, New Price policy, 108
Ninth Five-Year Plan of Industrialization of New and Renewable Energy, 70
Non-Carbon-based Fuel Portfolio (NCFP), 35–36
Not in my backyard (NIMBY), 21
Notice on Issues of Further Support for Renewable Energy Development, 103
Nuclear energy, 71
Nuclear power, 105–106 (*see also* Power)

Oil import dependence ratio, 42–43
Oil price
liberalisation, 136–137
policies on, 109–110
Oil supply crisis, 19
Organisation for Economic Co-operation and Development (OECD), 25

Particular matter concentration level emissions (PM_{10} emissions), 50*n*13
Patents, 48
People's Republic of China (PRC), 4, 75
Performance scoring, 59
Persuasion, 5
Plans on Medium-and Long-term Development of Renewable Energy Resources, 71
Policy relevance, 41
Political factor, 37
Power
plants and grids, 67
power-sector reform, 120–121
shortages, 147
Price reform and 'cross the price hurdle', 122–124
Pricing liberalisation, 72
Production Lump Sum Policy, 109
Property rights, 13
Provisional Regulations Regarding Energy Conservation Management, 91

Qualitative methodology, 165–170
Quantitative analysis of energy security in China, 39
4-As evolution, 59–72
data, 54–58
data coding, 58–59
formulation of indicators, 39–53
performance scoring, 59
Quantitative methodology, 163–165

Reasonable price, 3*n*2, 20, 34
Reform of energy enterprises, 76–77
Regulation on Management of Grid-connected Wind Farms (1994), 102
Reliability, 19, 34
Renewable energies, 101–105
Renewable Energy Law, 71, 90, 104–105
Renewable Energy Promotion Law, 70
Renewable energy share in energy and electricity, 51
Research Report on China's Energy Policy, 7
Response SIs, 37

Retail electricity prices, 52*n*16
Retail gasoline/petrol prices, 52*n*16
Ride the Wind Program, 102
Risk Assessment (RA), 37
Rural biogas, 103

'Scientific Outlook on Development', 143
Selection difficulty, 40
Self-sufficiency, 43*n*5
Sending Electricity to Townships, 103
Shannon-Wiener index, 35–36
Short-term energy security, 19
Simple energy security indicators, 34
Small and medium-sized enterprises (SMEs), 80
'Socialism with Chinese characteristics', 119–120
'Socialist planned commodity economy', 119–120
Soot emissions, volume of, 50–52
South Asia, BRI projects in, 154–155
Southeast Asia, BRI projects in, 158–159
Spatial scale, 39
Stability of electricity prices, 53*n*17
State Administration for Coal Industry, 128
State coalmines, 137–139
State Development and Planning Commission (SDPC), 102, 128
State Economic and Trade Commission (SETC), 70, 98, 127–128
State Electricity Regulatory Commission (SERC), 144
State Environmental Protection Administration (SEPA), 98, 129
State Petrochemical Industry Bureau (SPIB), 128
State Planning Commission (SPC), 81
State Power Corporation of China (SPCC), 14, 133
State Power Investment Corporation (SPIC), 158
State SIs, 37
State-owned enterprises (SOEs), 13, 89, 95, 114, 162
  energy sector under, 144–145
  reform, 132–133, 143–145
  reform in coal sector, 137
  reform in oil sector, 135–136
  reform in power sector, 134–135
Steel Industry Development Policy, 94
Supply of energy, 31
Supply/Demand Index (S/D Index), 36
Surety, survivability, supply, sufficiency, and sustainability ('five Ss'), 22
Sustainability indicators (SIs), 37, 40
Sustainable development factor, 37
Sustainable energy development, 163
Sustainable Energy Programs under Agenda 21, 97
Sustainable Energy Watch reports (SEW reports), 33*n*13

Tariff Reform Plan, 109
Technology, 20, 31, 46
  innovation, 20
Tentative Provisions on Pollution Charge, 96
Tenth Five-Year Plan for New and Renewable Energy Commercialization Development, 70
'Third Front' of China's industrial distribution, 80
Time scale, 39
Top 1, 000 *Enterprises Energy Conservation Action Implementation Plan*, 94
Total Load Control, 99*n*20
Total primary energy supply (TPES), 35, 43, 51
Town and village coalmines (TVCMs), 12–13, 66, 83–85, 117, 137–139

Township and village enterprises (TVEs), 97, 116, 117*n*5, 166
Traditional geopolitics, 2
Transmission and distribution (T&D), 135
Transport factor, 37
Turkmenistan, 153
Two-cent policy, 108
Two-tier pricing system, 12–13, 121–122

U. S. Energy Information Administration (EIA), 54
United Nations Department of Economic and Social Affairs (DSD), 33*n*12
United Nations Development Programme, 21
United Nations Work Programme on Indicators of Sustainable Development (WPISD), 37
User utility, 41

Volatility of coal prices, 53

Western development strategy and impact on energy sector, 139
  China's regional disparities and, 139–140
  energy sector under, 140–141
World Energy Council (WEC), 54
World Summit on Sustainable Development (2002), 45